Cajun Women
and Mardi Gras

Reading the Rules Backward

CAROLYN E. WARE

UNIVERSITY OF ILLINOIS PRESS

Urbana and Chicago

Library of Congress Cataloging-in-Publication Data
Ware, Carolyn.
Cajun women and Mardi Gras : reading the rules backward /
Carolyn E. Ware.
p.   cm.
Includes bibliographical references and index.
ISBN-13: 978-0-252-03138-0 (cloth : alk. paper)
ISBN-10: 0-252-03138-5 (cloth : alk. paper)
ISBN-13: 978-0-252-07377-9 (pbk. : alk. paper)
ISBN-10: 0-252-07377-0 (pbk. : alk. paper)
1. Carnival—Louisiana.
2. Cajuns—Louisiana—Social life and customs.
3. Women—Louisiana—Social life and customs.
4. Sex role—Louisiana.
5. Louisiana—Social life and customs.
I. Title.
GT4210.L8W37   2007
394.25082—dc22   2006015293

To the memory of
Gerald Frugé
Agnes Miller
Vories Moreau
Ella Ruth Young
and
Tom and Ann Ware

Contents

Acknowledgments

Many people have helped with this book along the way. First and foremost, I am indebted to the Mardi Gras runners, captains, cooks, and other helpers in the Mardi Gras communities described here. The entire Moreau family of Basile-Vories, Joyce, Wayne, Faye, Brandon, and especially Kim have contributed generously to my quest to better understand Mardi Gras. Helena Putnam and Debbie Andrus have been good friends, endless sources of insight, and close readers of my work. They, like their fellow *vieilles* Mardi Gras Susie Lopez, Snookie LeJeune, Gloria Miller, and Janell Ashford, have been inspirations to me, as was the late Agnes Miller. Potic Rider, Sandy Sonnier, and Berline Boone have been wonderfully helpful and supportive, and pointed out at least some of my mistakes, for which I'm grateful. Thanks also to the LeBlue family—Cassie, Junior, Laura, and Jenny; to the late Ella Ruth Young; to Gilbert and Nin LeBlanc; and to Pat and Geneva Comeaux.

In Tee Mamou, the Frugé family has been unfailingly generous and kind, and this book owes a great deal to Linda, Renée, Jeanette, Todd, Chad, Roonie, and especially the late Gerald Frugé, a *capitaine* par excellence and an ambassador for his community. Suson Launey has been a steadfast friend and adviser on all things Mardi Gras, always ready to drop everything and come talk to my folklore classes. Merline Bergeaux, Shirley Reed, and Patsy Simar kindled my interest in female Mardi Gras through their artful performances and their eloquence. Claude Durio and Don LeJeune also have been enormously helpful. I am grateful to Larry and Jackie Miller in Iota, who got me started on Mardi Gras fieldwork years ago and have continued to be sources of all kinds of information. My gratitude, too, to Georgie and Allen Manuel, Frozine Thibodeaux, Evelyn Frugé, Alice Janot, Janice Ashord, Ivy Deshotels, Theresa Seale and Norma Jean Miller, and Curtis Joubert.

Roger Abrahams introduced me to the study of festival through his course on display events, and I am deeply thankful for this, as well as for his support and guidance on this project. I thank Carl Lindahl and Karen Baldwin for their excellent and informed suggestions as outside readers; their comments improved the book considerably. Carl has been a valued friend and mentor for many years; I owe more than I can say to his insights on Mardi Gras, and perhaps most of all to his example as a stellar fieldworker. I have also benefited greatly from the help of numerous other folklore colleagues: Barry Ancelet, with his encyclopedic knowledge of Cajun culture and his wonderful photographs, has commented on various drafts, given countless pointers, and corrected my transcriptions of Cajun French. Maida Owens has always been generous in lending her photos, her wide knowledge of Louisiana culture, and any other resources I asked for. Thanks, too, to Dana David, Donna Onebane, Ray Brassieur, John Laudun, Mike Luster, Rocky Sexton, Sam Kinser, Susan Roach, Peter Jones, Marcia Gaudet, Nick Spitzer, Frank DeCaro, and David Estes, all valued colleagues who have contributed to my understanding in myriad ways. My thanks, too, to Philip Gould for the use of his photo on the front cover, Elemore Morgan Jr., Greg Wirth, and Bruce Morgan for giving me access to their photos during my research, and to Ann Savoy for leads on women to interview.

I am also deeply grateful to other colleagues and writing group members who helped me through the writing and revision process. This book is much stronger for advice and encouragement from Robin Roberts, Rosan Jordan, and Sharon Weltman. My former writing group partners at the University of Southern Mississippi—Shana Walton, Amy Young, and Misty Jaffe—were a great help with earlier drafts.

Louisiana State University (LSU) has generously supported my efforts in many ways: through a summer research stipend that enabled me to finish the manuscript, and a semester's research leave that gave me time to revise it. I am especially grateful to the College of Arts and Sciences and its dean, Guillermo Ferreyra, for funding to support the book's publication, and to Malcolm Richardson and Anna Nardo for their help. My thanks, too, to Clifford "Dupe" Duplechin, of LSU's cartography office, for patiently working to create accurate maps of Mardi Gras routes. At an earlier stage of the project, I benefited from a research fellowship at the Newcomb College Center for Research on Women at Tulane University. Many thanks to Beth Willinger and Susan Tucker for their friendship and support there.

I am very thankful to Judy McCulloh at the University of Illinois Press for her encouragement and patience over the years, and for her many, many indispensable tips on shaping and submitting a book manuscript. Thanks, too, to Cope Cumpston for her expertise on illustrations, to Angela Burton for guiding me through the publication process, and to Martha Ramsey for her meticulous copyediting.

Finally, I want to thank my family for their interest and belief in the project. My late parents, Tom and Ann Ware, supported me in numerous ways in this journey, though they didn't live to see its completion. My sisters Pat and Ginny, brother Tom, and brother-in-law Russ all contributed much to its success, and I thank them for not asking "Aren't you done yet?" when they must have thought it. Thanks for believing this was important.

INTRODUCTION

Les Mardi Gras
Come but Once a Year

"Once you've run [Mardi Gras], once you've come into
that community or into that family, it's very difficult to
stand on the sidelines and watch it. It's always been
a very emotional thing for me."

—Helena Putnam

"Whenever I die, you can put my mask, my
capuchon [Mardi Gras hat] and my suit with me."

—Merline Bergeaux

In the days and weeks before Mardi Gras, anticipation builds in small towns and country neighborhoods on the prairies of southwest Louisiana. Decorations, many in the purple, green, and gold of the New Orleans Carnival, appear in shop windows, on house fronts, and in yards. The haunting Cajun tune known as "La Danse de Mardi Gras" sounds from jukeboxes and bandstands, its percussion mimicking horses' hoofbeats.[1] The song describes and sets the stage for the local tradition of *courirs de Mardi Gras,* or Mardi Gras runs, that take place annually in more than twenty Cajun and Creole communities.[2] Soon, its French lyrics remind us, disguised riders called Mardi Gras will come from all over to make their once-a-year voyage through the countryside. Stopping at houses along their route, they will ask their hosts for *charité,* even if it consists only of a sweet potato or two, a skinny chicken, or *gratons* (crisply fried pork rinds). The riders then urge their *capitaine* to lead them to the next neighbor's house, but not before inviting the master and mistress of the house—and especially *les belles,* the pretty girls—to join them for a gumbo and dance that night.

The rural celebration is a cooperative performance that depends on involvement by both sexes. Women contribute in crucial behind-the-scenes ways: creating the men's colorful *suits de Mardi Gras,* running errands before and during the run, cooking and serving the chicken gumbo shared by the community at the end of the day, acting as hosts and donating food, drink, and money to the riders, and dancing with them at their *bal de Mardi Gras* that night. Women also teach their children about the tradition, ensuring its continuity. Yet, despite their importance, women's activities have received little attention.

Gender has always shaped how people take part in the country Mardi Gras. Traditionally, it has been men who run Mardi Gras by masking, roaming country neighborhoods or *voisinages* to beg for gumbo ingredients (and steal them if necessary), sing and dance for their hosts, play pranks, dance on horseback, and perform other comical and daring feats. Men also have served as the groups' unmasked commanders, or *capitaines,* responsible for leading the mischievous celebrants, keeping them in line, and ensuring that they offer an entertaining show without offending their hosts or damaging property. Robert Tallant, author of several popular books on New Orleans and its Carnival, wrote in the 1940s that "men . . . have most of the Mardi Gras fun" in the rural Cajun celebration, because "the natives are still inclined to be strict with their wives, sweethearts, and sisters, and seldom permit their women to mask."[3]

Other books and scholars have also characterized Mardi Gras in ways that did not seem to leave room for women. Post, writing about the same era, called running Mardi Gras "a man's sport."[4] Forty years later, in the 1980s, Nadine Fournier and Richard Guidry wrote that the Cajun festival remained "*le privilège des hommes,*" an exclusively male right.[5] Similarly, folklorist Nicholas Spitzer remarked on the "cowboy machismo" of Cajun Mardi Gras runs;[6] and Carl Lindahl described the Mardi Gras as an initiation rite into manhood, as "boys . . . become men through their adventures."[7]

But these descriptions no longer apply to all communities. Women still carry out many of their traditional Mardi Gras duties, but in at least half a dozen places, they also run Mardi Gras themselves. As they refashion once-male Mardi Gras roles, women offer their own critique of gender relations, suggest alternatives, and introduce new meanings to the festival. Women's Mardi Gras performances include a wide range of behaviors. Some engage in physical, often rough, horseplay, just as male Mardi Gras do; others devise new, less rowdy and more collaborative ways of clowning. In their Mardi Gras roles, Cajun women variously affirm, manipulate, and topple traditional gender roles.

This book describes Cajun Mardi Gras runs, with a particular emphasis on the crucial parts women play as backstage sustainers, creative artists, and public performers. Two points are central. First, I argue that women have always been, and are still, mainstays of the country Mardi Gras celebration. Women's work and men's festive roles are interdependent, and women clearly see themselves as part of the event. Second, I suggest that women's largely unnoticed performances as Mardi Gras clowns and captains enlarge and enhance our understanding of Carnival as a dynamic, gendered practice. Through their disguises and actions, women challenge the static, male-focused analysis of Mardi Gras and offer a model of creative appropriation of male festive traditions. The book, then, explores Cajun women's maintenance, reinvention, and reinvigoration of the Mardi Gras festival. It focuses closely on two rural communities, Tee Mamou and Basile, where women have now run Mardi Gras for more than three decades.

Mardi Gras and Meaning

In southwest Louisiana, the term "Mardi Gras" (literally, "Fat Tuesday" in French) holds several meanings. It refers to the holiday itself, the Tuesday preceding Ash Wednesday, and sometimes to the entire Carnival season. An individual masker is also called a Mardi Gras, although unmasked captains are not. As a group, the runners are *les Mardi Gras* or, in English, the Mardi Gras (pronouncing the "s"). And finally, a community run is also commonly referred to simply as the Mardi Gras, as in "the Eunice Mardi Gras."

For many Cajun women and men, Mardi Gras is not simply a once-a-year diversion; it is a deeply meaningful part of their religious, ethnic, regional, and community identity. Cajun women—whether or not they run Mardi Gras—say that they, too, feel a deep connection to the celebration. Several have told me that Mardi Gras is "in our blood." Berline Boone, a longtime Mardi Gras in Basile, says, "It's my life and a part of my heart and soul and most important my true heritage."[8] For Berline and others who faithfully mask each year, running Mardi Gras becomes a performance of cultural memory.[9]

One reason for the custom's importance in largely Catholic southwest Louisiana is its religious significance. Many Cajuns carefully observe Lenten abstinence, and Mardi Gras is the last time they will eat meat on Fridays, drink beer, and dance until Easter. At midnight, Mardi Gras festivities give way to Ash Wednesday, a generally solemn day. The observant attend Mass to have the mark of the cross traced in ash on their foreheads, a gesture of penitence. Almost all, even nonchurchgoers, make some symbolic sacrifice on Ash Wednesday, usually foregoing meat for that day at least.

But the local importance of Mardi Gras extends far beyond its place in the Catholic calendar. Cajun Mardi Gras runs have also become important symbols of ethnicity and region. Both prairie Cajuns and Creoles traditionally run Mardi Gras (though almost never together), but in recent years Cajun runs have largely overshadowed Creole *courirs de Mardi Gras,* which are generally fewer, smaller, and less public than Cajun ones.[10] Many Cajuns and the general public now associate the custom specifically with Cajun culture. The runs represent ethnic heritage, but also a specifically regional way of life: *prairie* Cajunness, in distinction from life in Louisiana's swamps, marshes, and cities.

Perhaps most important, Mardi Gras runs are an expression of community and reciprocity. Once Mardi Gras runs were part of a widespread system of exchange in the isolated settlements that dotted Louisiana's prairies. Rotating *boucheries*, where country families took turns killing a hog, ensured that everyone had fresh meat regularly. *Boucheries* were communal efforts; neighbors helped with the hard work of cleaning the hog, salting pork, and making sausage and cracklings, and in return they took home a share of the meat. When a community member needed help with hoeing, harvesting, or other farm work, others lent a hand. This custom of holding a "community workday" was often called a *coup de main*, and it combined labor with socializing and sharing a meal.[11] In the evening, farm families often made *veillées*, informal sorties to the homes of friends and relatives. *Veillées* typically included conversation and storytelling, card playing, perhaps singing or performing music, and eating.

Likewise, Mardi Gras runs pooled and redistributed resources during the lean winter months: everyone donated whatever ingredients they could afford, and everyone feasted on gumbo. Today, this reciprocity carries more symbolic than practical value, but its significance is no less powerful. Mardi Gras runs are still essentially a community-based tradition, even—some suggest—a form of community service. Russell "Potic" Rider, the president of the Basile Mardi Gras Association, told folklorist Carl Lindahl: "We're not doing this for us now. We're doing it for the people of Basile."[12]

Now, as always, Mardi Gras runs depend on community support and commitment. Although relatively few people mask, many more must be willing to "receive" the Mardi Gras at their homes and businesses, to donate gumbo ingredients, liquor, or cash, and to be picked at (teased) and pulled into the riders' performance as dance partners and foils. Mardi Gras runs are traditionally very territorial, and participants often express a fervent loyalty to their hometown run. Where you run Mardi Gras defines where you're from, and each Mardi Gras community is convinced that its own run is, if not the biggest, the best.[13] *Courir* routes symbolically sketch neighborhood boundaries that are recognized by locals but seldom found on maps. However, as Acadiana's landscape changes, Mardi Gras communities are redrawn. Many of today's runs include natives who have moved away to find work, or a few "adopted" outsiders who take part each year and feel a strong connection to their run and fellow Mardi Gras.

For core members, Mardi Gras runs also enact family loyalties and enduring friendships. The tradition is passed down through, and kept alive by, families devoted to Mardi Gras. Close *camarades* have long Mardi Gras histories together, and these friendships create deep emotional ties to community runs. Having fun together in such intense, even dizzying ways further cements bonds among friends, and the Mardi Gras group becomes an extended family—at least for the duration of the run, and often long afterward.[14] Helena Putnam, a French teacher and native of Basile, describes her longtime Mardi Gras comrades as "Mardi Gras sisters." Helena stopped running Mardi Gras in her hometown for several years because she felt uncomfortable carousing in front of her students; during that hiatus, she explained how painful this decision was: "Once you've run, once you've come into that community or into that family, it's very difficult to stand on the sidelines and watch it. It's always been a very emotional thing for me. I usually cry when the Mardi Gras come into the hall. Because I'm not a part of it."[15] Some years later, after taking a teaching job in neighboring Elton, she rejoined the Basile run—in part because she wanted to teach her students and her own daughters the importance of their traditional culture.

Mardi Gras runs define community by exclusion as well as inclusion. Some households and businesses, for example, largely Protestant or non-Cajun enclaves, have little interest in the celebration. And for the most part, Mardi Gras runs still reflect and reinscribe racial boundaries. Almost all Cajun and Creole Mardi Gras runs remain segregated, and captains take care that the groups do not meet during their travels. Cajun runs rarely stop at African American households, and black Creole Mardi Gras likewise avoid most white homes in their neighborhood unless specifically invited.[16] In recent years, some Cajun women and men have voiced objections to this pattern of racial exclusion, but change has been slow.

Local interest in the country Mardi Gras celebration has risen steadily over the last two decades, but not everyone in the region likes or approves of the tradition. One non-Cajun woman from Jennings marveled at the interest folklorists have recently shown in the tradition, assuring me that she grew up around it and "That's nothing." Many other locals would agree with her. Even those who enjoy watching the festivities may have no desire to run. Berline Boone says, "I think you're born a Mardi Gras. . . . Because I know a lot of people, my best friends over here, that's just as Cajun as I am, and they don't like that. They just don't like that. I mean they can't endure the dancing and [activity] all day long."[17]

For dedicated members, though, the connection to the Mardi Gras tradition extends throughout the year, and often throughout their lives. Proud parents dress infants in Mardi Gras suits and hats to greet the riders, and coach toddlers in the fine points of singing and dancing like a true Mardi Gras. Women, like men, sometimes risk health, jobs, and marriages to run each year. One Tee Mamou Mardi Gras masker carries nitroglycerin in her pocket, in case her chronic heart ailment causes her to keel over during the run. The late Ella Ruth Young, Basile's women's captain for many years, wept when heart disease forced her to watch, rather than lead, the Mardi Gras run. The following year, Ella Ruth's red captain's cape and hat were displayed beside her coffin at a local funeral home. Mardi Gras ties can carry over even beyond death. After *capitaine* Gerald Frugé's death from cancer in 1998, both the Tee Mamou women's run and men's run added a stop to their routes: a visit to a small country cemetery where they serenaded Gerald's crypt with their Mardi Gras song.

Researching Mardi Gras

My introduction to the Cajun Mardi Gras celebration came about by chance. As a University of Pennsylvania graduate student in folklore and folklife, I visited the University of Louisiana in Lafayette in 1988. During my semester there, I was invited to fill in for another, more experienced folklorist on a short-term research project. The Tee Mamou-Iota Mardi Gras Folklife Festival, then entering its second year, had received grant funding to hire two fieldworkers to research Acadia Parish Mardi Gras traditions and then create an exhibit and public programming for the festival. That fall, I spent several weeks trailing after Larry Miller, my guide and sometime translator, interviewing more than a dozen men and women about past and present Mardi Gras runs. From my first visit to the rural neighborhood known as Tee Mamou (a contraction of *Petit Mamou,* or Little Mamou) and my first interview with three Mardi Gras captains, I was captivated.[18] I soon discovered that what interested me most of all was the variety of roles women played.

On a cold Saturday in February 1989, I found myself joining the Tee Mamou women on their Mardi Gras run. Wearing the mask and suit I bought from a local artist, I climbed on the Mardi Gras' painted "wagon," a converted cattle trailer, ready to encounter the event firsthand. To my surprise, the first few hours dragged. It was rainy and freezing, and my feet were wet. The routine of getting off the truck, singing the Mardi Gras song, dancing, begging for coins, trying to find clever ways to clown, and then climbing back on the wagon for the next house visit was harder than I expected, and a bit monotonous. Then Suson Launey, a seasoned Mardi Gras who took me under her wing that year, offered me a few swigs from her bottle of schnapps. Suson likes to remind me of how, in her words, "You didn't do *any*thing" all morning long, until that drink. The next thing she knew, she says, I was sitting in a tree (a time-honored Mardi Gras trick) and ignoring captains' commands to come down.

Despite that moment of glory, I discovered that I'm not a very good Mardi Gras clown or beggar. Too shy, maybe, too inhibited, or just too much a Yankee. Five years later, I tried again. This time, I decided to get in the Mardi Gras spirit by drinking my first beer before eight o'clock in the morning and keeping up the pace throughout the day. By the end of the run, I could barely walk, sing, or dance, and didn't even notice that I had lost a contact lens somewhere along the route. I remember little of that day, but one Tee Mamou captain and Mardi Gras mentor periodically reminds me of my unladylike excesses. Although drinking is an accepted part of most Mardi Gras runs, becoming incapacitated is not; riders are expected to know their limits and respect them.

I learned a lot in those two runs, much of it how *not* to run Mardi Gras. My attempts gave me a deeper appreciation of the performance as a comedic and

Captains herd Basile women onto their Mardi Gras truck. After leaving the Town Park Barn at seven o'clock on Mardi Gras morning, the group makes a round of stops at homes and businesses in town, then heads into the countryside. Throughout the day, men and women ride on separate trucks, with the men's truck leading. Courtesy of Carl Lindahl.

physical art form, and great respect for those who do it well. Although peri- odically I say that I'll run Mardi Gras one more time—*next* year, when I'm in shape—I suspect that I've found my place trailing Mardi Gras runs and enjoying the show. Each year, I follow the Tee Mamou women on their weekend run, and over the years I've interviewed a number of maskers and their captains, some repeatedly. They may be surprised to see me still around for so many years, but the Tee Mamou women and men have been patient and forgiving of my field- work missteps.

My second Mardi Gras home is the nearby Evangeline Parish town of Basile. In 1991, Barry Ancelet and Carl Lindahl introduced me to the Basile *courir,* where men and women run Mardi Gras together. (At that point, Barry had been documenting various Mardi Gras runs for two decades. Carl Lindahl had ten years of Mardi Gras experience, and had recently begun doing research in Basile.) Through them, I met Helena Putnam and Vories Moreau, two of Basile's most skilled Mardi Gras, though Vories was largely retired by then. Vories and Helena in turn led me to other women and men in the Mardi Gras association, opening countless doors for me.

Basile maskers (called Mardi Gras) rush toward a house along their route. They dismount from their trucks only after a captain waves a white flag, the signal that a household has agreed to receive the group. Courtesy of Carl Lindahl.

Although I have yet to work up the courage to run Mardi Gras in Basile, I ride behind their Tuesday run (usually hitching a ride in a supply truck) and end my holiday at their *bal* that night. Members of the Basile Mardi Gras Association, like those in Tee Mamou, have always been extraordinarily generous in agreeing to interviews and making me feel welcome. One of my proudest professional moments took place when Carl Lindahl and I were named honorary members of the Basile Mardi Gras Association at the group's 1997 Mardi Gras dance.

The Cajun Mardi Gras research I began fifteen years ago was my first intensive folklore fieldwork project, and it has become my longest term and most

personally meaningful. Like other folklorists, I have found that fieldwork has led to friendships I prize greatly. My visits to Tee Mamou and Basile now include weddings, high school graduations, holiday dinners, too many funerals, and numerous other occasions. My partner, Kim Moreau, was born into one of Basile's most dedicated Mardi Gras families: his father Vories was a legendary Mardi Gras and captain, his mother Mary served as a women's captain and cooked the gumbo, and his older brother and sister ran at various times. Despite ruined knees and back, Kim unfailingly runs Mardi Gras in Basile each year, as does his son Brandon.[19] Through this second family and other Mardi

Gras friends, I've begun to understand the tradition's deeply felt connection to family and community.

Over the years, I've observed (sometimes with nostalgic regret) a number of changes in both the Tee Mamou and Basile runs, as captains die or drop out, routes shift, veteran Mardi Gras retire, and younger members are initiated. By necessity, I often generalize in my descriptions of these runs in the following chapters, but I also try to give a sense of their variability. My own perspective on women's Mardi Gras runs, too, has altered over time. I've found, for instance, that some aspects I focused on in earlier years are not considered important or typical by many participants.

I continue to research and write about Cajun Mardi Gras runs for many reasons. One is a conviction that both women's support roles and their innovative Mardi Gras performances deserve closer attention and analysis than they have yet received. A second reason is the emotional intensity that Mardi Gras runs hold for core members. To the Jennings woman who wondered why I study Mardi Gras and scoffed that it's "nothing," I would answer that it *is* something very important indeed to the women and men at the heart of it. Many endure hardship or inconvenience to run each year, get choked up when they talk about the celebration's importance in their own lives, and mourn when they are sidelined.

A final reason is my own reaction to the tradition: it makes me laugh, gives me joy, and often leaves me with goose bumps. Not every minute of every run—the customary chases after live chickens make me a bit queasy, and I find myself paying little attention to them. But each year, I am overwhelmed by moments of inspired comedy, the beauty of the Mardi Gras song, the palpable sense of camaraderie, and the vibration of dozens of feet stomping on a wooden floor as the Mardi Gras dance or "march" around the hall for each other, for their captains, and for us, their audience. It makes me cry, too.

Mardi Gras History

Mardi Gras runs derive from a centuries-old European tradition of masked begging processions, typically clustered around Christmas, New Year, and Carnival. These quests, known by various names, were widespread in medieval Europe.[20] Most were performed by young bachelors, viewed as marginal members of society, but occasionally, young women held their own festivities.[21] Postmedieval French celebrations are also significant antecedents to French Louisiana Mardi Gras runs. Descriptions of nineteenth-century enactments in Poitou, Berry, Bretagne, and other parts of France, for example, share many features of modern runs.[22] Midwinter festivals that still take place in some New World locales also share a strong family likeness to the Cajun Mardi Gras: la Chandaleur

Two female Mardi Gras admire a chicken captured in one of the day's many chicken chases. The Mardi Gras run is a quest for gumbo ingredients, and live chickens are among the most valued donations. Homeowners usually toss the bird into the air, and celebrants pursue it through muddy fields and drainage ditches. Courtesy of Bruce Morgan, Louisiana Office of Tourism.

Potic Rider, leader of the Basile Mardi Gras Association, gestures to hosts as he sings the Basile Mardi Gras song. The rest of the group kneels around him and chimes in on refrains, pumping their arms in the air. The song is performed during each house visit, after the group has danced for their hosts. Five or six singers take turns leading the song.

(Candelmas) and Mi-Carême (mid-Lent) in French Canada, la Guillonée (on New Year's Eve) in French Illinois and Missouri, Christmas mumming and similar celebrations in the Caribbean, African American Mardi Gras Indian processions in New Orleans, and German American Christmas house visits in south Louisiana.[23]

The early history of French Louisiana Mardi Gras runs remains undocumented. Most scholars suggest that the custom dates to eighteenth-century French and Acadian settlement in the region.[24] French-speaking Acadians came to south Louisiana from Canada, where they had settled a region of Canada known as L'Acadie, in what is now Nova Scotia. Expelled from their homes by the British in 1755, Acadian families were separated, herded onto prison ships, and exiled to various destinations, some of which refused to accept them. Some Acadians began trickling into Louisiana by the mid-1760s, and more followed over the next forty years. Here, their descendants, who called themselves Acadiens or 'Cadiens, became known as Cajuns among their English-speaking neighbors. In their new environment, the Cajuns created a new way of life and intermarried with other ethnic groups: Native Americans, Germans, Irish, Spanish, Continental French, and others. As some Cajuns moved westward from the rivers and swamps to the sparsely populated prairies, regional subcultures developed.[25] Today, rural Mardi Gras celebrations reflect these differences.[26]

By the late nineteenth century, and probably much earlier, Mardi Gras runs were well established in the sparsely populated prairie parishes. Brief newspaper accounts describe Cajuns and "Negro merrymakers" roaming rural neighborhoods, parading the streets of towns such as Iota and Church Point, and holding Mardi Gras dances in local dance halls.[27] Some runs were small, almost impromptu events, as young men got together to run Mardi Gras on horseback for a year or two, before disbanding or joining other neighboring groups. Other communities founded more lasting runs, whose histories stretched over decades and became, for many residents, an integral part of community identity.

The 1930s, 1940s, and 1950s saw a strong trend toward Americanization, and the Cajun French language and culture came to be stigmatized as backward, "country," and basse classe (lower class). Many Mardi Gras runs had reputations as disorderly and dangerous events, and their numbers declined as many households turned the riders away. Still, many rural communities maintained strong and resilient Mardi Gras runs throughout the prewar years. For poor subsistence farmers on the prairies, Mardi Gras runs and dances provided a rare break in a tedious routine, an important opportunity for socializing and courtship.

Prairie Cajun life in general, and Mardi Gras runs in particular, changed dramatically around the time of World War II. As the region shifted from subsistence farming to mechanized production, many people left the rural voisinages that supported Mardi Gras runs, finding work instead in small towns or on oil rigs. The war itself interrupted many (then all-male) Mardi Gras runs, as young men were called away for military service. A few runs made it through the war years without interruption, and others resumed as soon as possible afterward with only a handful of members. Rebuilding was slow work, and some runs never successfully regrouped.

Surviving runs saw a number of changes in the postwar years. Some groups switched from horses to trucks in the 1940s and 1950s, as the countryside emptied, stops became farther apart, and horses were scarce. Some Mardi Gras *courirs*, like Basile's, gradually began making most of their visits in town. Most runs also became more organized and regulated, as communities formed their own Mardi Gras associations to coordinate the event. Slowly, the image of the country Mardi Gras began to improve.

Still, membership in all-male Mardi Gras runs remained small in many communities during the postwar decades. Men's low level of participation provided an opportunity for women to take a more active role by forming their own "ladies' runs." The years from the mid-1940s through the 1970s—decades of enormous social change and shifting gender roles—saw a spate of women's Mardi Gras runs. These ladies' runs served as bridges, keeping the custom alive during a period of general disinterest. Eventually, some women's runs disappeared, and others merged with local men's runs. Only one community, Tee Mamou, continues to hold a separate women's run. Pioneering ladies' runs were transitional, granting women access to a tradition that routinely excluded them, but gradually giving way to more gender-integrated runs.

In the late 1960s and early 1970s, cultural activists sparked an ethnic pride movement aimed at preserving the local French language and culture. A second, more grassroots impetus followed in the 1980s.[28] Cajuns and Creoles began taking new interest in their traditional language, music, and foodways and other aspects of traditional culture. But even before these renaissance efforts, the country Mardi Gras run had become a pivotal symbol for cultural conservation. Revon Reed and Paul Tate revived the dormant Mamou run in 1951, as an early and major component of their project to revitalize the Cajun French language and culture.[29] The Mamou Mardi Gras run played an important part in nurturing Cajuns (Barry Ancelet, among others) who later became major figures in the renaissance.

Meanwhile, core members of several other community Mardi Gras runs had never lost their dedication to the tradition, and in many cases a few individuals and families had kept local *courirs* alive. Now they were joined by other, newly interested members. Horseback runs in Mamou, Church Point, and Eunice swelled to include hundreds of riders, many from other communities in the region. Other runs like those in Basile and Tee Mamou saw their membership grow on a smaller scale. Country Mardi Gras runs also began capturing the attention of television and newspaper reporters, folklorists, filmmakers, and tourists, further enlarging runs as well as audience size. Community runs and Mardi Gras street dances draw tourists to prairie towns such as Iota, Mamou, and Eunice.[30]

Today, the custom thrives among Cajuns and continues—though more tenuously—in several Creole communities. Its heart lies mainly in the prairie parishes west of Lafayette, in Acadia, St. Landry, Evangeline, Jeff Davis, and Allen Parishes. Over the last decade or so, long-dormant *courirs* have been reintroduced in Cajun communities such as Elton and Egan, based on oral histories of prewar runs. At least five towns also host children's runs on the weekend before Mardi Gras. Although the number fluctuates from one year to the next, as many as thirty runs, including men's, women's, and children's events, may take place during the Mardi Gras season. Internet websites and local newspapers make these events accessible to an ever larger audience, printing schedules for rural runs and posting photographs of previous years.

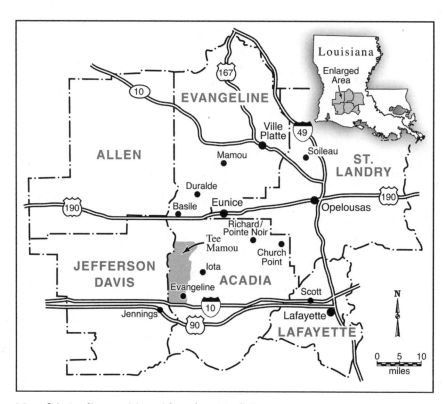

Map of six Acadiana prairie parishes where Mardi Gras runs are numerous.

About half of the Cajun runs taking place each year still bar women riders. Mamou and Church Point, perhaps the most famous horseback runs, steadfastly remain all-male, as do runs in Oberlin, Grand Marais, Elton, LeJeune Cove, and Grand Prairie. The number of mixed runs is rising steadily, giving women more Mardi Gras options than ever before. In Eunice, Basile, and Tee Mamou, women have run Mardi Gras for thirty years or more. The L'Anse Maigre run, once limited to men, began allowing women to join in 2003. New or revived *courirs de Mardi Gras* in Egan, Mermentau, Pecanière, Chataignier, and LeBleu include men and women, and sometimes entire families.[31] Perhaps more important, virtually all of today's children's Mardi Gras runs are open to girls and boys, training a new generation of Mardi Gras to carry on this key community festival.

Like all folklore forms, community Mardi Gras runs are conservative in many ways but constantly changing in others. Most, for example, have been influenced to some extent by the Carnival parades of New Orleans and other Louisiana cities. By the 1930s, improved transportation meant that a few Cajuns, at least, could occasionally visit Mardi Gras parades in New Orleans. Today, many small-town people watch, or even take part in, Mardi Gras parades in cities closer to home,

Mardi Gras surround a visiting photographer and untie his shoes, in a begging ploy that approaches extortion. Persistent Basile beggars will surround and immobilize a target until they receive enough coins or dollar bills to satisfy them. Courtesy of Carl Lindahl.

Basile captains and maskers return to town for a triumphant procession after a day of town and countryside visits. The maskers dance in pairs along Main Street, lined with people enjoying a street dance while they await the Mardi Gras. As their "march" ends, the group sings for and "picks at" (teases) the crowd. Afterward, many runners unmask to relax for a while.

especially Lafayette. For example, small-town high school marching bands are often invited to perform in urban Mardi Gras parades. Inevitably, Cajun runs have absorbed and appropriated some urban symbols: the green, purple, and gold Carnival colors, costume contests, strings of shiny plastic beads, feathered and sequined masks, and, in some places, Mardi Gras royalty, or "krewes," a New Orleans term for Carnival organizations.

Differences between urban and rural styles, however, are far more striking. New Orleans float parades are lavish spectacles passing along the city's main avenues, with tens of thousands of spectators. Cajun and Creole Mardi Gras runs are far smaller and more intimate; they meander along country roads and stop at farmhouses, putting on a show for a handful of watchers and followers. As Lindahl notes, the country Mardi Gras goes to the people, while New Orleans spectators travel to the parade route.[32]

The social dynamics of urban and rural Mardi Gras celebrations are also very different. De Caro and Ireland, among others, have noted the "aristocratic nature" of the New Orleans Carnival.[33] The oldest and most prestigious urban

Mardi Gras cooks Agnes Miller and Euta Young wait to serve the Basile Mardi Gras a hearty meal of chicken-and-sausage gumbo, their reward for a hard day of play. The group returns to their "hub" (now the Town Park Barn) in late afternoon, after their Main Street performance. The community is invited to come share the feast, after maskers and captains have been served. Courtesy of Carl Lindahl.

krewes are confined to the social elite who, riding high above the crowds, symbolically bestow their largesse on the masses. Those who run Mardi Gras, on the other hand, are often working-class members (once, mainly farmers) of small, tight-knit communities. Runs are organized not by exclusive and expensive krewes but by Mardi Gras associations with modest dues that most rural Cajuns can afford, generally between ten and twenty dollars.

*   *   *

Both Cajun women and men keep alive a key community tradition of running Mardi Gras. As women more actively engage in country Mardi Gras runs, powerful new readings of the festival emerge. This book describes the festive actions and presents the words of central female Mardi Gras performers—maskers and captains, as well as cooks and costume makers. It examines the complex meanings the tradition holds for them, and explores relationships between women's festive roles and their everyday lives. By looking closely at two very different Mardi Gras communities and their histories, this book also demonstrates how performance and meaning become localized and change over time. It demonstrates how and why women within the Cajun Mardi Gras tradition re-create the celebration, and their enterprise offers a splendid example of tradition and change.

1

Just Like Cinderella:
Women's Traditional Mardi Gras Roles

"That was the fun of it for the women. . . .
The cooking and then also making the costumes."
—Betty Pousson

"That was the big deal before Lent. So you lived it up
until midnight. Just like Cinderella."
—Betty Miller

The Cajun Mardi Gras celebration has often been described as a quint-essentially male event, staged by and for men. Popular author Harnett Kane commented in 1943 on the relative absence of women, calling the country Mardi Gras "a thing primarily for men and horses." Its "impromptu hell-raising," he reported, "has no place for the girls . . . although there is a happy *fais-do-do* [dance] in the evening."[1] And in fact Mardi Gras runs were—and still are to a great extent—displays of male prowess and mischief making. Running Mardi Gras allowed Cajun men to drink and carouse publicly, show off their horsemanship, chase chickens through muddy fields, "*faire le macaque*" (clown or make monkeyshines), and flirt with attractive girls.[2] Such no-holds-barred rowdiness might be acceptable for young men, at least on Mardi Gras, but it was definitely unacceptable behavior for girls and women during the period Kane describes.

Small wonder, then, that he noticed only men's performances. However, Kane gives us only part of the picture. Although girls and women did not mask and run Mardi Gras in most places, they were then and are still essential figures in the celebration. The Cajun Mardi Gras consists not only of men's public performances during house visits, but the gumbo and "happy *fais do-do*" that follow, as well as weeks of preparation beforehand. Each of these stages depends heavily on women's talents, energies, and resourcefulness.

Women's traditional contributions are often underestimated because they take place outside the limelight, part of women's "invisible culture" within their domestic realm.[3] In the Mardi Gras festival, as in everyday life, Cajun women have customarily been "supporters, sustainers and inspirers."[4] Behind the scenes, wives and mothers typically design and sew men's Mardi Gras costumes. They cook and serve *le gros gumbo* or "big gumbo," the late afternoon meal that nourishes and revives the exhausted riders, captains, and hosts and anyone else who wants to eat. Women are also drawn into the maskers' public performance during house visits: as hosts, as dance partners, as appreciative spectators, and as targets of practical jokes. Their presence is particularly crucial for the *bal de Mardi Gras* that night, a prime courtship opportunity. And finally, mothers and grandmothers instill the tradition in their children, coaching and supporting the next generation of Mardi Gras maskers and captains.

Women's prescribed Mardi Gras duties, drawing on their domestic skills, often involve hard or tedious work—but they also provide a valuable outlet for women's talents, imagination, and humor. Older women recall their pleasure in turning their needlework skills to making beautiful Mardi Gras costumes many years ago. Often they had little to work with but scraps and their own ingenuity. Generations of Cajun women have also taken pride in their ability to create a delicious gumbo under the challenging conditions of Mardi Gras. Mardi Gras cooks transformed drudgery into play by socializing and joking with each other, drinking a little whiskey, and playing tricks on the maskers. And Cajun women, married and unmarried, eagerly looked forward to the Mardi Gras dance, the biggest social occasion of the year, when they "lived it up until midnight, just like Cinderella," in Betty Miller's words.[5]

Women today will readily tell you that Mardi Gras is not just for the men's benefit; as a Tee Mamou woman asserted, "It's *our* tradition, too." Mardi Gras wives and mothers in Grand Marais, which hosts a men-only run, explained to folklorist Patricia Sawin in 1998 that women's and men's roles may differ, but both genders are equally engaged. One Grand Marais woman commented that when she was a child, "The way we were raised, that was [the men's] time" to mask and run Mardi Gras. But women "shared just as much fun," without the whippings that misbehaving male riders receive. She continued, "And you knew you were going to be chased around. The enjoyment was just made for everybody. . . . You had just as much fun as they did."[6]

This chapter explores how Cajun women mold the country Mardi Gras celebration through conventional and familial roles. (Chapter 3 describes women's more structured and official roles in Mardi Gras associations.) First, women's aesthetics and innovations forge the run's appearance, as they craft inventive and functional Mardi Gras suits, hats, and masks. Second, their culinary and organizational skills are central to the gumbo feast that, for many Cajuns, is the event's symbolic heart. Third, women's flexibility and humor come into play in their roles as audience members; women and girls readily hand over coins to the beggars, laugh at their pratfalls, and respond to teasing and chasing with good grace. Wives and mothers often follow the run throughout the day, assisting in countless unobtrusive ways and making sure the event flows smoothly. And finally, women's dedication to Mardi Gras ensures its survival; as women take their children to Mardi Gras dances or follow the riders along their route, they teach the next generation to value the community tradition.

To illustrate continuity and change, throughout this chapter I draw on women's descriptions of their roles in all-male Mardi Gras runs half a century ago, followed by accounts and my own observations of women's present-day involvement. In many ways, little has changed; women still perform many of their conventional duties, although technology has made their work easier. One key difference is that women now have more options for Mardi Gras participation. In addition to their behind-the-scenes work, some women now run Mardi Gras themselves and devise their own suits and masks, as well as their menfolk's. A few have turned their disguise-making skills into small businesses, selling dozens or more of their handmade masks to Mardi Gras runners, tourists, museums, and craft shops. Today, as fifty years ago, the country Mardi Gras is a vivid display of women's creativity and adaptability.

Life on the Prairies

For the first half of the twentieth century, most prairie Cajuns were subsistence farmers who lived frontier-like and often impoverished lives. Transportation was typically on foot or by horse and buggy, so they rarely traveled very far from home. Families were usually large, close-knit, and as self-sufficient as possible, with husbands, wives, and children all working together in the fields. Berline Boone, a sharecropper's daughter who grew up in the countryside near Eunice during the 1950s, recalls that farming was "hard work, but that's all we knew. Working in the cotton fields and digging sweet potatoes, because that was our way of life." Still, she calls her childhood a "wonderful life," in part because "there was a lot of time spent together with families, with kids and fathers and mothers."[7]

Girls and women were tied to home by necessity and custom. The late Agnes Miller of Basile, born in 1918, recalled that when she was young, "Women had their places at home, you know. You didn't go too much everywhere, years back."[8] Young girls in "olden times," as one observer wrote in the 1960s, were "always under the watchful eyes of their mother" and "exposed to few of the besetting sins of life."[9] Girls were closely chaperoned until they married in their early teens and began their own families. Married women were expected to be obedient wives, nurturing mothers, and frugal household managers. Cajun matriarchs typically kept a garden and a few hens, canned the vegetables and fruits they grew, made their own lye soap, and sewed their families' clothes and household linens. Typically, Cajun women's Mardi Gras activities were closely tied to their family lives, as they readied, fed, and supported husbands and sons who ran Mardi Gras. On Mardi Gras, women's domestic skills and responsibilities were recontextualized and became a crucial part of the festivities.

Making Disguises

One of women's most important Mardi Gras tasks has always been making Mardi Gras disguises. Farm wives in the past used their sewing skills to create multicolored, fringed Mardi Gras suits, hats, and sometimes masks for their menfolk. Mothers or other female relatives usually sewed a boy's first Mardi Gras costume, using whatever was at hand. As Elson Cart says, "It was the old mama had the job to do it. They'd have to do it the best they could."[10]

If a young man continued to run Mardi Gras after marriage, his wife usually took over making his suit. Evelyn Frugé, a native of Breaux Bridge, got involved with Mardi Gras after marrying Wade Frugé in the 1940s and moving to the countryside outside Eunice. She recalls, "He liked [Mardi Gras] so much, so I got interested in that, and I made a lot of suits."[11] Mr. Frugé described what kind of costume he wanted, and she bought material and sewed it. Like other wives, Evelyn Frugé took pride in creating "pretty suits" and matching *capuchons* (tall, cone-shaped hats) in bright colors such as red, yellow, or green, for him. Sometimes women had to make two suits: one for the daytime run, and a second for the dance that night.

During the Depression, rural Cajuns had little money to buy special fabric or decorations for Mardi Gras disguises. Inventive farm wives recycled whatever materials they had on hand to create memorable suits. Betty Pousson speaks proudly of her mother's ability to make suits of "anything she could get ahold of. . . . Everything she could think of."[12] Often, women sewed Mardi Gras suits—as well as everyday clothes and quilts—from the cloth sacks that rice, flour, and fertilizer were sold in. Sacks with printed designs could be used as they were, but plain white ones had to be dyed with beet juice or other coloring agents. Marion Courville, born in 1919, remembered his mother boiling plain sacks with colored clothes to make her husband's Mardi Gras suits.

> My daddy, when he was first running, you know, they had to make his suit with sacks. You know, long time ago, we used those white sacks of fertilizer. Okay, after we used the fertilizer, [my mother] goes and unsews all that string, you know. . . . And then she put them in a big old iron pot. . . . She put the water in there, and then she started boiling that water, and when it was really boiling good, you

know those days, when they buy a sweater, or a hat, anything, or skirt, anything they'd buy, it'd fade. It'd fade a lot, you know. They used to dye eggs with those things, too. And she put those sacks in there, you know. . . . [The dye would] bleed on it, and that's where she'd make the pants and the shirt. Oh, we was all excited with that, you know.[13]

Cajun women also created Mardi Gras suits by altering old clothes, including their own dresses. Mr. Courville first ran Mardi Gras when he was five or six years old, and, in his words, "We got a bunch of boys together" to run Mardi Gras on foot. In a 1992 interview, he recalled how his mother, Nora Courville, redesigned a straw hat and a long dress of her own to create a costume for her son. "She said, 'You can have my dress.' And she said I had to tie it up with the rope, you know, with a string, around [my waist], a big old long dress. And she had to kind of sew it a little bit so it wouldn't be too long, so I wouldn't trip. So I run on that. And then I had an old straw hat. What she did was she took an old cloth, you know, a red cloth, she put on top of my [hat]—and she sew it back on there. And that was my *capuchon*." Sometimes women simply added handmade fringe or colorful patches to everyday clothes to transform them into festive costumes. The late Vories Moreau remembered running Mardi Gras in Bayou Barwick as a boy in the 1930s, when an improvised suit was all his family could afford. In a 1991 interview with folklorist Carl Lindahl, he recalled: "When I was small, we were very, very poor. Everybody was poor back in the '30s because you know, it was the Depression then and my daddy was a cripple. And so my mama would sew me some—I had some coveralls—and she'd sew me some red strips of material and anything that she could find, she'd sew it on my pants and that's what I wore to Mardi Gras."[14] Vories, however, always envied the satin suits worn by a man named Renos Johnson, who always had "a pretty, pretty suit." As an adult, Vories ran Mardi Gras in Basile for many years and made sure that he always had a striking suit like those Renos had worn. "[The Johnsons] didn't have much money but he'd work and he'd make money so he'd buy his material. . . . He'd always have a pretty, shiny suit, like red and black or green and red. Man, I could see him for half a mile way back to the house, you know. I loved him and I admired him and I always thought it was so good, that suit was so good. And I'd say, 'When I get grown up, I'm going to work and I'm going to buy me some pretty material and I'm going to make me some pretty suits.' And brother, I did that. . . . I had some beautiful suits. Every year I had new suits—one to run in and one for the dance that night." A local seamstress, Ida Marcantel, made his suits for a while. When Vories married Mary Frugé in the 1940s, his mother-in-law Alita Frugé took over, with assistance from Mary. Like many prairie Cajuns of her generation, Alita Frugé spoke only Cajun French and had little or no formal education. And like other farm wives, she was resourceful; nothing went to waste and she was rarely idle. She learned to sew well, her grandson Kim Moreau says, because "You couldn't just go out and buy stuff [then], she had to make things." Alita also spun yarn, knitted, quilted, and wove rag rugs. Kim remembers, "She always had to be doing something with her hands."[15]

Mrs. Frugé possessed a remarkable talent for designing and sewing clothes, always working without a pattern; she could copy the latest fashions by studying store-bought clothes or pictures. Her grandson Kim says, "If she seen something, she could make it. If she couldn't make it by eye [by just looking at it], she'd take it apart" and figure it out.[16] Her sewing brought in a little extra money in her later years, when she made bridal gowns and bridesmaids' dresses for local women.

Alita's needlework skills were put to good use when she made Mardi Gras suits for her husband, Isaac, and son-in-law Vories Moreau. Vories described the kind of Mardi Gras suit he wanted, and Alita translated his vision into reality. Years later, Vories said of his mother-in-law: "She was a good seamstress. She couldn't speak English and she couldn't read and she couldn't go by a pattern and read what the pattern said, but she could just do it from up here [her mind], you know. She was a great seamstress. . . . And [she] made some of the prettiest [suits]." When daughter Mary and several grandchildren began running Mardi Gras, Alita made their suits as well. Kim, for example, first "dressed out" in a Mardi Gras suit created by his grandmother when he was two years old. Vories eventually became a *capitaine,* and Alita made his captain's outfit: a red satin cape and fedora covered in matching satin, both trimmed with black fringe and green sequins.

The entire Moreau family shared Vories's love of beautiful Mardi Gras suits. Never wealthy, they splurged on expensive fabrics that Alita transformed into one-of-a-kind masterpieces. She had a strong knack for design and color combinations, especially in fancier nighttime Mardi Gras suits. As her grandchildren reached their teens in the 1960s and 1970s, they requested even more elegant costumes, with intricate details: special collars, puffed sleeves, bell-bottom pants, or vests, for example. One of her most memorable suits for Mary Frugé had silver floral appliqués, hand-cut and sewn over pink satin. Mrs. Frugé spent months making as many as twelve suits a year for her family, according to Kim. He comments, "It wasn't just the suits, it was all the fringe. One suit might have a flat trim [fringe] and long trim, plus belt loops, pockets, [and] sashes to tie."[17] Many costumes were handed down from one Moreau to the next and are still treasured as family heirlooms.

For talented and creative women like Alita Frugé, making Mardi Gras suits was an artistic expression as well as a practical skill. Betty Miller of LeJeune Cove made suits for her husband, Hugh, in the 1940s and recalls that wives would "make a pride trying to make the prettiest costumes out of the bunch" for their husbands. Often, they invented distinctive designs to set their handiwork apart. A Mrs. Pousson of Acadia Parish is still remembered locally for putting together fabric scraps to create patchwork Mardi Gras suits in the prewar years. And older women can often describe, in detail, suits they made many decades ago.

Although wives and other female relatives made most Mardi Gras suits, sometimes men ordered custom-made suits from professional seamstresses, or paid a talented neighbor to make a suit. Alice Janot, born in 1906, is a longtime Eunice resident and a *traiteuse* (traditional healer) who held many jobs in her life, including seamstress. Mrs. Janot is gracious, hospitable, articulate, and proud of her handiwork. When I visited her at her comfortable brick home in Eunice, on April Fools' Day in 1992, we spent time looking at photographs of her family and the suits she created.

Over the years, Mrs. Janot made Mardi Gras suits for many male riders. In French-accented English, she spoke proudly of her work: "I'd make pretty Mardi Gras. I'd make *pretty* Mardi Gras. And I *loved* it."[18] She bought special fabric for her suits, and like Alita Frugé, she used no commercial patterns. Mrs. Janot explained: "You could go to town, and that was percale, what they called percale. On one side of the material it was natural, and on the other side . . . it was like a shine, like a satin or like that. And it was *cheap*. . . . And then you—well, there was no pattern. I had to take your height, shoulders, and I had my tablet, from shoulder to shoulder, your waistline, height, what size, what kind of suit you wanted. Understand? I'd put that down, and how long the waist had to come, that coat. Then the length of your pants. But as I did that, I'd have all your sizing." She then cut the pieces out, sewed them, and trimmed the suit in strongly contrasting colors. She invented unique details for her suits, depending on the style. Stars were one particular trademark, she says. "It's different styles [of suits], sometimes it was a big square collar I'd make with that, and I'd put a big star in the corner of the collar. That looked beautiful. Now, in the corner of the collar, I liked to put two stars, in the back there, and fringes all around it. . . . It was prettier than what they have today. Well, it was so different, anyway. I'm not going to say prettier because they do have pretty suits, you know. And I loved it. I loved them all."

Cajun Mardi Gras outfits usually included a hat covered in the same fabric as the suit. Pointed *capuchons* were the most common, but some Mardi Gras riders wore flat mortarboards or, less frequently, bishop's miters. Older men, for instance, often preferred mortarboards because they were less awkward than the tall *capuchons*. Whatever the style, women typically did all the sewing on Mardi Gras hats. A male masker might shape his own *capuchon*, twisting a sheet of cardboard into a cone that fit snugly on his head. The woman of the house then took over, sewing a fabric cover for it and attaching an elastic strap or fabric ties. The *capuchon* cover, which usually matched the *suit de Mardi Gras*, included a fabric drape to cover the wearer's hair, ears, and the back of his neck. Sewing a *capuchon* was (and is still) the most difficult part of making a costume; it required care and skill to cut out the shape all in one piece, hand-sew it inside out, and then invert and slip the fabric over the cardboard cone.

Trimming the hat was equally important, and women wound fringe, pom-pons, rickrack, or sequins around it. Alice Janot always made a little tassel on the top of her *capuchons*. The final touch was sewing bells on both suit and *ca-puchon*. Mrs. Janot said, "And then we have the Mardi Gras bells, you know, we had those then! And I'd buy them or I'd supply them with the bells . . . for the costume and for the hat. And when you'd shake, it would ding-a-ling-ding-ding, you know." Mrs. Janot's perfectionism, and her sense of herself as an artist, was evident as she recalled, "I'd make pretty Mardi Gras. . . . I enjoyed it. . . . And I was proud. I was a proud little woman." Her philosophy in making Mardi Gras suits was "When you do it, do it right or don't do it [at all]. . . . I even would make the blankets, to put over your horses. Yeah, a matching blanket. If you wanted to."

Mrs. Janot never actually ran Mardi Gras in the countryside, but later in life she began masking to ride in the Eunice Mardi Gras truck parade that precedes the horseback procession along Main Street. She also "dressed out" to compete for prizes at the city's Mardi Gras dance, investing the same care, creativity, and pride in her own suits as her commissioned costumes. She boasted, "I could show you some of my pictures, I won prizes and prizes with *my* own costume." Like many other Cajun women, then, Alice Janot moved into the Mardi Gras spotlight after many years behind the scenes.

Although piecing and stitching Mardi Gras suits and hats was traditionally women's work, making masks was not necessarily. Masks could be made from many different materials, which were more or less gendered: anything that re-quired sewing was likely to fall to women. Women, for example, typically made the fabric masks that some runners wore. One type was made of cheesecloth, stiffened with a flour-and-water paste and shaped to the wearer's face. Other fabric masks, made of oilcloth-like material, simply hung down in front of the face.

Women were less likely to make the wire screen masks popular with many male Mardi Gras, perhaps because stiff window screen was difficult to cut and shape. In the pre–World War II years, men often bought manufactured screen masks at local mercantile and grocery stores.[19] Alice Janot recalled, "At that time you could buy [wire screen masks] for a dime, for fifteen cents." Some masks already had features painted on them, but older residents also recall buying an undecorated screen base and painting it themselves.

Other men chose to make their own wire masks, cutting and bending pieces of door and window screen to conform to their faces. Usually they painted features on the mask, or in some communities, stitched decorations such as corncobs, horsehair, or chicken feathers onto it. Wives usually added finishing touches on screen masks, sewing a fabric border around the edges to cover stray wires. Sometimes they lined the mask with fabric or an old nylon stocking to make it more opaque. Alita Frugé, for example, used material that matched her husband Isaac's suit to line the mask he made from a screen door.

Women did sometimes make entire wire screen masks for sons or husbands. Marion Courville recalls the day in the mid-1920s when his mother made his first (undecorated) screen mask from start to finish. "I had pulled out a screen door—they didn't have too many screens those days. Anyway, [my mother] finally found a piece. Then she put it on my face like that and then she punched it [out] like that . . . for my nose, you know. She made a little place where my nose [fit]. . . . And put a little thing around so it wouldn't blister me, you know, cut me. *Mais* [but] boy I loved it. . . . She didn't paint nothing [on it]. It was just the screen. They couldn't recognize you."

Today, making Mardi Gras suits remains an almost exclusively female task, and women still make suits for their husbands and sons. But in some communities, they also make disguises for themselves. Sewing the suits is easier and faster than it once was. Women can cut their fabric out with the help of a commercial pajama or clown suit pattern, and stitch it on sewing machines. They can also choose from a much wider variety of materials. In the weeks before Mardi Gras, women search local stores for distinctive fabric and trim. Most women prefer bright prints, often juxtaposed with contrasting solid colors.

Sewing may be easier today than it once was, but finding time to sew is a problem for many modern women. Making costumes, whether their own or their husbands' and sons', is likely to be squeezed in between work schedules and other family responsibilities. Berline Boone, who runs Mardi Gras in Basile, remembers staying up all night one year to finish her gorilla costume, after getting off work at midnight. She finished the suit just in time to run Mardi Gras the next morning.

Sandy Sonnier, also of Basile, does not run Mardi Gras herself. But like generations of women before her, she makes Mardi Gras suits for the men in her family. Most years, she creates a new suit or mends an older one for her husband, Russell ("Potic") Rider, and her son Shane Lavergne. At times she has also made suits for her two grown stepsons and for Shane's young daughter.

Years ago, Potic's mother and aunt made his suits, beginning right after New Year's day. For Sandy, who works six days a week at the Basile Post Office, sewing and hand-cutting strips of fabric into fringe is usually a last-minute task. Sewing a basic suit is not very time-consuming, but hand-cutting material into a fringe does take some time. (The hardest and most frustrating job, Sandy says, is cutting out fabric for the *capuchon*.) Although Potic may describe the basics of what he wants in a suit, the details are up to her. Sandy recalls, "One year I put ... all color of rickrack, and I cut out little squares [of fabric]" to create a patchwork effect.[20] Her more elaborate suits take days to create, however. In 2003, she used two hand-pieced quilt tops she inherited from her grandmother to make Shane's suit, which she lined and reinforced with stronger fabric. Another year, she spent many hours cutting apart Crown Royal whiskey bags to make a special purple flannel Mardi Gras suit her stepson requested.

Most Mardi Gras suits are homemade, but professional seamstresses also custom-make suits and *capuchons*. Another alternative is to buy an entire ready-made Mardi Gras disguise, complete with screen mask, from a local maker. These are available from several shops in Eunice (though locals are likely to find the prices there exorbitant, geared to tourists), or from a handful of local women who make and sell disguises from their homes.

One major change in Mardi Gras disguise is that more women are now directing their imaginations and talents to crafting masks, especially in communities that require handmade masks. Women's masks often resemble local men's masks, but they also reflect women's own aesthetics, priorities, and senses of humor. Although women's masks are highly individual and differ from one community to the next, they share certain characteristics. For one thing, they must be comfortable as well as striking; female Mardi Gras do not want their faces torn or mashed by poorly fitting masks. As a result, women mask makers experiment with a variety of new materials, tools, and techniques. Another common feature of women's mask making is its improvisational and whimsical nature. Makers recycle everyday objects in unlikely ways, often drawing on symbols of domesticity and femininity: feather dusters, shoulder pads, pantyhose, yarn, and sewing notions, among others. Lou Trahan of Egan, for example, uses hosiery stuffed with cotton to create absurdly long noses and fat lips, a trick she remembers seeing when she was a girl. Hattie Freeman of Eunice makes masks out of plastic milk jugs, turning the handle into a nose. Women mask makers, like other women artists, value the process as much as the product. Some view their masks as works perpetually in progress, adding a touch here and there over the years. The creative process often becomes collaborative as friends suggest additional details.

Many communities have inventive mask makers, both male and female. But the Tee Mamou women's Mardi Gras run has produced a disproportionate number of creative artists, perhaps because handmade masks are both mandatory and, by community tradition, highly adorned. When women began running Mardi Gras there, they found that wire screen masks rubbed and irritated their faces; as Suson Launey comments, "A woman's face scratches easy."[21] The community's female mask makers have solved the comfort issue in various ways.

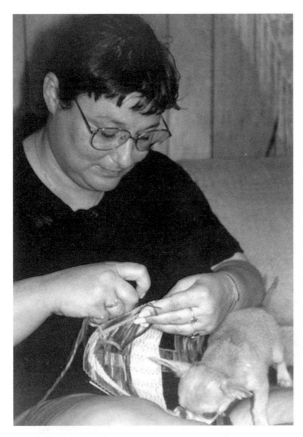

Suson Launey stitches a needlepoint mask at her home in Iota. Suson began crafting masks upon joining the Tee Mamou women's run almost twenty-five years ago. Now she is perhaps the region's most prolific mask artist, and her imaginative creations are prized by other Mardi Gras runners and by collectors. Courtesy of Maida Owens.

Jackie Miller devised a double-layered mask with a stiff screen on the outside to hold the mask's shape, and a lightweight mesh behind it for comfort. Renée Frugé Douget binds the edges of her screen masks with hot glue to cover stray wires, and then liberally pads the edges with foam rubber.

Suson Launey's needlepoint masks are an excellent example of how women are artfully redesigning Cajun Mardi Gras disguises, making them more comfortable in the process. Suson, who once considered an art career, began making her own masks and suits when she joined the Tee Mamou run twenty-three years ago. Like many women, she found that metal screen masks gouged her as she clowned and tangled with captains. She says, "Our group is rough. To run with a screen mask, my face would look like hamburger—it gets all scratched up."[22] As a solution, she began stitching yarn masks onto flexible plastic screen. Not only is her needlepoint mask more "wearer friendly," she says, but also "it was something to hold true to the tradition of a screen mask."[23] Soon other revelers asked her to make masks for them; some women—and at least one man—started

Tee Mamou woman wearing a needlepoint mask, a style invented by Suson Launey in her search for more comfortable masks. Suson's innovations in mask design have helped shape the appearance of her community *courir,* and needlepoint masks are now a hallmark of the Tee Mamou women's run. Courtesy of Barry J. Ancelet.

making their own versions. Needlepoint masks have become a hallmark of the Tee Mamou women's run, and are seen in smaller numbers in the local men's run. Suson now makes hundreds of masks, both screen and needlepoint, each year for fellow Mardi Gras, tourists and collectors, and museum collections. Although she still paints occasionally, mask making has become Suson's primary aesthetic expression, as well as a source of income.

Some communities prefer simply painted wire screen masks, but Tee Mamou Mardi Gras like plenty of three-dimensional decoration. Tee Mamou women's masks in particular reflect many of the artistic modes common to women's art. Like the women's altars Kay Turner describes, they tend toward certain "aesthetic principles" such as layering, accumulation, and embellishment.[24] Tee Mamou women imaginatively combine scraps of fabric, fur or hair, yarn, pipe cleaners, feathers, plastic insects, miniature animals, and costume jewelry to create multilayered and multitextured designs. Their collage-like creations reflect what feminist folklorists have termed "femmage"—women's creative combination and juxtaposition of fragments, "bits and pieces of materials that signify specific moments and relationships in the life of the creator," into an artistic whole.[25]

Suson Launey tries to whip captains with a water hose during the Tee Mamou women's run. Suson, a role-player par excellence, is among the run's most mischievous participants. She says that to be a good Mardi Gras, "You've got to be bad"—and she comments, "I'm very good."

Suson Launey exhibits her Mardi Gras masks at the 1991 Louisiana Folklife Festival in Eunice. Suson, like a few other mask makers, has become a spokeswoman for her community run, part of its public face. She frequently demonstrates mask making and talks about running Mardi Gras at festivals, museum programs, and other public events. Courtesy of Greg Wirth.

Most Tee Mamou women learn to make masks by watching others and then experimenting. Janice Ashford, like many Tee Mamou Mardi Gras, began making her own masks soon after she started running Mardi Gras in the 1980s. She says: "I just sat and decided to try it. And from seeing others. You know, in fact the very first one that I made, I had made out of—it's like the hardware cloth, it's the real soft stuff. And that didn't work real well. So I went and got the regular [wire] screen and put tape around it so it wouldn't scratch my face, and then I went with the bias tape. And then I lined [it] because you could see through it, and painting it would have defeated the purpose because air couldn't get through it. So I put like a cheesecloth backing so the air could still get through . . . and you still couldn't see [my face]."[26] Janice's masks reflect the whimsy typical of Tee Mamou women's masks. Her earliest mask has huge stuffed ears, big satin lips, a polka dot fabric nose, and wig hair. She says, "And I have no idea why I stuffed the ears, I just did."

Women's masks are a reflection of spontaneity and creativity, incorporating almost anything to create a weird or "ugly" effect. The makers may have a general design in mind when they begin a mask, but for the most part they improvise. Linda Frugé Doucet says, "When I was putting a mask together, whatever would come to mind, I'd do it."[27] Similarly, Janice Ashford recalls of the masks she made, "There [isn't] really any plan to it, you just look at it and go from there. I guess it's like a painter. You know when you get started, you just don't know where it's going to stop. . . . And nothing matches." As women borrow ideas from each other, a particular innovation can quickly show up on many masks, as Suson Launey's needlepoint technique did.

One of the most notable features of Tee Mamou women's masks is their fanciful humor. Although masks are supposed to be "ugly" and even scary, the effect is often more comical than frightening. Plastic spectacles rest on the nose of a wildly hairy mask, a rubber rat or alligator sits on a protruding tongue. Women sometimes personalize masks for friends by incorporating private jokes or references. For instance, Suson Launey remarks, "I made one for a friend of mine, his nickname is Frog, so I made it green and it looked like a frog. . . . One time I made me a mask that had a big old mouth with a tongue sticking out. That's me, you know, a big mouth. If you make it personal, you pick something that works and go with that."[28]

Many women make masks for their own use, but a handful of Tee Mamou women make masks on a larger scale to donate or sell to other riders, and to sell at craft shops and festivals. Suson Launey is one example. Renée Frugé Douget is another prolific mask maker, although now, as a wife and new mother, she has less time for her craft than she did some years ago. Renée grew up in the country Mardi Gras tradition: her father, Gerald, was Tee Mamou's head *capi-taine* for many years. Her mother, Linda, who ran Mardi Gras for two decades or more, usually got together with a friend to make their masks. Renée first ran Mardi Gras in 1989 at thirteen and started making masks soon afterward. She developed her own tastes and techniques partly by watching her mother and partly by trial and error.

Renée still prefers wire screen masks because she considers them the most traditional style, but she uses a galvanized wire screen that can be cut with scissors. She cuts the screen freehand, without a pattern, and explains "I just kind of judge it, like with cooking."[29] Like other female mask makers, Renée has explored ways to make her masks more comfortable. At first, she folded the edges of the screen twice, but then she discovered that she could bind the cut edges with hot glue from her glue gun. The glue not only prevents unraveling but also gives the edges a transparent finish so they don't need a cloth border.

One of Renée's favorite materials to work with is colored silicone gasket maker, which she remembers her mother using. She says, "I remember Mom making a mask [for me] . . . and I remember the silicone because she made this big wart on my nose, and I loved the way it felt, I thought it was so neat. So I looked all over for silicone, [and] I finally found it."[30] Today she rims her masks' eyes with silicone, and sometimes creates long pointed noses. One of her own innovations is casting noses and mouths from hot glue, using store-bought plastic "gag" features as molds. Once the glue is dry, she paints the features with at least three coats of paint. The glue lips and noses are not only cheap to make but also adhere better to the masks; any drips that form during casting only add to their ugliness. Renée also favors popular craft materials such as puff paint, which she dries in the microwave or with a hair dryer.

Renée, like many Tee Mamou women, likes wire screen masks made opaque with glued-on fur, feathers, scraps of burlap, and other materials. She says, "I find that a lot of the masks I sell, [the Mardi Gras] like to be hidden behind it. That way, they like to go behind someone they know, and stand right behind them. That way, whenever they turn around, [we] can look them straight in the eyes, you know, and we can have a big smile on our face, and they can't tell who we are. And they're sitting out there trying to figure it out."[31] Her masks, like many Tee Mamou masks, have a feral look, with snouts, fangs, and beaks as well as abundant hair. After seeing the 1993 documentary film *Dance for a Chicken: The Cajun Mardi Gras,* which suggests a link between medieval "wild man" imagery and today's animal-like masks, Renée felt she had found one possible explanation. In a 1996 interview, she commented that "I always made mine kind of resemble animals, and I didn't know why [then], but I just did."[32] Among her favorite masks are those covered with wig hair, because they are scariest.

Renée commented in 1996 that she decorates masks with "whatever Mom has hanging around the house."[33] Often she raids her mother's sewing box for inspiration, and she has incorporated zippers, rickrack, and an empty thread spool in her designs. She also stocks up on commercial items such as miniature beer cans, rubber ants and spiders, and plastic eyes. Some of her most unusual masks have been inspired by discount store finds: cheerleading pompons from Toys R Us, and a bag of fabric flowers from Wal-Mart.

Renée, like other women mask makers in Tee Mamou, enjoys the process of making masks. She comments that once the mask's main features are in place, she adds other details, often until she gives away or sells the mask. She says, "This is something else I do—I add later" as finishing touches occur to her or a friend suggests a new detail.[34]

Tee Mamou women mask makers, then, find imaginative new uses for domestic materials such as sewing supplies, pieces of women's clothing, and junk jewelry. The masks also reflect aesthetics, skills, and processes traditionally associated with women. Somewhat ironically, the region's most prolific mask makers now are women, and several have successfully built cottage industries around mask making. Today more than ever, then, women's handiwork in making suits, *capuchons,* and masks provides the celebration's central images.

Le Gros Gumbo

Another aspect of the Mardi Gras run that depends heavily on women's talents is the community feast that concludes the daytime run.[35] For many participants, the gumbo is the celebration's real focus, an expression of cooperation and reciprocity among neighbors. As the *Basile Weekly* reminded readers in 1990, "The traditional gumbo is as much a part of the celebration as the 'Run.'"[36] Decades ago, prairie Mardi Gras runs ensured that everyone in the rural *voisinage* survived the lean midwinter months. Each family contributed whatever ingredients they could afford, and everyone filled up on bowls of gumbo.

Most Cajun men are just as skilled as women at making a good gumbo, but women are typically the main cooks on Mardi Gras day. (Older men no longer able to run sometimes help out, especially with cleaning and cutting up chickens. In one or two places, men are completely in charge of the gumbo.) Mardi Gras gumbo preparation is especially demanding, as the cooks make and then serve huge quantities of chicken-and-sausage gumbo, rice, and, in some Acadia Parish runs, potato salad to accompany the thick soup. Often they work over butane burners in improvised kitchens (and in the past, on open fires outside). The task relies on women's organizational skills and flexibility as well as their culinary skills, as they must carefully judge when to add various ingredients, making sure that the meal is ready but not overcooked when the riders arrive. In years past, male riders' mothers or wives were expected to help with cooking and serving. Often, the *capitaine*'s wife was in charge, and the feast was prepared at her house. Later, most gumbos moved to community or church halls, many with kitchens.

Betty Miller remembers helping to cook the gumbo for LeJeune Cove during the 1940s. She had little involvement in Mardi Gras—beyond going to the dance as a young girl—until she married Hugh Miller, an avid Mardi Gras. The wives, she says, cooked on an open fire outside the captain's house. They used huge cast-iron pots, normally reserved for boiling clothes on washday or for *boucheries.* Mrs. Miller says: "Every Mardi Gras would have a wife or mother that helped. As many men that were doing Mardi Gras, there was that many women who were preparing the meals. The captain's wife took over. Whoever had it at her house, she directed. But I mean there wasn't too many instructions because they all knew what they had to do. So everybody just pitched in and did the gumbo." Making the gumbo was a difficult and time-consuming chore. The women had to meet the riders along their route, pick up the chickens they had collected so far, and then kill, pluck, scald, and cut them up before adding them to the gumbo. Betty Miller describes the tedious process: "And the chickens had to be scalded and cleaned because they gave you live chickens and you had to come back home. About noon that day they would have a certain place where the wives would meet the Mardi Gras and [the riders] would pick up everything they had picked up that morning and bring it back to the captain's house and prepare the chickens and the sausage and whatever else had to be gotten. Maybe in the middle of the afternoon they would meet in another spot [to collect the remainder of the day's spoils]." Farmers often saved their oldest hens or roosters for the Mardi Gras, and the tough meat took hours of cooking to tenderize.

Despite the hard work, women made cooking the gumbo into a festive social occasion. The daughter of a former Tee Mamou *capitaine* remembered women gathering at her mother's house to cook the gumbo. As they prepared the gumbo and awaited the riders' return, the women "took a nip" of whiskey and talked and laughed together. The maskers, hungry but "full of vim and vigor," arrived and joked with the women, who often reciprocated with practical jokes of their own. She said: "When the Mardi Gras said, 'Oh, we had a good time today,' Mother said, 'Well, we did too. We made gumbo . . . and we had a little nip here and there. . . . But boy, we had a terrible accident. A big old rat came and fell into the gumbo.' But she said she couldn't get over the look on their faces when she said that, because they were starving."[37] This, she commented, was "the fun of it for the women. . . . The cooking and then also making the costumes."

Today, the Mardi Gras gumbo's community function is largely symbolic—few people are in danger of starving. Still, the meal remains at the heart of the run. In towns like Eunice, preparing the gumbo has become a much larger-scale undertaking than in the past, as hundreds of riders and spectators must be served. Although a few larger runs now hire cooks, in the majority of community runs, women and some men continue to volunteer their time and skill.

Agnes Miller, affectionately known to everyone in Basile as "Miss Agnes," was a head gumbo cook for many years for the Basile Mardi Gras Association. When they added a children's run on the Sunday before Mardi Gras, she made the gumbo for that as well. In a region full of good cooks, Miss Agnes was known as an exceptionally skilled one. She helped support her family at various times as a short-order cook, and worked (more for pleasure than necessity by then) at Basile's popular Chunky's Drive-In until shortly before her death in 1998.

On Mardi Gras morning, Agnes Miller arrived at the Woodmen's Hall (in later years, at the Basile Town Barn) soon after the riders had departed. Throughout the day, as the Mardi Gras sang and begged their way through town and the countryside, Miss Agnes and coworkers Euta Young and Alida Young were kept busy in a small kitchen. Surrounded by electric rice cookers, they gradually put together two forty-eight-gallon pots of chicken gumbo to feed dozens of Mardi Gras, onlookers, and musicians when they returned at four o'clock.

When Agnes Miller first volunteered to make Basile's Mardi Gras gumbo, the cooks still had to scald and clean the captured chickens. Mrs. Miller recalled in a 1991 interview, "The first year I cooked that for the Mardi Gras . . . oh, I thought we'd *never* get through plucking them so we could cook them."[38] These days Basile, like many communities, buys many of its gumbo ingredients in advance, including jars of commercially made roux, and as many as forty pounds of chicken already cleaned and cut up. Still, the task requires considerable planning and coordination. Describing their work, Miss Agnes explained, "We have to wash all that meat, you know, and then dissolve that *roux*. And cut some onions to put in that gumbo, and fix the tables, hoping [the Mardi Gras will] come in [soon]." During the day, volunteers brought the cooks any donated sausage, rice, onions, or chicken quarters, and the women added them as needed to the gumbo or saved them for after–Mardi Gras suppers.

Miss Agnes and the other cooks knew each other well and worked together smoothly and cooperatively. But Miss Agnes explained that she had the final word: "It depends on *my* say-so to put whatever is to be put in the gumbo . . . because I have to say how much or when." Part of the art of gumbo making is knowing just when to add each ingredient. If chicken is cooked in the roux too long, it falls off the bone. The group prefers mature laying hens or roosters to young chickens, because they hold up better in the cooking process. Mrs. Miller said, "I don't put my meat before two o'clock. Because the hens that I'm cooking, they'll be cooked enough. Because they've had times before that somebody has cooked [the hens] and the meat was all undone, you know. . . . So I usually say when the meat goes in the juice."

While the gumbo simmered and rice pots steamed, the women set up their serving tables with bowls, cutlery, napkins, and saltine crackers. (For many years, Basile used real crockery, and the cooks had to wash dishes as well. When the group's gumbo moved to the Town Barn, they switched to plastic plates and utensils.) As they worked, according to Miss Agnes, the cooks were "kind of anxious for [the Mardi Gras] to come to the building." When the maskers finally arrived in the late afternoon, the riders danced around the hall, two by two, in a special "march" for the cooks before lining up to eat. Miss Agnes and her helpers worked as a team to serve bowls full of gumbo, first to the maskers, captains, and musicians, then to the public. One year, so many people came to eat gumbo that none was left for the musicians playing the dance that night, and Mrs. Miller had to make another pot at the last minute.

Agnes Miller understood the importance of her contribution to the celebration. Each year, organizers called on Miss Agnes; she says, "'You'd better be ready,' they'd tell me, you know, they want me to cook. And so I always end up cooking, me and some other women. . . . It makes you feel good when you hear them say, 'Boy, the gumbo was good.' And I love to cook." In appreciation for her work, the Basile Mardi Gras Association awarded her a plaque in 1987; in 2003, the group again honored Miss Agnes, this time posthumously.

Since Miss Agnes's death, a younger generation of women and men has taken over Basile's Mardi Gras gumbo, but it is often a scramble to find enough volunteers. Many local women now work or run Mardi Gras themselves. Peter LeBlanc, whose mother, "Nin," was once a Mardi Gras captain and cook, is usually in charge of actually cooking the gumbo, with help from at least one assistant. However, almost all of the ingredients are processed in advance: chickens are cut up, the *roux* comes in a jar, and the captain's wife has already diced the onions, green onions, parsley, and so on.

By mid afternoon, the gumbo servers arrive and begin organizing their folding tables. A trio of women—Sandy Sonnier, her sister Nanette, and Carolyn Bertand—have developed a well-choreographed assembly line approach to serving over the years. By the time the maskers return to the barn, the women have plastic cups of Coke, Diet Coke, Dr. Pepper, and Sprite lined up in rows on one table, and rice pots, plastic bowls and spoons, and paper napkins each holding a few saltine crackers on another. Chicken meat and sausage have been spooned out of the gumbo pot and placed in a large metal bowl on the serving line. When the Mardi Gras arrive after their street dance on Main Street, Carolyn spoons a mound of rice in a bowl, Nanette places chunks of meat in the bowl, and Sandy ladles "juice" or broth over it. Typically they serve about two hundred people, some of whom come back for seconds and thirds. After everyone has been served, the cooks and servers finally sit down at picnic tables to enjoy their own gumbo. In 2004, Nanette, Sandy, and Carolyn received a plaque of appreciation from the Mardi Gras association in thanks for their service, just as Agnes Miller had seventeen years earlier.

As Mardi Gras runs have evolved into larger and more public events, women's responsibility for preparing the gumbo has taken on an ironic twist. While women prepare everyday meals, it is usually men who do festive cooking.[39] On Mardi Gras, women take over what is essentially the male performance of public cooking, in an odd kind of role reversal. A further inversion took place when women first began running Mardi Gras: in some places, at least, their husbands made the gumbo. Years ago, for example, when the Basile women's run took place on the weekend before Mardi Gras, men in the local Mardi Gras association cooked and served their gumbo feast.

House Visits

Many of women's traditional Mardi Gras roles are relatively private and closely connected to their domestic domain. But women also routinely get pulled into the men's public performance, as house visits bring the celebration to their doorsteps. Wives, along with their husbands, serve as hosts and offer the riders customary gifts of gumbo ingredients or money. In the past, the woman of the house might offer the hungry riders a snack of baked sweet potatoes, homemade doughnuts, *boudin* (a rice and pork sausage), boiled eggs, or hot chocolate. Most of the foodstuffs that maskers stole or received—chickens, eggs, and garden produce—were products of women's work and sources of their income. House visits, then, were symbolic raids on women's traditional domestic realms—although captains and maskers politely thanked *le maître* and *la maîtresse* for their generosity before leaving.

Half a century ago, and still today, entire families often stood on the porch for these house visits. Girls and women of all ages enjoyed watching the maskers sing, dance, clown, and chase live chickens. Anne Marie Leger recalls, "We gave them a chicken when they come [to our house], you know, and that was the fun of it, [watching them] chasing up the chicken."[40] More important, Mardi Gras visits gave young men a chance to mingle and flirt with the household's unmarried girls.

Girls and women were often targets for the masqueraders' mischief, as the men tried to find an attractive dance partner. If they couldn't find a willing partner, the men resorted to trickery. One older Mardi Gras describes how one or two men would clown and divert the captains' attention, while others picked out the girls and women they wanted to dance with. Maskers might chase a reluctant young woman, grabbing her and sweeping her into a dance. These symbolic abductions were brief and generally playful, but they reinforced traditional notions of men as sexual pursuers and women as the pursued.

If women met up with the Mardi Gras away from the safety of home, they were vulnerable to rougher treatment. Kane wrote in the 1940s, "On the road, when [the Mardi Gras] met a lone . . . woman . . . she was the object of fulsome attention. One of the clowns requested the honor of the dance. The lady might decline, but she was danced with whether she liked it or not."[41] An elderly Acadia Parish man recalled watching a male Mardi Gras waylay a woman and child in a horse-drawn buggy many years ago, grabbing the horse's bridle, spooking it, and almost overturning the carriage.

Not surprisingly, women generally avoided meeting the revelers on the road, and frequently kept their distance during house visits. Agnes Miller remembered that when she was a girl, her father didn't want her to associate too closely with the masqueraders, so she watched from the safety of her porch. She explained, "They'd dance and we'd get out on the porch to see them, but we didn't go mix with the Mardi Gras."[42] Shy or frightened young women hid in the house and refused to come out. Vories Moreau says that when he ran Mardi Gras in the 1950s, "I think [homeowners] were scared, they'd keep them [women] . . . in the house. They'd look at you through the windows and stuff like that, you know." He adds, "But boy, if you could get you one outside for you to dance with, that was a big thing, you know. It's true, you'd grab her and boy, then the other Mardi Gras would want to dance with her and you didn't want [them to], and it was a big hullabaloo."[43]

Mardi Gras were strictly forbidden to enter houses masked and uninvited; doing so was grounds for expulsion from the run, or even violence by the home-owner. However, then, as now, the riders played with the house façade, stopping just short of going inside. Elson Cart, who ran Mardi Gras in the prewar years, likes to tell the story of an attractive young woman who refused to leave the safety of her home one year during the group's visit. He rose to the challenge and surprised her by kissing her through an open window. Later, he married her. In this case at least, the run worked just as it was supposed to, helping men to find and win wives. At the end of each house visit, the riders invited their hosts, especially those with eligible daughters, to their gumbo and the Mardi Gras dance later that evening.

Today, women still provide an appreciative audience and foils for the Mardi Gras' clowning. Girls and women not only await the riders at houses along their route but also follow them in cars throughout the day. Women onlookers, like men, are active participants in the Mardi Gras performance, although they are usually assigned the role of straight man (or woman). Now, as fifty years ago, male Mardi Gras show off for, amuse, chase, and tease young women during house visits. Today symbolic abductions are more explicit than in the past: a young man is likely to playfully toss a pretty girl across his shoulders and run off with her, forcing captains to rescue her. Male Mardi Gras' macho attacks, though largely playful, can still unsettle the women they target. Helena Putnam, a sea-soned Mardi Gras herself, stumbled upon a small, all-male horseback run near Evangeline a few years ago. As the rowdy men's horses crowded her, she clung to a stop sign, unexpectedly overwhelmed and terrified by the encounter.

Most of the sexual clowning between male Mardi Gras and female spectators is mild, and both parties enjoy the joke. In a recent run, for example, a pair of Mardi Gras threatened two women with a "panty check," and the women laugh-ingly evaded them. Occasionally the play is more overt—Carl Lindahl recalls a male Mardi Gras briefly pulling down a woman's pants one year, for instance, but this is a rare instance.[44] More often, men "pick at," or tease, young women by untying their shoes, or hanging onto their legs until they hand over coins. Au-dience members sometimes play pranks themselves, for example, tying money high in a tree for the Mardi Gras to retrieve. A female spectator recently turned the tables on male Mardi Gras outside Trapper's Bar in Tee Mamou; around her waist she wore a towel that she periodically lifted to reveal an enormous cloth phallus. In this case, she appropriated not only the Mardi Gras' trickster role but their anatomy as well. As spectators, women can choose to play a very active role that enlivens and enhances—or sometimes subverts—the maskers' performance.

Women also play important support roles during daytime Mardi Gras *courirs,* as they run errands for the riders and follow them in cars. Patricia Sawin notes that wives of male maskers in Grand Marais become a "support staff" and provide a "protective bubble" around the men during their run; they watch out for rule violations and monitor safety, among other things.[45] Women in Grand Marais, as in other places, are often just as knowledgeable about the celebration's rules and conventions as the men performing. In numerous, though often invisible, ways they ensure that the run proceeds smoothly, safely, and correctly.

Le Bal de Mardi Gras

Decades ago, the *bal de Mardi Gras* marking the end of Mardi Gras runs was the year's biggest and most eagerly anticipated social event for rural Cajuns. After all, it was the last dance before Ash Wednesday and six weeks of Lent. Betty Miller explains that Mardi Gras was "the big deal before Lent. . . . So you lived it up until midnight." Entire families attended Mardi Gras dances, held first in homes—usually the *capitaine*'s and his wife's—and later at dance halls or clubs.

For Cajun girls, Mardi Gras dances were a chance to meet and dance with potential husbands. The Mardi Gras *bal* allowed young, unmarried Mardi Gras to "participate in social interaction with females, to dance with, court, and ultimately marry the girls and women who . . . witnessed and admired their holiday feats."[46] Women often went to great trouble to attend the Mardi Gras dance, even if this was their only participation in the celebration. Berline Boone remembers her two older sisters walking five or six miles into Eunice for Mardi Gras dances in the 1950s. Wives went to watch their husbands' performance and perhaps dance with them, and mothers went to chaperone their daughters. Ann Marie Leger recalls, "The mama and the daddy came, and it was not like the dances we have nowadays. The mamas sat around and the little kids were on their laps and they'd visit, while the girls danced."

For these dances, the male Mardi Gras riders remained masked and costumed, while guests went undisguised. In many communities, the men danced into the hall in what was known as a "march," and then sang their Mardi Gras song. All the while, Hugh Miller says, they were looking for unattached girls to dance with. "When we'd get to the hall we'd start singing and we'd go in the center of the hall and we'd just try to pick out the partner we was going to dance with. . . . But we'd finish singing the song and they'd start playing a song . . . something that was peppy and you'd go and pick out [a partner]. . . . It was a hell of a dance." Married maskers might dance with their own wives or with other women. Alice Janot has vivid memories of a Eunice-area Mardi Gras dance decades ago. The revelers—disguised so well that "their own wives could not recognize them," she said—entered the hall, six or eight at a time, to dance with the women there; afterward, they went back outside. Mrs. Janot says, "And they'd go invite you, who[ever] they wanted—and if it was your husband, you didn't know who it was. . . . They'd pass [do] three dances, and off they'd go."[47]

If running Mardi Gras was a rite of passage into manhood for young riders, attending the Mardi Gras dance was an equally important transition for girls. It could inspire both excitement and fear. Betty Miller recalls the thrill of going to Mardi Gras dances as a young girl, and her mixed emotions on being asked to dance by anonymous men. "The Mardi Gras [would] want to dance with you, you know, and you were scared to dance but yet you'd dance. And sometimes they'd whisper who they were, and they'd tell you who they were. . . . But it was fun. It was anticipation. That was a big deal before Lent. And so everybody just lived it up that day." Betty Miller wasn't the only woman intimidated by the attentions of masked, often drunken partners. Anne Marie Leger described her feelings in a 1988 interview. "But you would come to the dance, you know, and they'd let [the Mardi Gras] go in, they had one particular time when they'd all let them loose and they'd all run and try to find a girl for dancing. And I was petrified, I tried not to show them how scared I was, but I was. And it was usually someone I knew but behind that horrible mask, you know." Her husband, Allen, assured me, "But they wouldn't do you nothing, just dance." Mrs. Leger, though, refused to discount her own reaction to the experience and insisted, "No, but I was afraid."

The Mardi Gras were determined to remain anonymous as audience members tried to guess their identities by their disguises, hands, shoes, and mannerisms. The guessing game became a contest of wits, and maskers often switched suits, hats, and masks with each other to increase the confusion. It was especially gratifying to fool those who knew them best, including the wives who made their costumes. Mamie LeJeune, of LeJeune Cove, remembers being fooled into kissing a stranger in her husband's disguise when he came to dance with her. Hugh Miller pulled a similar prank on his wife, Betty. Together, the Millers recount a Mardi Gras *bal* years ago at the old Four Corners Club, when Hugh traded disguises with another Mardi Gras and sent him to dance with his wife. Betty had anticipated such a switch and thought she was prepared, but she recalls, "I was [fooled] because, you see, I thought 'I'm going to recognize his shoes.' And this fellow had on his shoes. But then, there was something [odd] about it, you know. So when [Hugh] came back, he said, 'It wasn't me, it was so-and-so.'" These deceptions, and the confusion they caused, were in keeping with the mischievous spirit of Mardi Gras and Cajuns' general appreciation of practical jokes. Symbolically, though, they represented a temporary breakdown of familiarity and marriage, as husbands became indistinguishable from strangers. (On a similar note, several present-day Mardi Gras have jokingly told me, "No one's married on Mardi Gras.")

Mardi Gras dances are still important events in community life, though not to the extent they once were—rural Cajuns today have plenty of other entertainments available. *Bals de Mardi Gras* are usually held in local bars, American Legion or VFW halls, or church halls. Men, women, and children flock to them, paying a small entrance fee and lining the hall as they wait for the Mardi Gras's processional entry. Frequently wives, mothers, and girlfriends videotape or photograph the march. Spectators come to admire the maskers' disguises and performances, and usually stay to dance to the live Cajun music. Mardi Gras dances are still an excellent opportunity for single women and men (and sometimes married ones too) to meet and dance with potential partners. Most now end well before midnight, however, because many of the revelers have to work the next day.

Passing It On

One of women's most pivotal, though often unrecognized, Mardi Gras roles is transmitting their Mardi Gras knowledge and dedication to the next generation. Women have used many different means to teach their children about the celebration over the years: they dressed infants in Mardi Gras suits to greet the riders, for instance, as Kim Moreau's mother and grandmother did. By "receiving" the Mardi Gras run at their homes, Cajun matriarchs taught their sons and daughters about the performance and its various roles; the children not only watched the maskers but inevitably became performers themselves as they were chased and teased. Women also took their children to Mardi Gras dances. A Tee Mamou woman now in her fifties described her family's involvement in Mardi Gras when she was a young wife and mother: "We looked forward to the Mardi Gras dances and watching them run, because we wanted to show our kids what we were born and raised with."[48] Mothers sometimes organized their children or grandchildren in small, informal Mardi Gras runs through the neighborhood in the days before Mardi Gras. Shirley Reed and her sisters-in-law did this in the 1970s, soon after they began running in the (then new) Tee Mamou women's run. She explained: "We had a couple of years that we ran the children around the neighborhood. . . . And they had enjoyed it, we did it once or twice. . . . It was just around the neighbors, you know. Because they would see us have such a good time, that they wanted to do it, too, and we figured, well, that was a good way to get them started into it, you know, so when they get older we'd still have Mardi Gras left in the area."[49]

Women continue to instruct their children in these and other ways. Mothers and children often trail after a community Mardi Gras run in cars or trucks, enjoying and photographing one performance after another. In places where women run Mardi Gras themselves, mothers often induct their teen-age daughters into the run. Women are also active in organizing and leading special children-only runs that take place annually in at least five prairie neighborhoods. (I discuss women's roles in children's runs more fully in chapter 2.) And in some small towns, women and men also visit local schools to demonstrate and talk about their Mardi Gras traditions.

Women, then, have always been indispensable to the country Cajun Mardi Gras. Their handwork molds the celebration's distinctive look, their cooking creates its taste, their interactions with male maskers provide much of its humor and zest, and their encouragement ensures its survival. Although their traditional festive roles have tended to keep them out of the Mardi Gras limelight, women are beginning to receive more public acclaim, both within and outside their own communities. One example is Basile's naming of five former gumbo cooks—several of whom had also served as women's Mardi Gras captains—to their Mardi Gras Hall of Fame in 2003, followed the next year by an appreciation plaque for the current three gumbo servers. Before her death, Basile's Agnes Miller was named grand marshal of the town's 1993 Louisiana Swine Festival, in part because of her contributions to the community as a Mardi Gras cook. As she served bowls of gumbo to out-of-town visitors and locals, Miss Agnes became "one of Basile's ambassadors," in the words of the *Basile Weekly,* and people across the state remembered and asked about her.[50]

On a larger scale, a handful of Cajun women who make Mardi Gras masks, *capuchons,* and suits have become well-known figures on the folklife festival circuit, demonstrating and talking about the Mardi Gras tradition to thousands of people. For instance, Georgie Manuel, who makes wire screen masks with her husband, Allen, is a frequent exhibitor at festivals and craft fairs throughout the year. During the Mardi Gras season, she becomes an especially public figure in her hometown of Eunice, appearing on radio and television shows to talk about Cajun Mardi Gras. Georgie's masks, like those of several other women in the region, are displayed in museums, books, craft stores, and private collections throughout the nation and abroad. For many visitors to the region, Cajun women have become the public face of the rural Mardi Gras.

2

Not Just the Work:
Cajun Women's Masking Traditions

"We wanted in on the fun, not just the work all the time."
—Linda Frugé Doucet

"We'd make noise like little kids. We was enjoying ourselves.
Each was telling a story about where we could find some pretty
men, what we would do when we get to the hall, and we was
planning everything, you see."
—Frozine Thibodeaux

Cajun women, barred from running Mardi Gras for many years, generally accepted their situation as part of the status quo. When I asked Agnes Miller, who grew up in the 1920s and 1930s, if she and other girls felt excluded from the daytime run, she said, "Well, in a way we did, because it'd be like all the boys had the fun. But it wasn't a custom that we did run."[1] Many women found great enjoyment in supporting the celebration by making Mardi Gras suits for their menfolk, cooking *le gros gumbo,* and then attending the dance that evening. Betty Pousson commented of her mother's generation during the Depression years, "That was the fun of it for the women."[2]

Not all women, however, were so sanguine about their circumscribed Mardi Gras roles. As cultural ideas about gender roles gradually began to change, especially in the latter half of the twentieth century, some women decided that they too would mask. In Linda Frugé Doucet's words, "We wanted in on the fun, not just the work all the time."[3] Women used a variety of tactics to experience the pleasure and freedoms of masking—sometimes openly, at other times through subterfuge.

One way to briefly assume the Mardi Gras role was to infiltrate an all-male Mardi Gras run during their *bal de Mardi Gras.* Another was to mask for public masquerade dances during the Mardi Gras season. The next step was to actually run Mardi Gras, by demanding to join established men's runs (*courirs de Mardi Gras*), by taking part in special family runs, or by creating independent women's runs. In deciding to mask, women—as Reid Mitchell remarks of the New Orleans Carnival—"claimed Mardi Gras as a time and space for women's performance, assertions, and enjoyment."[4] Over the years, women increasingly "inserted themselves into a holiday traditionally dominated by men"[5] and adapted it to suit themselves.

Cajun women's early masking performances were, first and foremost, an assertion of power. Masking gave women access to public liberties not normally associated with women: they could roam the streets unrecognized, flirt and dance with men who were not their husbands, beg strangers and friends for money, clown, act "crazy," and play practical jokes. The act of masking was itself empowering, as men (the usual maskers) were left puzzling over the women's hidden identities and even their gender. A woman who stood next to me inside Basile's Exxon station as we watched the Mardi Gras guisers through the window commented that she used to run Mardi Gras; when the masked crowd drew closer, she told me, "The mask is power. You feel invisible. You can do anything you want to."[6]

Women's masking was subversive, temporarily erasing the everyday relationships that defined women as wives, daughters, and mothers. It was also a barometer of gender dynamics and women's changing images of themselves. And finally, pioneering women maskers created new female roles that transformed the rural celebration as a whole; they paved the way and set precedents for female Mardi Gras today.

This chapter traces rural Cajun women's early transition from supportive roles to public performance in the country Mardi Gras festival. Women's masking, and especially their Mardi Gras runs, emerged most often during times of social upheaval. The events I describe range from the 1920s through the mid-1980s, but the main focus is on the three decades following World War II, when rural Cajun women's lives and Mardi Gras roles changed dramatically. In many ways, women's growing involvement in the "privileged time of carnival" reflected broader social changes.[7] The battle of the sexes taking place in American society played out in a very physical way in Mardi Gras runs. But, at times, women's Mardi Gras actions preceded larger cultural changes and suggested new ways of acting for women. Women's festive play symbolically toppled an everyday social order that tied women to the domestic world of home and family. Female maskers presented their own points of view and images of themselves as energetic, fun-loving, comical, ambiguous, and often unruly.

Masking at Mardi Gras *Bals*

Before the advent of women's Mardi Gras runs, women found other, backdoor ways to experience the freedom of masking. The Mardi Gras dances that ended all-male runs offered one opportunity. The male Mardi Gras riders, still masked and costumed, usually danced a waltz and two-step for onlookers, and then left the hall. After their performance, many men left their suits and masks outside and returned to dance with their wives or sweethearts. Others switched disguises with friends and sent them to dance with unsuspecting wives. Occasionally, though, women turned this trick to their advantage by borrowing a discarded suit and mask and infiltrating the Mardi Gras. Then the choice of partners, male or female, became hers. Alice Janot reminisced about a long-ago Mardi Gras dance: "Back then womens didn't run Mardi Gras. If some of these women felt excited, and they thought it was fun, they'd get some of these costumes and they'd change and their husbands didn't know who they were either. And they could invite who they wanted [to dance]. . . . The women would dance with womens or with men, whatever. But you didn't know who you were dancing with."[8] On other occasions, women dancing with each other was common; women inviting men to dance was not. Even today, older people often ask permission to dance with someone else's spouse, because dancing can imply courtship. Mardi Gras anonymity allowed women to take the sexual initiative (however mild or brief), breaking everyday social rules and inverting their usual gender roles.

Even after separate ladies' runs were formed in some communities, women still occasionally crashed men's Mardi Gras dances just for the fun of it. In the 1970s, Linda Frugé and her friend Carol Reed, both members of the Tee Mamou women's run, decided to mask and join the local men for their dance. Unknown to Linda's husband Gerald, the group's *capitaine,* the two women mingled with the male maskers. Linda recalls it as a frightening experience: it was, she says, "just [a] whole different atmosphere. You could feel the roughness once we started going around and sang the song and everything. And then when everybody scattered out, I thought, 'Oh hell, what did I do?' . . . I mean . . . you could just feel it around you, the roughness. Kind of like when you go into a bar and there's a fight getting ready to start and they have that atmosphere. . . . Never again."[9]

Public Mardi Gras Dances

Public dances sponsored by local dance halls, the American Legion, Woodmen of the World, and other civic organizations provided a more open chance for women to "dress out" during the Mardi Gras season. These masquerade parties, inspired by urban Mardi Gras celebrations, were very popular by the 1950s and 1960s, when Mardi Gras runs themselves had temporarily fallen out of favor in many communities. Married couples dressed up in elaborate thematic disguises for these dances, competing for prizes awarded to the "most original and 'eye catching' costumes."[10] A common device was for a husband and wife to switch roles by crossdressing as a *vieille femme* (old woman) and *vieux homme* (old man). A 1966 newspaper account of a Knights of Columbus Mardi Gras dance in Basile, for instance, reports that Mr. and Mrs. Willie Arnaud, disguised as an old man and woman, took second place in a competition for best costume.[11] (First place went to a couple dressed as penguins.) Georgie Manuel's mother told a story of dancing with an "old woman" who turned out to be her father-in-law at a Eunice-area dance many years ago.

These dances, then, were a socially acceptable way for women to openly mask and engage others in the guessing game central to Mardi Gras disguise. Several have described to me the exhilaration of going undetected, despite close scrutiny. Agnes Miller, known to everyone in Basile as "Miss Agnes," made the gumbo every year for Basile's Mardi Gras run for many years, but never had the chance to run Mardi Gras herself. Even after a local women's run was founded, she always had to work during the Mardi Gras season. Her husband was disabled, and Miss Agnes's income from cooking at a local restaurant supported her family for many years. However, she remembers the excitement of dressing in her husband's old clothes one year and joining her friend Thia LeBleu (who did run Mardi Gras) for a Mardi Gras dance at a Basile club. "We got dressed one night and went. . . . Right in back of the bank, there was a bar. They call that Quincy's. And we went there all dressed up. And I had a straw hat, I remember. And I had put me an overall, one of my husband's overalls. And I had put a stocking on my face, a silk stocking. And they recognized . . . Miss LeBleu, some of the people recognized [her]. And they couldn't recognize me. And . . . a man asked me to dance, and all that time it was my brother-in-law. He said, 'Well, I'd like to find out if you're a man or a woman.' . . . But we had fun that night."[12] Women obviously enjoyed escaping recognition by those who knew them best, but their actions also had a deeper symbolic significance. Their identities and even gender obscured, women were transformed into strangers who could no longer be defined by their roles as wives, mothers, daughters, and sisters—or sisters-in-law. They blurred the lines of everyday social relationships, the very relationships women are usually responsible for nurturing.

Early Women's Mardi Gras Runs

Masking at dances gave women a chance to briefly try on the Mardi Gras role without actually running Mardi Gras. Deciding to take part in a Mardi Gras run was the next step, although it was sometimes a controversial progression. Many men, and some women, felt strongly that there was "no place for the ladies" in the rough, often drunken horseplay and "impromptu wildness"[13] of traditional Mardi Gras runs.

Women who tried to join existing men's runs were usually rebuffed. For many Cajuns, even in the shifting social climate of the 1950s and 1960s, the prospect of mixed-sex runs was highly improper. As the late Vories Moreau, a longtime Mardi Gras and captain in Basile, told folklorist Carl Lindahl in 1991, "Thirty, forty years ago, it was a lot different than it is now. It wouldn't have been considered very nice for the men and the women to run together."[14] Objections were often voiced as moral concerns; the potential for "anonymous carousing" among drunken riders was especially troubling.[15] Male participants also invoked tradition and chivalry, arguing that they wanted both to preserve the tradition unchanged and to protect women from its debauchery.[16]

Many men disliked the idea of female maskers running Mardi Gras with them, but women also could be vocal critics—especially the wives of male riders. The town of Mamou ("Grand" Mamou, in distinction to Tee Mamou) tried including female Mardi Gras in 1952 and 1953, soon after Paul Tate and Revon Reed revived the dormant men's run and "tried to render [it] respectable and relatively safe."[17] The experiment ended after an inebriated female rider arrived back in town, her clothing disheveled, at the end of the day. The next year, a delegation of Mardi Gras wives told Paul Tate they would not let their husbands run unless women were excluded.[18]

For women determined to run Mardi Gras, two other tactics proved more successful than trying to integrate all-male runs. Women could mask as part of a family run, or they could establish their own single-sex runs. Both were means of sidestepping some, though not all, of the moral and cultural obstacles to women's full participation in Mardi Gras.

Family Runs

One of the most socially acceptable ways for women to take an active part was through their children. Both before and after World War II, a number of rural prairie communities hosted small, informal family runs. In Ossun, Scott, Vatican, and other Lafayette Parish neighborhoods, family groups masked and rode in buggies from house to house.[19] Parents who wanted their children to experience Mardi Gras firsthand might organize and lead a neighborhood run, often with the help of grandparents. Maskers ranged from young children to teenagers and older adults, and sometimes included friends and neighbors as well as family members. Households reluctant to offer hospitality to an adult Mardi Gras run, for fear they might damage property or be too raucous, sometimes welcomed family runs. These events tended to die out in a few years as children grew up, lost interest, or found other opportunities to run Mardi Gras, and as adult organizers dropped out.

During the postwar decades, family runs filled a gap in communities without separate children's runs. For boys, they were a training ground, a chance to learn how to run Mardi Gras before graduating to a men's *courir*. For girls and women, though, family runs often were their only opportunity to run Mardi Gras. Participating in a family run, centered around children and domestic relationships, was essentially an extension of a woman's maternal role. Cajun women have traditionally been responsible for imparting many cultural practices within their families, and teaching their children about Mardi Gras fell within this domain. Family runs emphasized "good, clean fun," in Maude Ancelet's words, and avoided most of the disreputable behavior associated with adult runs.[20] Thus, women encountered little resistance to their involvement in family runs, because on the surface, at least, the events reinforced conventional gender roles.

Family *courirs de Mardi Gras* still take place in some communities, although children's runs in Eunice, Basile, and Tee Mamou now offer boys and girls other opportunities to mask. The Ancelet family held a neighborhood run in Scott annually for about eight years, until 1998. It included three generations of Ancelet women, men, and children, along with friends and a few strangers, on horses and trailers. Now, the Ancelets' adult sons, young boys when they started running, are talking about organizing the run themselves. A recently revived run in Mermentau also includes men, women, and children together.

Women's Mardi Gras Runs: The First Wave

In years past, women who wanted to run Mardi Gras had another alternative to family runs: they could organize separate women's Mardi Gras runs, or "ladies' runs," as they are usually called. Although at least one ladies' *courir* took place in the 1920s, women's Mardi Gras runs are largely a post–World War II phenomenon. Their heyday was from the mid-1940s through the 1970s, when women's Mardi Gras runs sprang up in a number of rural neighborhoods and small towns on southwest Louisiana's prairies—Pointe Noire, Eunice, Duralde, Basile, and Tee Mamou, and perhaps other communities as well. In addition, the war had meant suspension of most all-male runs, and membership was often slow to rebuild. Women's Mardi Gras runs helped fill this void and keep the tradition alive.

Most of these women's Mardi Gras runs were relatively small and loosely organized, created when a small group of female friends and relatives decided they wanted to run Mardi Gras. Like many early men's runs, ladies' runs had no official names; they were simply associated with whichever rural neighborhood their members lived in. Almost invariably, they emerged in places that already hosted an established men's run. Mardi Gras runs depend on community support, and some enclaves (those that were predominately non-Cajun or Protestant, for example) were simply not interested. Neighborhoods that already supported male Mardi Gras runs were more likely to be receptive to ladies' Mardi Gras runs.

Like family runs, women's Mardi Gras runs often found a warm welcome at households that refused to accept poorly disciplined or "rough" men's runs. Many all-male groups had (and still have) a "mystique of toughness reminiscent of the American Wild West."[21] Drunken male riders sometimes scared the women of the house by forcing them to dance, carelessly trampled flower beds, and fought with each other. Lady Mardi Gras, on the other hand, were generally considered to be better behaved, less prone to vandalism and violence.

Some women's runs were probably inspired by precedents in other communities. Often, though, founders say they had no idea that women ran Mardi Gras elsewhere. "We decided we wanted to run Mardi Gras and the men wouldn't let us, so we decided to just form our own," one woman says.[22] Evidently, women in a number of communities felt a strong desire to run Mardi Gras and came up with the same solution.

Female Mardi Gras modeled their own runs on local men's runs, adapting the tradition to their own needs. Each community *courir* took on its own characteristics, but most early women's runs, and even some today, shared certain features. First, lady Mardi Gras were typically mature women, settled wives and mothers in their twenties and thirties, and some were much older. (Many men, in contrast, began running Mardi Gras as children or teenagers.) For the first half of the twentieth century, and some years beyond, it was unthinkable for impressionable, unmarried young girls to run Mardi Gras. Mothers strictly chaperoned and protected their daughters, closely guarding their reputations until they married as teenagers and began their own families. No responsible Cajun parent would allow an unmarried daughter to take part in the public drinking, dancing, flirting, and raucousness associated with Mardi Gras runs. Although women became subject to their husbands' control upon marriage, some seem to have found a measure of independence. Their respectable status as wives and mothers allowed them to engage in the license of running Mardi Gras.

Second, founding members typically belonged to families deeply immersed in the Mardi Gras tradition: their husbands, fathers, brothers, and sons ran. In most Mardi Gras communities, certain families were known for their passionate devotion to Mardi Gras and played a crucial part in the celebration's local survival. Girls and women in these families often shared this commitment, taking part in customary female ways such as making costumes and cooking gumbo. They were also among the most likely to organize women's runs. Men who loved Mardi Gras themselves—and were invited to take part by "captaining" or driving the truck—evidently supported, or at least tolerated, their wives' desire to mask.

Third, most of the earliest lady Mardi Gras were country women, farm wives who worked in the fields alongside their husbands. Rural families with few luxuries had to create their own entertainment, and Mardi Gras was a highlight of their year. As Hugh Miller says of his own Mardi Gras experience, "We were just poor people having a good time."[23] The countryside was for many years the heart of the Cajun Mardi Gras tradition, before urban migration emptied many *voisinages* in the postwar years. Over time, some women's runs, like men's, came to be more closely associated with towns than with the country.

Fourth, most (but not all) women's groups chose male *capitaines* to lead their runs. Usually, they recruited husbands, other male family members, or neighbors who were seasoned maskers or Mardi Gras captains. In some places, captains carried whips—riding whips or braided burlap *quoits*—to keep the maskers in line; in others, they didn't. The determining factor seems to be whether or not whips were present in the local men's runs.

The few ladies' runs with female captains usually rotated the role of captain—more a duty than an honor—each year. This egalitarian approach ensured that no one woman wore the mantle of authority for long. It is not surprising that women hesitated to adopt the role of "temporary despot" among their peers.[24] (Many men were, and are, also reluctant to be captains.) Cajun Mardi Gras *capitaines* are traditionally strict disciplinarians capable of commanding respect, and fear, if need be, among their followers. For women, wielding this paternal authority ran counter to gender expectations; in many ways, it was a more profound role reversal than masking as a Mardi Gras. On the whole, then, women seemed to prefer male captains—perhaps because they believed men could exert control more effectively, or because they were simply reluctant to forgo the fun of "cutting up" and acting silly in exchange for the captain's responsibilities.

Fifth, female Mardi Gras typically rode on farm wagons or trucks rather than horseback. Men's runs demanded considerable horsemanship as the often-inebriated Mardi Gras rode long distances between houses, mounted and dismounted dozens of times throughout the day, charged homes at full gallop, and even danced on their horses' backs.[25] In everyday life, Cajun men routinely traveled on horseback throughout the nineteenth and early twentieth centuries, but women rode in horse-drawn buggies. Horseback riding, then, was not a skill commonly associated with women. Indeed, Agnes Miller suggests that one reason women didn't run Mardi Gras in her youth was "because it was on horseback, you know."[26] Traveling on wagons, and then trucks, made the tradition more accessible to women.

And finally, women's runs were frequently held on the Saturday or Sunday before Lent, days often associated with children's runs, to avoid competing with men's Tuesday runs. Women's runs that did fall on Tuesday followed different routes from local men's runs. For one thing, most hosts could not be expected to welcome, and donate to, two groups in the same day. For another, Cajun Mardi Gras runs were, and remain, very territorial, as the event "defines group territory" by its route.[27] Male riders took great care not to cross paths with other community runs; when they did, fights usually broke out.

Female Mardi Gras feared running into "rough" all-male bands of revelers, not because of fist fights but because women were considered fair game for merciless groping. A member of the Tee Mamou run in the 1950s recalls the group visiting the town of Eunice and encountering a masked woman: "There was one woman Mardi Gras, you know, and she was on the street and all that, and the fellows got after that woman and . . . ganged up on her. . . . I'm pretty sure that woman got pawed pretty bad. . . . We [captains] had to get them away from her."[28] Frozine Thibodeaux of Pointe Noire similarly recalls, "You know, the men's Mardi Gras, they're tough. And if they catch a lady, that's hers [she's in trouble]. That's the end. . . . And [the men] drink and they think they're animals. So the ladies had to run on Sunday."[29]

Necessity may have played a large part in women's decisions to run on the weekend, but claiming their own day also worked to women's advantage. Not only were husbands more available to help out, but ladies' runs were seen as relatively nonthreatening because they did not intrude on the men's festivities.

A history of Cajun women's Mardi Gras runs must be pieced together from oral accounts of individual runs, family snapshots, and a few scattered newspaper descriptions. (Many rural Cajuns were illiterate in the early twentieth century, and the early written history of the Cajun Mardi Gras tradition in general is poor.) Gaps and discrepancies abound, and dates are rarely exact, as women use their children's ages or family events as reference points. Women often recorded their performances through photographs and, later, home movies as part of their personal and family histories but gave little thought to a larger cultural significance. As Tee Mamou's Linda Frugé Doucet says, "[Years ago] I never thought of culture, or keeping up a tradition or anything. [Running Mardi Gras] was just a way to celebrate before Lent began and a time of penance and sacrifice and all that. A time to let loose one last time."[30]

In part, then, this gap reflects broader community attitudes toward Mardi Gras runs in general: They were often dismissed as commonplace. Berline Boone says of her hometown Basile, "Mardi Gras around here is just an everyday thing, you know." A longtime member of Basile's women's run, she points out that it never occurred to her that what she was doing merited much notice, much less formal documentation. She says, "I really never thought that was important. We took stuff like this for granted."[31]

There are other reasons women's Mardi Gras history has received so little notice. Until recently, ethnographers rarely focused closely on individual Mardi

Gras runs and the people who took part in them; instead, they described Mardi Gras in terms of a single, male model. Nor did they pay much attention to the event's recent history or participants' memories. Gender bias has also played a part. Community members, journalists, and folklorists have tended to describe Mardi Gras as an almost exclusively male practice. Ladies' Mardi Gras runs, like women's sports, or indeed, any aspect of women's culture, are often seen as secondary to men's *courirs*. Women's runs are still few, and their origins more recent than many all-male runs; thus, they are frequently trivialized, described as less traditional, and treated as novelties.

In recent years, as interest in the Cajun Mardi Gras has grown, so has attention to its complexity, variety, and dynamic nature.[32] This more microscopic approach has extended to women's participation. Scholars are beginning to recognize ladies' runs as a significant piece of Mardi Gras history, and women as creative artists.[33]

The remainder of this chapter traces the history of seven women's Mardi Gras runs in six different prairie communities, founded between 1920 and the early 1970s. Some of these *courirs* were short-lived, perhaps because of competing demands such as child rearing and other family responsibilities. But some lasted a decade or more, and three continue today, although in somewhat different form. Arranged in rough chronological order, the following accounts draw on participants' own stories and words. These narratives reveal the various ways women adapted the traditionally male Mardi Gras role to suit themselves, and how their festive play changed over the years.

Mardi Gras Pioneers: The Soileau Run

Marion Courville, born in 1919, provided a description of one of the earliest women's runs, in the countryside near Soileau, Louisiana. He grew up listening to the stories his mother, Nora Frugé Courville, told about running Mardi Gras in the early 1920s. Nora's husband, Delmas, was a tenant farmer and an ardent Mardi Gras himself. Mr. Courville said, "I guess [my mother ran] when my daddy was running, about 1921, something like that."[34] Drawing on his own memories of his mother's tales, Mr. Courville described a small group of women traveling the countryside in a farm wagon, climbing fences and tumbling as they chased chickens for their gumbo. They dressed in long skirts and sunbonnets that even then were old-fashioned. "Well, they'd dress in long dresses and the old bonnets ... the *garde-soleil*, you call it. And ... they run in a wagon, you see. They put benches in the wagon. That's the wagon [that] had those sides like that, where they'd put the cotton when they went to the cotton gin.... She said they had to make a ladder with wood ... so they could get in the wagon. And they'd sit down, and they'd get to a house and they'd get down and they'd go and sing [the] Mardi Gras [song] and dance, you know. My mother loved to dance. And I used to dance with her, that's how I learned to dance, with my mother." Mr. Courville remembered that the women's hosts would "give them chickens, ducks, whatever they had. Oh, the ladies was chasing [chickens], yeah. [My mother] said, 'Sometimes we would fall about five times before we can get the chicken, [but] we'd get it.'"

Mr. Courville believed that the group (unlike many early women Mardi Gras) chose one of their own members to act as captain each year. He said, "One lady was the head of it, you know. They'd pick one up, say 'You going to be the captain.' Yeah. That's the way they worked it, you know." The run consisted of six to twelve women at most, and lasted only a few years. Maternal duties and economic difficulties may have made it difficult for farmers' wives to maintain their run for long. As Mr. Courville pointed out, "You know, times was kind of hard those days," and his family relocated several times during his childhood as his father sought employment. Or perhaps the women lost interest in running for other reasons; it was not unusual for small men's runs to disband after only a few years, too.

The Pointe Noire Women's Run

Whether or not this 1920s-era Soileau run was an isolated phenomenon remains open to speculation. (So does the significance of its timing—soon after World War I, a period of great social change, especially for women.)[35] But the years following World War II, when women gradually entered the public domain in other areas of life, saw a spate of new women's runs.

This period was also a turning point for the country Mardi Gras tradition itself. By the 1930s, interest had diminished in many communities, partly because maskers sometimes behaved disreputably. Most surviving men's runs were interrupted during the war, and began slowly rebuilding in the late 1940s and early 1950s. Others were never successfully revived. During the 1950s, 1960s, and 1970s—decades marked by a continued trend toward Americanization and stigmatization of French Louisiana culture—community Mardi Gras runs often struggled to continue.[36] Ladies' runs, then, served as a bridge during a period when membership in all-male runs had dwindled.

One notable women's run took place for at least a decade in the rural Acadia Parish community first known as Pointe Noire and later as Richard. Pointe Noire, like most other communities with women's runs, also hosted a horseback men's run that was well established long before the women began running in the mid-1940s.

Frozine LeJeune Thibodeaux, known to her friends as Zine, is a Pointe Noire native and *traiteuse*, or healer. A second cousin to Cajun music legend Iry

LeJeune, Zine was born into a family of twelve children in 1920. Like most country Cajuns of her generation, she grew up speaking Cajun French as a first language, and still speaks English with a strong accent. She married Hilton Thibodeaux in 1936, when she was sixteen and he was nineteen. Hilton farmed cotton and corn, and the couple regularly hosted "French" (Cajun) music parties in their garage for many years. Frozine Thibodeaux says, "We had a time to work and we had a time to play."[37]

Frozine grew up with some family connections to the local Mardi Gras celebration, because her brothers ran. She recalls, "They liked that. Oh, they enjoyed that." These ties grew stronger when she married Hilton, a devoted member of the local men's run. As his wife, Zine sewed his Mardi Gras suits and helped cook the men's gumbo.

Soon after a group of neighborhood women founded their own run, they recruited Frozine. She was about twenty-six years old, a wife and mother known for her love of dancing, joking, and (in her own words) acting "crazy." She says, "When I got married, I never did run Mardi Gras before. But a few years after that, maybe ten years after that, we started. They was running and running and they was begging me to run because I was always acting silly and I liked to joke and tell jokes and stuff like that. So [a friend] said, 'You would make a good Mardi Gras.' So, 'Okay, I'll try.' . . . And we did have a good time." She adds, "My sisters never ran. There was only me . . . that was crazy enough to run, I guess." All of the other riders were also married women and mothers. Frozine recalls, "There was not one girl. . . . My daughter ran with us one year, after she got married." Among their female peers, and away from husbands, the women were free to be "crazy"—they could act silly and make noise, dance with abandon, make outrageous jokes, talk about meeting "pretty men," and unabashedly have fun together. The license of Mardi Gras not only sanctioned but rewarded this unladylike behavior.

Through their disguises, the lady Mardi Gras adopted a range of personas. Some chose to become idealized feminine figures such as brides—what Olga Supek (writing about Croatian women's carnivals) calls "metaphors of women."[38] Others transformed themselves into exotic female characters: gypsy fortune-tellers, and Indian or black women.[39] Still others dressed like men (the bride's groom, for instance), just as some male Mardi Gras have traditionally masked as women. Several women favored the traditional fringed pants and shirt (*suit de Mardi Gras*) and conical hat (*capuchon*) many male Mardi Gras wore. Most of the women liked commercially made plastic masks, because an opening near the mouth allowed them to drink without unmasking. Mrs. Thibodeaux says, "With that you could take a little can and drink. That's why they liked that."

The women usually held their run on the Sunday before Lent. About fifteen masked women rode in the back of a pickup truck driven by Zine's husband

Hilton. Their *capitaine* was usually Orell "Snow" LeJeune, who was perhaps seventeen or eighteen at the time. He was chosen as captain, Mrs. Thibodeaux says, "because he wanted to be with the ladies all the time. And . . . we [all] saw him raised." His mother, Annie LeJeune, was a neighbor and a member of the ladies' run. Snow, like captains in many men's runs, carried both a flag to signal stops and a whip to keep the riders in line. He seems not to have been the autocratic leader typical of many all-male runs, however. Frozine Thibodeaux says that their captain "had his whip but he didn't use it" on the women. The whip was mostly for show, representing an authority that was perhaps more symbolic than real—or simply not needed.

Throughout the day, the women joked and played practical jokes, or *niches,* on each other. Having a young, male captain (even one they had watched grow up) provided fodder for much teasing and sexual innuendo. Frozine recalls, "But there's two of the ladies that got real drunk. . . . And we was hateful a lot because we laughed at them and said they wanted [Snow] to raise them up and carry them. It was just a joke. We had a good time with that."

The run began and ended at Richard's Catholic Church. In an interview with folklorist Donna Onebane, Frozine Thibodeaux recalled, "We stopped everywhere we thought they would enjoy us and give us something like some eggs and some money and some chickens."[40] However, they were more interested in visiting businesses in nearby towns—cafes, stores, and especially bars and dance halls—than homes in the countryside. She explains, "We didn't want to go house to house because we didn't care about the money. All we cared about was drinking and having a good time." Traveling by truck made them more mobile than horseback runs, and their quest for a good time took them far afield—not only to the nearby town of Eunice but also to Mamou, more than twenty miles away. The Pointe Noire women traveled an equally great symbolic distance, as they left behind the familiar domestic world and moved into public spaces such as bars and dance halls, which historian Karen Leathem calls "territory that catered to male vices."[41]

Alcohol was an essential ingredient, as it is for most Mardi Gras runs, although Mrs. Thibodeaux says, "I never did drink much." The women brought their own wine onto the truck, and businesses they visited gave them whiskey and more wine. As they rode from one stop toward the next, the women drank, laughed, and sang. Frozine Thibodeaux remembers, "We'd make noise like little kids. We was enjoying ourselves. Each was telling a story about where we could find some pretty men, what we would do when we get to the hall, and we was planning everything, you see."[42]

When they arrived at a club, the group waited outside while their captain approached the owners. Mrs. Thibodeaux says, "Then the *capitaine* went in front and asked if we could go in, you see. . . . And when we was accepted, we could go in." The women circulated among the bar patrons, entertaining them by singing and clowning, and inviting them to dance. "Oh yes. I promise you. We were singing and dancing and cutting up. . . . And we would dance with the people at the bar and in the club and everywhere. . . . They would dance with us. . . . As soon as they seen it was some ladies they didn't care [mind]. They knew we wasn't going to be mean, you know. So they would dance with us and we would dance between us [with each other] too. They would play the music for us." Like all good Mardi Gras, they begged onlookers for money. Their targets, Frozine says, "didn't have no chance. Just might as well leave the money right there." At the end of the day, the ladies shared chicken and sausage gumbo in the church hall, and later that night they "had a little dance" there, she says.

Mrs. Thibodeaux remembers running regularly for about five years, and intermittently for a few more. In its later years, the run became a family event with women, men, and children running "*tout ensemble*" ("all together"). She remarks that her husband didn't mind her running Mardi Gras with her friends because he loved it so much himself. He usually helped by driving the truck or

Women and children mask to run Mardi Gras in Pointe Noire, circa 1950s. Courtesy of Frozine Thibodeaux.

sometimes acting as captain, but accepted her participation even when he wasn't involved. She says, "Oh, he was okay. He didn't care, he was in the [truck], you know. But I ran a few times by myself, [when] he was not the captain or he was not running with us."

Running Mardi Gras in all-women groups was an expression of close female friendships and a statement of autonomy; it was a chance for women to get away from their husbands and enjoy themselves raucously together. As Frozine Thibodeaux says of her friend Mrs. LeJeune, "That's the only time she could get away from the old man, was when she ran Mardi Gras. And that's why she enjoyed herself so much." Men were there primarily as helpers and supporters, and seem to have interfered little with the women's fun and "craziness."

The Eunice "Maw-maws' Run"

By the early 1950s, a band of older, respectable country women was running Mardi Gras near Eunice, a relatively large St. Landry Parish town that now has about twelve thousand residents. As in other places, the local men's run had been interrupted by World War II. Immediately after the war, local men regrouped, but the run was slow to rebuild. In 1946, the first postwar run had only six members.

Eunice women, like those in other rural communities, chose to run on the weekend before Mardi Gras. On Sunday, the women rode through the countryside on the back of a farm truck. The late Cecilia Manuel was a longtime member of the "masked maw-maws" (grandmothers), as her granddaughter later dubbed the group for a newspaper story.[43] Mrs. Manuel's description suggests that this was a larger run than the one in Richard: "We were about 35 of us. Some dress like the men, some dress like the women."[44]

Photographs from 1965 and 1966 show many of the same disguise motifs as the Pointe Noire and Soileau women's runs. Some women are dressed in traditional Mardi Gras suits and *capuchons,* and a number of others wear men's clothing. Others wear the long skirts and sunbonnets associated with Cajun ladies in *les vieux temps* (the old times). Two women are disguised as a bride and her groom. As a humorous touch, the bridegroom sports a straw hat left over from a political campaign, bearing the endorsement "McKeithen for Governor."

Cecilia Manuel's printed recollections of the run evoke images of playful but headstrong women, just barely under the control of their male captain. She says, "My husband, Témon, was the *capitaine,* and let me tell you he had a hard time with all those women, because we would take a little taste of whiskey with our pop when we got thirsty, and when we got to town, Témon, he could hardly keep up with us."[45]

Georgie Manuel, a Eunice-based mask maker and active Mardi Gras today, is

Helena Putnam makes a *capuchon,* or traditional Mardi Gras hat, by shaping poster board into a cone and taping it, and then covering it with fabric and fringe. Helena has been active in the Basile Mardi Gras run since the mid-1970s. One of her many Mardi Gras roles is costume maker for herself, her grown daughters, and sometimes their friends. Courtesy of Carl Lindahl.

Cecilia Manuel's daughter-in-law. She recalls both her own grandmother and Mrs. Manuel running Mardi Gras in 1954 or 1955, when she was a girl. "They had a big old cattle truck for which they built a ladder so that the ladies could climb in. They also had seats (benches) built along the sides for them to sit. They also had some live musicians to ride with them. There was no electrical system, just the sound of the instruments and the singing. They would cover the top of the truck with those old smelly, oily army tarps. That was how they ran."[46] The Eunice women's disguises were much like men's Mardi Gras costumes during their daytime run. But for their evening dance at a local club, the women wanted to be pretty. They changed into ultrafeminine homemade satin dresses, decorated with lace, sequins, and tinsel, to compete for the "best dressed" prize. The run continued annually for about fifteen years, ending when it "eventually became too much for the carefree grandmothers."[47]

Eventually, all of these early women's runs disappeared, as families moved, women got too busy or too old or lost interest. But they set the stage for later runs and helped keep the tradition alive at a time when men's participation had dropped.

The Second Wave: 1960s to 1980s

The 1960s, 1970s, and 1980s saw even more dramatic changes in Cajun culture and in women's lives. In the countryside of southwest Louisiana, as elsewhere, gender roles and family dynamics had begun to change, though these changes were often slow and uneven in rural communities. As Eula Fontenot of Mamou told a group of French Canadian ethnographers in the early 1980s, "Tu peux voir comme notre petite communauté est. Les femmes sont pas égales à l'homme, elles sont toujours amarrées avec les petits à la maison." ("You can see how it is in our little community. The women aren't equal to the man, they're always tied with the children to the house.")[48]

Still, women's roles did change. Rural Cajun women became less homebound than their mothers had been, for a variety of reasons: education, urbanization, technology, smaller families, the civil rights movement, and higher standards of living, among others. More women began working outside the home than ever before, sometimes in male-dominated fields, and significant changes in gender roles took place within Cajun society. Although rural French Louisiana has been slow to embrace the feminist movement, and few female Mardi Gras during these years would have identified themselves as "women's libbers," nevertheless women lived more independent and public lives than their mothers had. The rural Mardi Gras celebration felt the impact of these social shifts. During these years, a second wave of women's Mardi Gras runs emerged. These were similar in most ways to earlier runs, and even overlapped them in time in some cases. But their histories also reveal differences—most significantly, a slow but steady progression toward gender integration.

A New Eunice Ladies' Run

A second Eunice ladies' Mardi Gras run was formed in the early 1960s, a time when the city's "maw-maws' run" was probably winding down. Members of this later run, however, recall being unaware of any precedents. A group of friends, most in their early thirties, simply decided that "We wanted to run Mardi Gras, by God," as one says.[49] They, like earlier pioneers, met with resistance from the local men's run. In a 1991 interview, Norma Jean Miller explained, "And the men wouldn't let us, so we decided to form our own, you know." Norma Jean Miller and her sister-in-law Theresa Miller Seale (nicknamed "Chief") were early members. Their husbands agreed to help by providing the gumbo.

This event differed from other early women's celebrations in several important aspects. Its founders, like those of most pioneering ladies' runs, were mature
wives and mothers in their thirties or older. However, they were not poor farm
wives. Most were relatively well-to-do, educated, and socially prominent women,
the wives and daughters of landowners and prosperous cattlemen—what one
Eunice resident describes as *la crème* of local society. Like many others of their
generation and social class, they grew up speaking English, rather than French,
as a first language. Indeed, some would not have described themselves as Cajuns, once a derogatory term used to refer to poor, rural French Louisianians, in
contrast to more genteel and urban "Acadians" or non-French "Americans."

Another striking difference was that the women took turns being captain
for a year, instead of inviting husbands or male neighbors to lead them. Their
run took place on Mardi Gras day, as did the Eunice men's run, so the women's
route covered a different part of town and nearby countryside.

A final distinction was that their run was on horseback. A few of the thirty
to forty women traveled on a flatbed trailer, but most rode horses. Their decision to ride horses was based partly on local custom—the Eunice men's run
continued on horseback even as some neighboring communities moved to
trucks—and partly because it was "more fun," they say. (And—unlike some
townspeople—they had access to horses, usually borrowed for the day.)

Horses lent the run a certain drama but made it all the more physically demanding. Founders remember that one woman was such a skilled equestrian
that she could catch a chicken on horseback. But most members rode infre-
quently and were sore by the end of the day; Theresa Seale jokes, "We couldn't
walk for two weeks afterward." Women on horseback sometimes switched places
with a friend on the trailer halfway through the run. Norma Jean Miller says,
"Well, to begin with, we wasn't used to riding horseback. And [when] you drank
[it got harder]. . . . I remember one year, it was late in the day, and I don't know
if I was just tired. [But when I tried to remount] I was playing Hopalong Cas-
sidy—went right over the horse, ended up in the gravel on the other side." She
adds, "But I still say, it's a lot more fun riding a horse." The women point out
that, unlike some male riders, they didn't charge houses at a gallop. Mrs. Miller
says, "We didn't do like some of them old boys that run their horses and they're
all lathered by the time they get to town."

Running Mardi Gras gave the women permission to act silly in public, and
their children's mortification only added to their fun. Theresa Seale recalls,
"We'd go to the schoolyard, all of our kids were in school, right there at St. Ed's.
And all of the kids were just so embarrassed. . . . And we'd do it on purpose."
One year, she rode a reluctant donkey that had to be pushed and pulled across
the schoolyard and along Main Street.

The role of captain rotated among members of the run each year. Leading
the group was hard work, often an unwelcome responsibility. Theresa Seale

says, "It was a job to keep everybody in line." The captain (like male captains in other ladies' runs) had to watch for excessive drinking, which caused most problems. For the most part, there were few serious discipline problems; the riders were longtime friends who helped each other out as needed. Mrs. Miller says: "You knew most of them very well, and you knew what they were like after they drank a few drinks. With the captain . . . usually what they had to do was to watch them. . . . If Theresa came over to me and said, 'So and so looks like she's getting pretty crocked,' others would help out . . . We wanted everybody to have a good time but we didn't want anybody to get hurt, and get too wild or anything like that." As women, they faced some concerns male Mardi Gras did not. For instance, they had to guard against strangers (especially men) trying to attach themselves to the group during stops at clubs along their route. Norma Jean Miller says, "And the Mardi Gras day, you know, you got all these characters running all over the place, you got to kind of be careful. . . . We didn't pick up anybody on the way—whatever started out, that's what we had on our run. . . . We kept it to where we knew everybody." She adds that it helped that "most of us were masked, so [male bar patrons] didn't know we were women. . . . We wanted to have a good time and we didn't want to have any trouble." Although earlier groups often found it to their advantage to be recognized as women—it gave them entree to places where men were no longer welcome—in some circumstances, letting people assume they were men kept them safer. Many bar patrons would have considered a group of anonymous women, unaccompanied by a man, fair game for sexual overtures.

Eventually, the leader of the Eunice men's run invited the women to join a parade through town at the end of their run. According to Mrs. Miller, "He told us that . . . if we [were] in town at the same time they have their parade, well they would let us get in the back of the parade." The women agreed, despite their clearly second-class status. Norma Jean Miller jokingly compares their situation to African Americans being required to sit in the back of the bus during segregation, but adds, "Sure we said yes. I ain't proud." From then on, the women and men rendezvoused at three o'clock at the Blue Goose, a Eunice dance hall, for the parade.

In 1972 or 1973, the men's and women's runs combined because there were so few men interested in running Mardi Gras, the women say. (The late Hillman Smith, longtime captain of the Eunice run, told interviewers years later that the women's persistence led to the change. He said, "They kept after us to make only the one run. Finally a few years ago, we let the women join our run.")[50] That first year, women Mardi Gras outnumbered male riders. Once more, women played a pivotal role in the continuity of the local Mardi Gras tradition, just as women elsewhere, and Eunice's own earlier "maw-maws," had done soon after the war.

Today, many young women take part in the Eunice run, often riding on trailers or doubling up with a boyfriend on horseback. With the addition of women and, later, tourists and other visitors, the Eunice run grew dramatically. Today, it is by far the largest Mardi Gras run in the region, attracting many hundreds and even thousands of male and female riders on horseback, wagons, and trucks. Members seem to agree that the nature of the coed run is different from that of the earlier single-sex runs. Curtis Joubert, a former mayor of Eunice, suggests that the presence of women has "added a lot of class" to the event. The riders' behavior, he feels, is "aided tremendously by having women on the run." He says, "Let's face it, the ladies are there and the men have to adjust their behavior accordingly."[51]

Theresa Seale suggests that both the size of the event and the presence of men have changed the women's experience. The focus has shifted from a small group of female friends clowning and enjoying themselves to young women vying for male attention, in a crowd so large that most riders no longer even dismount during house stops. She says, "They're not having a good time like we had. They're just sitting on these flatbeds and drinking or riding horses with the men or the boys, or whatever. And that's all they do."

Women's Runs in Duralde and Basile

Neighboring Evangeline Parish also was home to a ladies' Mardi Gras run—or two successive runs, depending on your perspective. In the 1960s, a small bunch of women, led by a male captain and traveling by farm truck, ran Mardi Gras near rural Duralde.[52] Most of its members were drawn from the countryside between Duralde and the small town of Basile, though some lived in Basile itself. Berline Boone, now Basile's first elected female mayor, remembers getting her first taste of running Mardi Gras in Duralde when she was fifteen. In a 1994 interview, she recalled: "They used to have a Mardi Gras group in Duralde, a community . . . about fourteen miles from here. And I ran with them a couple of years . . . at least twenty-five [years ago.] . . . It was quite a few older women from Basile that did run. Most of them are deceased [now]. You know, I was one of the young ones. And they had their dance in their church hall out there."[53] Eventually, the Duralde group either disbanded or became associated with the town of Basile. (Opinions vary on whether the Basile and Duralde ladies' runs were actually different runs covering much of the same terrain and including some of the same women, or the same run with a shift in territory.) Its history can be traced through participants' stories, the local newspaper, and Mardi Gras association ledgers (available from 1974 to the present). However, there are occasional discrepancies in these accounts.

Oral histories point to the origin of a local ladies' run in the mid-1960s.[54] However, the countryside run may not have been specifically identified with

Basile until 1970, when the *Basile Weekly* announced: "This year an extra touch of excitement will be added because the women of our area will be 'running' Mardi Gras on the Sunday prior to Mardi Gras. They will have a 'Free gumbo' for the public at the Woodmen Hall Sunday evening and have a Big French Dance that Sunday night."[55] A week later, the paper declared the run's success: "A truckload of women ran Mardi Gras Sunday, February 8, and went all around the countryside. A large group of people waited to see their parade down Main Street despite the rain which postponed it until an hour later than scheduled. There was a free gumbo and a dance at the Woodmen Hall that night."[56] In many ways, the Basile ladies' run resembled other early women's runs. The community already had a well-established men's run, although it suffered periods of declining membership. Folklorist Carl Lindahl notes that the ladies' run was born during one of these slack periods, and that "women are credited with reviving the entire Basile Mardi Gras in the 1960s after the men's run had been discontinued."[57]

Like earlier women's runs, Basile's run was founded by older, married women, many with husbands and sons active in the local men's run. One significant difference was that a few teen-age and preteen girls were allowed to join the older women, especially if their mothers or other relatives were running. The social climate had changed considerably, and it was no longer shocking for an unmarried girl to take part in Mardi Gras. Still, younger members were closely watched and tutored by older ones.

The ladies' run, then, trained the next generation of lady Mardi Gras, just as men's runs had traditionally done. Several mainstays of the Basile women's run started running as schoolgirls, thirty or more years ago. Debbie Andrus grew up watching her father play music for the men's run, and later older neighbors and relatives took part in the women's run. Debbie got her own chance in 1968, when she was twelve. By that time, she believes, the older women had been running at least three or four years. "I was in seventh grade when I started. I was twelve . . . I started running with the older crowd back then. . . . I guess they were somewhere in their thirties and forties. . . . And there were some maybe a little bit older, in their fifties and sixties. And the reason I started [was] because the men always ran Mardi Gras at that time. And I can remember my father getting up to go and run. . . . So I wanted to run Mardi Gras."[58]

From its earliest years, the Basile ladies' run has been associated with the local men's run. Many Mardi Gras families—the Moreaus, Riders, Bellons, and Richards—were closely involved in both. Lady Mardi Gras, like men, became dues-paying members of the Basile Mardi Gras Association, which organized the runs. (In 1974, thirty-nine men and nineteen women each paid dues of $3.50 to cover the expenses of purchasing liquor and gumbo ingredients, hiring musicians, and other operating costs.)[59]

Debbie Andrus remembers that the women's run was much the same as the men's. She says, "We'd do the same, what the men did, we'd go out in the country, we'd go out in town, we'd chase the chickens, we had our own gumbo when we'd come back to town, and we had our dance." The lady Mardi Gras were accompanied on their truck by an accordion player who played music at house visits and along the route. (Berline Boone laughingly recalls the awkwardness this lone male presence caused the women, who had only a bucket on the truck as a toilet. They solved the problem by shielding each other with coats for privacy.) Male members of the Mardi Gras association stayed behind at Basile's Woodmen of the World Hall to clean chickens, cook, and serve their gumbo.

Basile, like most other women's runs, was initially headed by an experienced male captain. Often he was assisted by a cocaptain (usually simply called a captain), also a man. Basile captains like Dewey "Badeye" Bellon, Vories Moreau, and Enos Richard were known as no-nonsense leaders, and they treated the women strictly. Captains used their whips freely when needed to bring disorderly riders back into line. Some used pliable burlap whips for the women's run, but Berline Boone remembers *capitaine* Enos Richard carrying a leather bullwhip. She says, "It used to be a lot rougher than what it is today. . . . And if you was misbehaving, and he'd see you, he could really cut you. . . . And you really don't notice it until, you know, you go home that night and undress to take a bath."[60]

The women, however, were not intimidated. Berline says, "We would keep the captain busy, I mean he had to do his job."[61] Debbie Andrus recalls, "We had some wild women in our group. . . . We climbed trees and we got whipped a lot." The captains' willingness to use harsh discipline suggests that they took their female charges seriously—or that the women, by behaving rambunctiously, demanded to be taken seriously.

By 1975, the ladies' run began including a female captain, although the reasons for this change are murky today. Almost always, she was accompanied by a male captain—a husband or a seasoned *capitaine*.[62] The group often had difficulty recruiting women captains. Susie Lopez, a core member who joined the run as a young girl in the 1970s, recalls "It was more or less someone different every year. Whoever they could kind of pull in for a year to handle us, you know."[63] Early female captains like Judy Ardoin, Mary Moreau, Agnes Vidrine, and Esther (Nin) LeBlanc were usually middle-aged or older, and they rarely captained for more than two or three years at a time. In 1984, Ella Ruth Young became the first long-term female captain and served until illness forced her to retire twelve years later.

Past female captains say that the rambunctious maskers sometimes tried their patience. Nin LeBlanc, a cocaptain for at least two years, recalls that women

Mardi Gras always wanted to go into houses along their route to use the bathrooms; this required unmasking and asking permission of homeowners, and slowed down the run considerably. She says that women's captains often pulled in husbands or other men to help control the Mardi Gras. Nin quit soon after an incident in which a drunken female Mardi Gras jumped into a swimming pool during a house visit. When Nin tried to invoke the traditional punishment for serious misbehavior—making the disobedient woman unmask and walk home—the Mardi Gras appealed to the male helper for clemency, and Nin was overruled.[64] Even women Mardi Gras, it seems, had little respect for female authority and paid more attention to a male leader.

For years, the Basile women rode on an old rice truck without steps. Berline Boone comments that the physical demands of running Mardi Gras were hard on the older women, and a few had trouble getting down from the truck. "When I started running, I can remember some that couldn't even get out of the truck anymore. . . . They'd come with us, but they wouldn't get out of the truck, because it was high, you know. [Running] is very hard on your legs, stomping all day long, all day long, you know. And so they wouldn't even get out of the truck, and they'd just bring their stuff up there, but they were *with* us. You know, it helped us."[65] Drinking made getting on and off the truck even harder, and women sometimes fell off during the day. Eventually, the women began riding on a lower, more accessible, and practical trailer.

The women's run, like the men's, typically began and ended at Basile's Woodmen of the World Hall, where the gumbo and dance were held later that evening. Women and men alternated routes each year: one group rode north toward Duralde, through the Evangeline Parish farm land, while the other headed south to Tepetate, in Acadia Parish. There was no lack of willing hosts, and many people contacted the captain in advance to make sure the run would visit them. Berline Boone says, "Now used to, we just had to take names down to go from house to house, because everybody accepted you back then."[66]

Basile's early female Mardi Gras were aware that they had to prove their ability to run Mardi Gras, especially to men. Susie Lopez recalls that some people "from the older tradition" would "kind of look down on the ladies' run." The women, on the other hand, were convinced that they not only had the right to run Mardi Gras but could do it just as well as—or better than—the men. An undercurrent of competitiveness underlies some of their stories. Basile Mardi Gras pride themselves on their skill as beggars, for instance; a good Mardi Gras should be able to talk his or her hosts into donating chickens, rice, money, or whatever else the group needs. Berline Boone notes of the women, "I felt that we collected more than [the men]."[67]

Several longtime riders describe a bitterly cold Mardi Gras years ago, when the women outlasted the men despite the weather. Berline recalls, "One year I remember they had to come get us in Duralde, we was on that side. And it was raining so bad they had put a tarpaulin on top of the truck. And it was raining and it was icing. They had to get us off the road, you know, because that's how bad it was. Oh, we wouldn't never stop, you know. The men had stopped at noon, [but] we stopped at two."[68]

This story, similar to one told by rival community runs about themselves, reflects traits many male Mardi Gras value: toughness and a dauntless determination to run Mardi Gras, despite serious discomfort. For Basile's women, the story is an answer to all of those from the "old tradition" who felt that women could not perform well in this formerly male role.

In 1978, the Mardi Gras association decided to move the women's run to Tuesday, the same day as the men's, although the two runs remained separate for the most part. Both groups met at the Woodmen of the World Hall and left together at seven o'clock in the morning, but then each went its own way. Men and women still alternated routes through the countryside, and now they also split Basile. Debbie Andrus says, "The ladies would run on one side of town and the men would run on the other side of town. Because they didn't want to combine the women and men together."[69] A local business, Gene's Food Store, divided the town's east and west sides. In the afternoon, both groups of riders met in town to parade on foot along Main Street, and shared a gumbo and dance later that night at the Woodmen's Hall. The impetus for the change was economic: staging two separate gumbos and dances cost too much time and money.

Basile's male and female runs, much like Eunice's, were eventually combined, although the transition took place in fits and starts. As in Eunice, declining membership was a key factor. Attendance at a 1979 planning meeting, for example, was so low that the run's survival was in doubt.[70] Six years later, a Mardi Gras association ledger entry notes, "Men and women ran together since they were so few."[71] The next year, in 1986, the women and men ran separately in town, but "both met together at noon and ran in [the rural] Tepetate area."[72] Stops in the countryside, once plentiful, became fewer, and the run's main focus gradually shifted to the town.

Officers made the change permanent in 1987, deciding finally that "Men and women will run together but in separate trucks."[73] Once again, practicality dictated the decision. The number of riders in the men's run had dwindled, and money was tight. The association decided it was cheaper and easier to combine the two runs and "make a bigger and prettier Mardi Gras," current Mardi Gras association president Potic Rider says.[74] Today, Basile men and women continue to run Mardi Gras together, although each group still rides on its own trailer.

Inevitably, mixing the Basile men and women changed the dynamics of the run, as the Eunice women also discovered. Men once feared that a mixed *courir* might ruin their Mardi Gras fun; in Basile, women—especially those initiated

A Mardi Gras masker "picks at" Helena Putnam by holding her over a hill of stinging ants during the 1992 Basile run. Helena, a Cajun insider, is intent on documenting Mardi Gras culture in various Creole and Cajun communities. Here she was photographing her home-town run when she was pulled into the comic performance. Courtesy of Carl Lindahl.

in the early women's run—seem to feel its effects most. Women sometimes feel overshadowed by male Mardi Gras, for example. Mary Jane (Snookie) LeJeune, a longtime core member, says, "Naturally when a bunch of women get together, you say things and you do things on your own. While when the men are there, they kind of tend to take over the show."[75] And women who previously "cut up" (clowned and joked) freely among their female peers may censor or dampen their own Mardi Gras rowdiness in front of husbands and boyfriends, because it is considered unfeminine.

Berline Boone pointed out in a 1994 interview that not all women initially wel-comed the change. "Whenever they combined the men and the women, we did *not* want it. . . . But it was less trouble, you see . . . to have the dance the Tuesday night and the gumbo and everything all together instead of two different nights. It was a lot less trouble for the people that was organizing all this stuff."[76] She commented that in the all-women's run on Sundays, "We done it better. . . . I guess maybe because we might have wanted to prove a point, [it] was better."[77] But ten years after that first interview, she sees the merger as a positive move: "I think we should all run together because it's for the same thing. I didn't mind

Helena, wearing a wire screen mask, triumphantly holds up a chicken she has captured during the 1993 Basile run. After a number of years doing behind-the-scenes work to support her community run, Helena returned to running Mardi Gras that year and was voted Best All-Around Woman Mardi Gras. Courtesy of Carl Lindahl.

it at first when we did run separate because, you know, you just didn't *do* it [run together] back then."[78] Times have changed now, and Basile women and men generally say that combining the two *courirs* has benefited both groups. In Basile, then, women have twice played an important part in reinvigorating the community Mardi Gras tradition: first by forming their own run, and later by merging with and strengthening the men's run.

The Early Tee Mamou Women's Run

By the early 1970s, women were also running Mardi Gras across the Acadia Parish line, in a country neighborhood known as Tee Mamou. Several of the earliest members belonged by birth or marriage to the Reed family, well known for their love of Mardi Gras. Merline Reed Bergeaux, her sister Patsy Reed Simar, and their sister-in-law Shirley Reed grew up in the countryside, watching brothers and other male relatives run. All can speak Cajun French, the traditional language of the rural Mardi Gras celebration, because older relatives spoke only French. Asked about their first memories of Mardi Gras, Patsy says that she (like many children) was frightened of the masked men, but Merline and Shirley remember feeling envious. They all say they looked forward to the men's *bals de Mardi Gras.* As young wives and mothers, they brought their children to the dances because, they explain, "We wanted to show our kids what we grew up with."[79] They also supported the local men's run in various other ways, such as cleaning chickens for their gumbo.

Because they considered Mardi Gras a family tradition, deciding to run themselves was a natural step. Merline Bergeaux says, "Well, in my family, everybody ran Mardi Gras, whenever I was growing up. And I decided I'd keep the tradition in the family, and I started [running myself]."[80] Merline, then in her twenties, couldn't participate in the first women's run because she was pregnant. "Besides that," she says, "I would have been there."

The women asked a local man named Ivy Deshotels to help organize the event and be their captain. Mr. Deshotels, who ran Mardi Gras for fifteen years and then served as a cocaptain for the Tee Mamou men, agreed. He recalled in a 1992 interview that he stipulated that the women would have to do what he told them. His rule for captaining, he said, was "Leave me alone, do what I ask you to do, and we'll get along fine."[81]

Patsy Simar and her sister-in-law Shirley Reed, a mother with small children at the time, ran that first year. They recall a neighbor, Curvis Clement, helping Mr. Deshotels. On the Sunday before Mardi Gras, the men led about a dozen women around the countryside in the back of a farm truck. This first run was highly successful; Shirley Reed remembers that local households were "just very welcoming." She says, "Some places, where the people did not want the men, that they were so rough," gladly accepted the women Mardi Gras.

Ivy Deshotels, on the other hand, recalled in a 1992 interview that the women could be a handful. He commented, "*Mais* the women, they're mean too, yeah." Some "drink a little bit" and then "it's no use you holler at [them]," he recalled.[82] Under his leadership, the run had about fifteen women. Many of the women had family connections to Tee Mamou's all-male run. One of the most indomitable members was Emedine Vasseur, Patsy's and Merline's grandmother, then in her seventies.

When Mr. Deshotels decided not to continue as captain, the women were determined to keep running. Shirley recalls, "We wanted to run again because we had enjoyed it. So we were bent on it." The following year, the women recruited husbands and relatives so they could continue. Shirley says: "We talked Sam [her husband] and Tout-Blanc [Merline's husband] into doing it, you know, and they ran us around the neighborhood in pickup trucks. And we had our dance at the Ponderosa Club. . . . And then . . . the next year we had our dance in Basile, I believe it was. And then the following year Larry Spears went overseas to work, and . . . Sam didn't want to do it by himself, and Tout-Blanc didn't have a pickup, so he didn't want to do it." Still intent on continuing their run, the women decided to approach Gerald Frugé, who had recently assumed leadership of the troubled Tee Mamou men's run. The women already included the Frugé house in their Mardi Gras visits. Gerald later recalled, "They'd run in pickup trucks, and they'd come around the neighborhood, and they'd even come here. . . . [There were] I guess, six to ten [women]."[83]

A delegation talked to Gerald at a pre–Mardi Gras meeting of the Tee Mamou Mardi Gras Association, which organized the local men's run. Shirley Reed says, "So we decided when they had the men's Mardi Gras meeting, at the Four Corners [Club], we were going to go and tackle Gerald. So Merline, and me, and Pat, and Darlene, and Grandma [Emedine Vasseur] . . . we went and tackled Gerald [to] see if he wouldn't take us on as a group, and run us. . . . And so he said, 'Yeah,' he would try it, and it was such a success the first year." Years later, Gerald Frugé admitted that he was doubtful at first about the women's proposal—"I couldn't imagine how in the world I could handle that"—but after some thought, he agreed.[84] Soon afterward, his wife Linda became a core member of the run.

Under Gerald Frugé's leadership, the event became far more structured than its informal beginnings. Merline Bergeaux says that the women's run "has improved a hundred percent" since its earliest years.[85] Indeed, some consider Gerald's involvement the start of the official Tee Mamou women's run. Women, like men, joined the Tee Mamou Mardi Gras Association, paid its dues, and attended planning meetings in the weeks before Mardi Gras. This affiliation had many advantages. Because their runs took place on different days, women and men could share many resources—they rode on the same painted trailer and had many of the same male cocaptains, for instance. At first, the women followed the same route as the men, but Gerald Frugé soon decided to carve out a separate route, west of the men's traditional territory. The women's run also moved to Saturday, because few people were home to receive the Mardi Gras on Sundays.

The Tee Mamou women, like other groups, ended their day with a public gumbo and *bal de Mardi Gras.* Initially, they held both at the Four Corners Club in Tee Mamou, the traditional site of the men's gumbo and dance. When the club burned down, they moved from place to place: the Knights of Columbus hall; Mike's, a local grocery store with a dance floor in the back; clubs in Lake Arthur and other communities; and later a church hall in Iota.

The Tee Mamou *courir,* like Basile's, reveals several trends in the second wave of women's Mardi Gras runs. These shifts reflect broader social changes over the past thirty years or so, as women redefined the boundaries of feminine behavior. One trend was a wider age range among participants, as young girls began joining older women. Tee Mamou's earliest lady Mardi Gras, like those in other women's *courirs,* were married women. Merline, Shirley, and Patsy were in their twenties, but several women were much older. Emedine Vasseur ran for almost twenty years, beginning when she was past seventy; she retired only when she could no longer get on and off the truck.

Eventually, though, Tee Mamou (like Basile) allowed girls as young as thirteen to accompany their mothers. By the 1970s and 1980s, women's runs were no longer just for settled wives and grandmothers; teen-age girls also had a chance to engage in the "impromptu wildness" of Mardi Gras, which no longer carried the social stigma it once had for girls.[86]

The Tee Mamou women, like the Basile women, could be unruly and impetuous charges. Ivy Deshotels's daughter, Janice Deshotels Ashford, then married and in her twenties, joined the run for three or four years in the early 1980s. Raised in a Mardi Gras family, she says that "Mardi Gras was always there for me.... [But] when I was young, the women didn't run. Of course that was before they had women's lib and everything. I mean women didn't do anything but stay home and have babies."[87] Once she did start running, rowdiness came easily to her. Janice recalls that Merline Bergeaux was "one of the wild ones," and she was another. She laughs, "There's nothing we wouldn't think of doing. . . . [And] if we'd think of doing it, we'd do it."

By the 1970s and 1980s, many rural Cajun women were working outside the home, sometimes at two or three jobs, out of necessity. For Tee Mamou's female Mardi Gras, especially those in service industries, work schedules complicated their participation. Shirley Reed says that her job prevented her from running every year, for instance. Janice Ashford did not work on weekends, but she comments that the run, and the drinking that went along with it, took their toll; she usually had to take Monday off to recover, and often Tuesday and Wednesday as well.

Another trend was more physical and unbridled "cutting up" by some female Mardi Gras. In earlier ladies' runs, women acted "crazy" by drinking in public, playing jokes on each other, riding a donkey along Main Street, and dancing with strangers. In Basile and especially in Tee Mamou, some female maskers rivaled the men in drinking and rough horseplay, as they climbed trees, jumped into swimming pools, stopped cars on the highway, and tangled with captains. Accounts of the women's rowdy performances, as they teased and tested their captains, evoke images of what historian Natalie Zemon Davis (writing about medieval Europe) calls "the disorderly woman . . . who gives rein to the lower in herself and seeks rule over her superiors."[88] At times, their play included a comic sexual note, as women "kidnapped" married men and carried them onto their Mardi Gras wagon.

Captains, faced with this unrestrained play, no longer carried their whips mainly for show. Tee Mamou's male captains used braided burlap whips to keep the women in line, just as they did for the local men's run. Often they found the women harder to control, because female Mardi Gras were willing to use any ploy to gain an advantage. Janice Ashford, whose husband, Danny, was a cocaptain for both women and men, says, "[Captains] had to be careful [with the women]. And the women didn't care. You just did whatever you could just to get the best of them. . . . And that's the truth. You know, the more you could do to get at them, [the better]." Their captains, she says, let the women get away with more misbehavior than the men, because they *were* women. Still, she recalls, "We'd have whip marks for a week. That was the fun of it." Bruises proved competence; the women had played the role of mischief maker well enough to draw a vigorous whipping.

A final trend has been greater integration of female and male Mardi Gras. Unlike the first wave of women's runs, three women's runs founded in the 1960s and 1970s have survived. In Eunice and Basile, they adapted by eventually merging with local men's runs. By that time, it was no longer unthinkable for men and women to run Mardi Gras together, and coed runs increased membership and saved money and labor.

The Tee Mamou women's run has taken a different path, adamantly retaining its identity as a women's run. Women and men have offered several theories on why. Linda Frugé Doucet notes that under her late husband's leadership, both Tee Mamou women's and men's *courirs* remained strong; membership never declined to the point that combining the runs seemed advantageous. As it is, the two groups share many of the same resources, such as their Mardi Gras wagon, captains, and drivers. A larger, combined group would require larger or more wagons. Linda also comments that male captains' battles with female Mardi Gras are among the run's biggest attractions, for spectators and Mardi Gras alike. Suson Launey, who joined the women's run in the early 1980s, says that the women continue to hold their run on Saturday "out of respect for the men. . . . We respect their right to run on Mardi Gras day [as they always have]."[89]

Still, men and women in Tee Mamou now perform together more often than not for public programs inside and outside the community. Female and male Mardi Gras mix for pre–Mardi Gras performances at D.I.'s Restaurant, at local nursing homes, and for restagings at festivals around the state. And every year since 1988, Tee Mamou's women Mardi Gras have met the men's run on Iota's outskirts to parade (on a separate trailer) along the town's main street, much as Eunice's lady Mardi Gras once rendezvoused and paraded with their local men's run.

*   *   *

Cajun women today have more Mardi Gras options than ever before. Three generations of women have now run Mardi Gras in Eunice, Basile, and Tee Mamou. In addition, women and men ride together in five newer or revived community *courirs* in Egan, Pecanière, Chataignier and Mermentau (both of which also include children), and L'Anse Maigre—a once-male horseback run that began allowing women to ride in 2003. Perhaps most important, today's children's runs include both girls and boys, even in communities with men-only adult runs. Girls today are trained in the Mardi Gras performance from a very young age and can easily make the transition to a coed or women's run as teenagers.

Women's own words reveal how meaningful Mardi Gras is to them. Several say that Mardi Gras is "in our blood," a key part of who they are. The celebration is closely bound up with their identity as prairie Cajuns and as members of a particular community. Merline Bergeaux said in 1988, "Whenever I die, you can just put my suit, mask, and *capuchon* with me." Sixteen years later, sidelined by a heart attack, she stood on her porch and wept as the Tee Mamou women's run—her run for three decades—visited her home.

Carl Lindahl describes the importance of the "remembered past" in present-day Mardi Gras runs; vivid memories and stories of past performances mold the actions and feelings of today's creative maskers.[90] Younger members, he argues, learn to run Mardi Gras not just by watching senior members but also through these stories, retold around Mardi Gras time. Young women now have their own legendary Mardi Gras figures to emulate, their own remembered festive past, as well as a "vitally enacted present."[91] The Mardi Gras pioneers described in this chapter, along with many others, were instrumental in creating, maintaining, and adapting the female roles that have transformed the celebration as a whole.

3

Organizing Mayhem:
Country Mardi Gras Associations

"I still get all excited when the time
gets nearer to Mardi Gras."
—Berline Boone

"When Mardi Gras comes around, the hair raises up
on the back of my neck. And you just get that feeling,
you know. You just can't wait for it."
—Russell "Potic" Rider

Today's Cajun Mardi Gras runs are larger, more expensive, and more public than in the past, and preparations are far more complex. Most planning takes place within local Mardi Gras associations, volunteer organizations that provide crucial infrastructure. Rural Mardi Gras associations make *courirs de Mardi Gras* possible in a changing world. They not only fund and produce the events but also make the group accountable to the larger community, ensuring that people continue to accept them. Most important for this book, Mardi Gras associations also serve as public forums and vehicles for change, including a stronger voice for women.

All community Mardi Gras associations manage essentially the same responsibilities: they handle the group's finances; purchase food, soft drinks, and alcohol; chart routes and schedules; book music for the *courir* and the Mardi Gras dance; register and train new members; and solicit volunteers to help with various chores before, during, and after the run. They also work to safeguard the group and its members from potential lawsuits over injuries or damages. Membership typically includes everyone who registers for the local Mardi Gras run and pays its modest dues, averaging between ten and twenty dollars. In places where both women and men run Mardi Gras, they belong to the same Mardi Gras association.

As in many volunteer organizations, a handful of men and women usually do much of the organizational work and end up making many crucial decisions for the group. Roles within the Mardi Gras association, like those in Mardi Gras families, generally fall along traditional gender lines. Most often, men hold the primary leadership positions as presidents or head *capitaines;* they decide policy, preside over elections of officers, round up volunteer helpers, and schedule and lead meetings. Women, whether or not they are elected officers, are often responsible for fundraising, purchasing food and other supplies, and record keeping. Women are also active in public outreach and educational activities such as children's Mardi Gras runs and school programs.[1]

In chapter 1 of this book I described women's traditional behind-the-scenes Mardi Gras work within family and friendship networks. This chapter, on the other hand, focuses on women's activities in, and influence on, rural Mardi Gras associations in Basile and Tee Mamou. Exploring the festival's organizational work helps us understand not only the mechanics of Mardi Gras staging but also how Mardi Gras associations have become another portal for women into a male-dominated celebration.

The Basile Mardi Gras Association

The Basile Mardi Gras Association dates back at least to the 1960s, though the local men's run is much older. When Basile women founded their own Sunday run, they, too, became members. Until the mid-1970s, the Ladies' Mardi Gras Association was nominally discrete from the men's association, and each had its own president and vice-president. However, the two groups held pre–Mardi Gras meetings and membership drives together, and worked together to organize their *courirs.* By the late 1970s, the twin associations had become a single organizational entity, with one set of officers, and a few years later, the runs themselves merged.

Today the Basile association elects a president, vice-president, secretary, and treasurer each year, although the latter two positions are frequently combined. Often the same people are reelected year after year because no one else wants to serve. In addition to officers, the association approves selection of two sets of captains: one for the men and one for the women, a holdover from the days of separate runs. These positions, too, are rarely contested; if a captain agrees to continue serving, she or he is almost automatically reappointed. Each captain then chooses his or her own assistants or cocaptains.

These two leadership hierarchies—Mardi Gras association officers and captains—have different but overlapping purposes. In theory, the association's president is in charge during the organizational process, and captains are the bosses during the run itself. Often the two structures converge when a member serves as both a captain and Mardi Gras association member. However, despite the group's formal structure, who actually does what depends mainly on gender, willingness and availability, and family or friendship ties.[2]

The Basile Mardi Gras Association's undisputed head is its president, a position traditionally held by a man—often a former *capitaine*. Presidents, like other officers, are elected for a year, but they usually serve multiple terms. Potic Rider has been Basile's president for two decades.[3] Charismatic and dedicated to Mardi Gras, he is described by many as the heart and soul of the Basile run. After so many years of leadership, he wields considerable authority in the organization, and captains and other officers defer to him.

The group's vice-president also is usually male. The sole female vice-president, in 1979 and 1980, was Berline Boone, who had earlier served as Ladies' Mardi Gras Association president in 1975.[4] Berline, however, later asked not to be nominated again in any capacity because, in her words, being an officer is "a lot of headache, when you're supposed to be having a good time."[5] Since Berline's short tenure, all vice-presidents have been men.

If men have dominated the association's top leadership, women have almost invariably been its secretaries and treasurers, often holding both titles simultaneously. (Women, it seems, are assumed to be good with money and at writing things down.) Although not as powerful as the president, the secretary/treasurer is nevertheless an essential figure. She works closely with the president on planning and organizing the run, collects donations, and orders supplies. She keeps not only the group's financial records but also its written history in minutes for pre–Mardi Gras meetings.

Few people want the position of secretary/treasurer, which involves lots of work and little prestige. (Few people want to be the association's president, either, but that office brings considerably more public recognition and authority.) Several of the run's core women have taken their turns, and Snookie LeJeune held the office for many years because, as one member joked, the association "wouldn't let her quit." Although being an officer may be more obligation than privilege, it does offer women an important avenue for involvement, even when work and family life temporarily prevent them from running. As a newlywed in the 1970s, Debbie Andrus sat out two years of the run, but remembers still doing the group's bookkeeping. Holding office, then, is one way Basile women have wielded influence in the Mardi Gras association, and by extension the celebration as a whole.

Cassie LeBlue is the current secretary/treasurer, as well as the women's *capitaine* since 1996. Together, she and Potic Rider handle most of the run's organizational chores. Cassie sees no line between her duties as captain and officer; for her, it is all part of "captaining." Her position demands not only organizational skills and attention to detail but also a great deal of flexibility and stamina. For

Cassie LeBlue, women's captain and vice-president of the Basile Mardi Gras Association with daughters Jenny (*left*) and Laura LeBlue. Laura frequently serves as Cassie's cocaptain for the children's Sunday run and the adult run on Tuesday.

instance, Cassie is usually one of the last to leave the Town Barn—the group's hub—on Mardi Gras night because she stays to wash and load up gumbo pots. After a recent run, she remained there until almost one o'clock in the morning, fixing a plumbing leak.

Getting ready for Mardi Gras, Cassie says, is by far the most demanding part of her job. Her work begins soon after the group's first meeting in January and continues well past Mardi Gras. She says, "It's hard before [the run]. Because I have to do everything."[6] Her prescribed duties include keeping the Mardi Gras ledgers up to date, balancing the association's bank account, making grocery lists, and shopping for supplies. As head captain, Cassie is also in charge of registering girls and women for the children's and adults' runs, making sure they sign release forms, and collecting their fees.

Finances and Purchasing

One of the association's most crucial tasks is raising money for both the adult run on Tuesday and (since 1986) a children's run on the preceding Sunday. The association counts on membership fees to offset costs, but most riders sign up and pay dues only on the morning of the run. Meanwhile, the group must pay for many supplies in advance. Liquor alone for the adult run costs about fifteen hundred dollars; ingredients for two gumbos and miscellaneous other expenses can bring the group's pre–Mardi Gras outlay to twenty-five hundred dollars or more. While this is cheap compared to the cost of a New Orleans parade, it is a considerable amount for most Basile residents. In 2005, membership fees for the adult run increased from fifteen to twenty dollars per person, in an attempt to keep up with rising costs. Like other Mardi Gras associations, the Basile group maintains a bank account with enough money for initial expenditures, and later replenishes it with Mardi Gras income.

The association also depends on donations of cash and goods from local businesses to meet the cost of two runs. Basile has tried different fundraising strategies over the years, including a special donations committee chaired by Berline Boone. These days, treasurer Cassie LeBlue solicits and collects donations. In the weeks before Mardi Gras, she visits stores in Basile, Eunice, and Elton, but comments that donations have dwindled in recent years. (A number of customary supporters—the local rice dryer, several bars, and a Basile grocery store—have gone out of business.) Only one business contributes cash to the organization, but several businesses offer in-kind donations of beer, onions, rice, and sausage, either before or during the run.

Cassie also takes care of most of the association's purchasing. She buys almost three dozen trophies for maskers in both runs, and orders engraved plaques for various helpers and Mardi Gras Hall of Fame inductees. One of her chief pre–Mardi Gras tasks is buying groceries for two gumbos, and then helping find volunteers to cook it. Gumbo hens (or sometimes roosters) must be specially ordered from Eunice Poultry a month or more in advance, and then picked up shortly before Mardi Gras weekend. Cassie also places an order for homemade andouille sausage and pork-and-rice *boudin* from Tee Bay's Sausage or other local makers, and travels to Eunice to buy nonperishable gumbo ingredients such as jars of roux and boxes of salt. Liquor, which Cassie and Potic get from local merchants a few days before Mardi Gras, is the most expensive purchase. They typically buy three bottles of whiskey, several of sweet wine and flavored liquor mixes, fifteen cases of Budweiser beer, and fifteen of Miller Lite or Schlitz, along with cases of soft drinks. During the run itself, leaders restock the liquor supply as needed at local stores and bars.

Pre–Mardi Gras Performances

A series of pre–Mardi Gras events also requires considerable time from officers and captains, as well as from a core of veteran Mardi Gras members. Most years, the Basile Mardi Gras Association is invited to put on special shows, or "marches," at local clubs, nursing homes, and other venues such as Eunice's Liberty Theatre; they may perform as many as six marches in two weeks. Cassie LeBlue comments that the week before Mardi Gras is her busiest, because the group "runs" almost every night at a different club, and she accompanies them as a captain. Members enjoy these shows, seeing them as a public service, a way of thanking supportive business owners, and promotion for their Mardi Gras run. Marches at clubs also bring in a little money, as the association is either paid a fee or allowed to keep any money they beg from patrons. Still, the schedule can be exhausting for association leaders who coordinate and lead each performance, and for the women and men maskers who perform.

Basile's greatest pre–Mardi Gras commitment of time and resources, though, is its Sunday children's run. The kids' run (as it's usually called) was founded in 1986 to help preserve an endangered community Mardi Gras tradition, especially its song. Girls and boys coached in the festive performance would in time join and reinvigorate the adult run. Debbie Andrus commented in 1991: "We decided . . . if we wanted to keep it [Mardi Gras] going, you know, in the community, then we would [have to] keep the younger ones. Because it got to where hardly anybody knew the Mardi Gras song any more. I'd learned it from the older [women]. . . . And it got to where a lot of the little kids didn't even hardly know French anymore, or the Mardi Gras song, or what Mardi Gras was all about. So we decided, well, let's run the little ones and maybe hopefully they will pick up our culture and they will continue keeping on the Mardi Gras."[7]

Women have often been described as conservators of French Louisiana domestic life and religion. Although men generally held the lead roles in public traditions such as running Mardi Gras, women often made active, if more private, contributions to their children's Mardi Gras performances.[8] It's not surprising, then, that Basile women today play a prominent part in the local children's Mardi Gras run. By the time the children's run was founded in the 1980s, Basile women had themselves been running Mardi Gras for more than fifteen years. Participants registered their own daughters and sons in the run, and volunteered to help as captains and cocaptains, coaches, and general helpers. Susie Lopez explained in a 1991 interview, "Some of the older Mardi Gras that run with [the children], chaperone them, we're more or less like cocaptains. . . . And [we're] just more or less showing them what it's all about. And kind of taking them through it, going from the house and chasing chickens and begging for the ingredients and stuff."[9]

On the Sunday before Mardi Gras, Potic Rider, Cassie LeBlue, and other regular captains (carrying burlap quoits instead of leather whips) lead the children on their five-hour run. Frequently the group includes over a hundred children, ranging from toddlers to preteens. A dozen or so veteran Mardi Gras, both women and men, ride with the children. Dressed in Mardi Gras suits but no masks, they circulate among the children during house visits, teaching them how to sing the song properly, stomp their feet as they dance, pump their arms to the music, and beg. Debbie Andrus, one of Basile's most adept and dedicated "old" Mardi Gras, usually helps lead the singing. Many of the women and men active in the early children's run now have grown children but still help out regularly.

Although the children's run is shorter than the Tuesday *courir,* it is no less intense or fast-paced. Indeed, it often includes more in-town stops than the adult run, because grandparents and other relatives insist on receiving the children. At two o'clock, they return to the Town Park Barn to perform a march for the crowd of parents and friends that has gathered, sing their song once more, and then are divided into categories (according to gender and age) for "jurying." Captains and helpers judge each division for prettiest, ugliest, and most original costumes, as well as for best all-around Mardi Gras.

Basile is proud of its successful children's run, which frequently attracts more revelers and community followers than the adult run. Many women and men view the kids' run as their tradition's future, looking forward to it even more eagerly than their own run. The late Ella Ruth Young, former women's and children's captain, told me years ago, "I tell you what, it's even more fun than the grownups."[10] One thing the children's run has accomplished is recruiting and training young girls to run Mardi Gras; nearly as many girls as boys participate. As some of these girls join the adult run at thirteen, they help to close a marked gender gap. The junior run also helps keep the association's finances afloat. Fees are only five dollars per child, but the event is relatively cheap to produce because it includes no alcohol.

The children's run, members say, is also achieving its educational goals. Training children who speak little or no French is difficult, but association members try to teach them at least a few words of the Mardi Gras song. Although only one or two women take the lead in singing the song during the adult run, they work hard to teach it to the next generation. Ella Ruth Young said that she distributed tapes of the song to children and added, "They know it more than the grownups do." Debbie Andrus commented that teaching the song is usually a "last-minute deal" but "we always teach them a few words." She noted, "I find that the ones that started off [running Mardi Gras] when they were younger, they're still running. They're picking it up more and more. Little by little. And some of them that run . . . come from parents that have all [run] before, so they're kind of picking it up. But they all know" the song.

The children's run is one form of outreach aimed at teaching children about their Mardi Gras heritage and, by extension, about their folk culture as a whole. Women have also been active in another initiative, special Mardi Gras programs in elementary school classrooms. By the late 1970s, members of the Mardi Gras association had begun visiting Basile's W. W. Stewart Elementary School to familiarize children with the local Mardi Gras custom.[11] Kim Moreau notes that one purpose at the time was to teach children not to be afraid of the Mardi Gras.[12]

At first these programs were cohosted by the Parent Advisory Committee, part of a French language program intended, according to the local paper, to "teach the children the customs of their French ancestors." Children in kindergarten and first, second, and third grades "dress[ed] tacky in old clothes put together at home" and made masks for a Mardi Gras party, where Mardi Gras association members judged their disguises.[13]

Soon the party expanded to demonstrations of singing and dancing by the association's women and men. Debbie Andrus told me in 1991, "Now when it gets around Mardi Gras time, we put on a little demonstration at the school. Some of them get to go and talk, and some of us get to go dressed out, and they play the Mardi Gras song, and usually someone sings the song for them, or shows them a couple of the words." Mardi Gras school programs have not taken place for the last few years, perhaps in part because core association volunteers, those most involved in early school programs, no longer have school-aged children themselves. A more compelling reason may be that the successful children's run makes school programs redundant.

Basile's Meetings

Basile, like most Mardi Gras communities, holds a series of meetings to assign duties and ensure readiness for the run. Meetings begin in early January with a "roundup" and end the week before Mardi Gras with a final "assembly" to ensure that everyone has done their appointed jobs. These open meetings—announced in the *Basile Weekly* and held in the town hall—are an important public forum, a chance to air concerns and negotiate power. Many changes that led to women's integration into the tradition took place at past meetings. Decisions to combine the men's and ladies' Mardi Gras associations in the 1970s, and finally the merger of the two runs in the 1980s, were all discussed and voted on during association meetings.

Nevertheless, Mardi Gras meeting attendance has always been low in Basile. Typically, only association officials, captains, and, on a good night, a handful of regular riders attend meetings. Accordingly, a few people—mostly officers—make the majority of decisions. Much of the group's business is ratified at the year's first meeting. Elections for officers and captains are held then, finances are discussed, and requests are made for volunteers to handle various tasks.

One of the most important pieces of business is choosing recipients of various honors presented during the Mardi Gras dance each year. For some years, the Basile Mardi Gras Association has awarded appreciation plaques to helpers such as gumbo cooks and truck drivers. In 1993, the group also formed the Basile Mardi Gras Hall of Fame to recognize those who have "helped to organize, promote, and enhance the continuing of the Basile Mardi Gras run."[14] Each year members (or more accurately, officers) select two or more Hall of Fame inductees to honor at the Mardi Gras dance.

The majority of Hall of Fame members have been men, most of them former *capitaines.* Women have only gradually gained access, perhaps because they rarely hold the highest Mardi Gras leadership roles. In 1998, women's captain Ella Ruth Young was posthumously inducted, along with her husband and co-captain Jim Young. Ella Ruth remained the only female honoree for five more years, until five pioneering women captains and gumbo cooks, all now deceased, were inducted as a group.[15] Still, male honorees far outnumbered women, and their contributions as *capitaines* and association presidents still hold higher (or at least more public) value than women's activities. The 2005 Mardi Gras ceremony made considerable inroads in balancing the Hall of Fame, however, with the induction of women's *capitaine* Cassie LeBlue (along with her husband, Junior, and brother-in-law Ronald), and six core women runners: Debbie Andrus, Janell Ashford, Berline Boone, Snookie LeJeune, Susie Lopez, and Gloria Miller. Helena Putnam was named to the Hall of Fame the following year.

Meetings for Basile's Mardi Gras have become fewer in recent years, and its power base has shrunk. The association seems caught in a spiral: officers, especially the president, determine many policies, because few members take part in meetings and elections. Some longtime members, on the other hand, no longer attend meetings because they feel their voices are ignored in the decision-making process. In 2003, the first public meeting was also the last, suggesting that the Basile association may be losing its most public forum. The "roundup" the following year was more encouraging, with six or seven younger members volunteering to become more active. One of their requests was that the association hold more meetings in the future.

For many years, a small core of men and women, now in their forties and fifties, has been the backbone of Basile's Mardi Gras association. But these mainstays have "done their tour of duty," as Potic Rider says, and say they are ready to hand over some responsibilities to a younger generation that includes their own sons and daughters. At the first 2004 meeting, Potic Rider told the younger members, "We need some young people to start learning this so y'all can take it over."[16] Men often outnumber women at meetings, but a few young women are taking an active interest in the organization. In recent years, as Cassie LeBlue has suffered heart trouble, Cheryl Young has become her apprentice, assuming many of her secretarial and bookkeeping duties, running errands, and helping out as a cocaptain. Cassie's daughter Laura, another cocaptain, is also learning from and assisting her mother. These and other young women are poised to take increasingly active and public roles, opening the Mardi Gras door even wider for women.

The Tee Mamou Mardi Gras Association

In Tee Mamou, as in Basile, the local Mardi Gras association offers women a wedge into a traditionally male celebration. Both women (who perform in a separate Saturday run) and men belong to the local association and help organize the two community runs.[17] Unlike Basile, the Tee Mamou association has no elected officers or formal structure; it is, says former cocaptain Don LeJeune a "ragtag, put-together kind of organization" that exists "only in theory."[18] According to Don, the group purposely has no elected officers because they might be singled out for legal liability. Instead, the association's hierarchy is the same as that of the run: the head *capitaine* is in charge, assisted by cocaptains—all men. The association's list of rules reminds members: "Your participation in this organization is solely at the discretion of the Captains. Eligibility to participate is regulated by the Captains."

Tee Mamou women contribute in similar ways to those in Basile: they handle secretarial chores such as registering members and keeping records, ordering and purchasing supplies, and helping sketch out routes and schedules for both runs. Here, too, women's organizational abilities and adaptability—and sometimes their flexible work schedules—are invaluable. And Tee Mamou women, like those in Basile, have creatively used pre–Mardi Gras meetings and performances to advance their own agendas.

As head *capitaine*, Todd Frugé juggles many logistical tasks himself, but delegates others to cocaptains and helpers who chip in as needed. Todd assumed leadership in 1999 after the death of his father, Gerald, who had "captained" for the men's run since the late 1960s and the women's run for almost as long.[19] During his tenure, Gerald and his cocaptains drafted the association's first set of official rules—its charter, in effect. Now Todd is responsible for maintaining and revising the group's policies.

Tee Mamou women have carved out their own areas of responsibility in organizing Mardi Gras. One contribution is helping captains sketch out Mardi Gras routes and schedules for the men's and women's runs. The Saturday before the women's run, the association holds a barbecue and work day at the Frugé barn, the group's Mardi Gras hub. While captains and male helpers set up the painted Mardi Gras wagon, one or two women make the rounds of local homes and businesses, asking if they will accept one or both runs. For years, veterans Suson Launey and Linda Gatte took care of this task, and then worked with captains to put together a route.

When Todd Frugé became *capitaine,* he asked his sister Renée, a Mardi Gras

Capitaine Todd Frugé, standing on the steps of the Tee Mamou wagon, reads the Mardi Gras rules aloud before the Saturday ladies' run. Visible in the background is the Frugé barn, the group's headquarters. After the rules are read, the assembled women climb, one by one, onto the wagon as Todd calls roll.

Tee Mamou women, masks propped up on their *capuchons,* clown by hanging over the sides of their painted Mardi Gras wagon. As the truck carries them along their countryside route, the women drink beer and wine, chat, and sing along with the blaring recorded Cajun music.

since she was thirteen, to help him make the route. Renée, who worked full-time until recently, sometimes contacts hosts by telephone rather than trying to track them down in person. The majority are longtime Mardi Gras hosts; usually, there is little change in routes from one year to the next. Renée notes that "We really have our same places [we always go]."[20] Most agree to accept the Mardi Gras again, but a few decline because they are ill, will not be home, or decide that hosting the runners is too much trouble. Renée creates a list of confirmed hosts for each run, outlines timetables, and distributes schedules to local businesses such as Trapper's Bar and the Quick-Trip grocery. Written schedules are increasingly important, as many tourists, folklorists, and local residents want to catch up with and follow the runs during the day.

Tee Mamou women, especially Renée and her mother Linda, also buy some of the supplies needed for each run. Here, as in Basile, beer is one of the principle purchases. Renée, who worked as an assistant manager for D.I.'s Restaurant (owned by her aunt and uncle) until her daughter was born, orders all the beer for the women's and men's runs, and for the group's pre–Mardi Gras shows, through restaurant suppliers. This is not only convenient but also gets the Mardi Gras association a better price. She also stores the beer in the restaurant's walk-

Arms linked, Tee Mamou women approach a house as they sing their Mardi Gras song in unison. Once the head captain receives permission from homeowners to visit, with a blast on his whistle he signals the women to dismount from their wagon. The maskers form a column, four or eight abreast, to make an orderly procession toward the house.

in cooler until it is needed for pre–Mardi Gras shows and the two runs. When Gerald was captain, his wife, Linda, always took care of buying emergency supplies, such as aspirins and Tylenol, Band-Aids, and safety pins for the *capitaine's* truck. Now, she does the same for her son Todd.

In many ways, then, work within the Tee Mamou Mardi Gras Association falls along gendered lines. Women's tasks frequently draw on organizational and financial skills they develop through managing a household and through employment. But women also volunteer to help out with jobs that are traditionally "men's work." For example, men usually take care of moving the Mardi Gras "wagon" onto a gooseneck trailer, nailing on its wooden sides, and preparing it for the runs. Recently, however, Renée and Todd's fiancé, Jennifer, helped refurbish and repaint the wagon. Renée says, "Last year we actually . . . painted everything. That was a job. We had to do all the letters [spelling out "Tee Mamou" on both sides]." Young women, then, are moving into nontraditional roles in their Mardi Gras association activities as well as in their festive performances.

Pre–Mardi Gras Performances and Meetings

Tee Mamou, like Basile, has a busy pre–Mardi Gras schedule of costumed visits to area clubs and nursing homes in Jennings and Lake Arthur. In addition, the association typically "makes" ten marches—two per night for five days—at D.I.'s Cajun Restaurant, ending on Mardi Gras night. Women and men perform together for these public programs, with the exception of Saturday's march at D.I.'s (the women's official postrun dance) and Tuesday's (the men's *bal de Mardi Gras*).

On nights when the Tee Mamou Mardi Gras Association is scheduled to perform, D.I.'s Restaurant is jammed with visitors and local residents, eating dinner while they wait to watch the Mardi Gras dance, sing, beg, and wrestle with their captains. Each march can last over an hour, because maskers customarily end their performance by refusing to leave the dance floor, hiding under tables, or climbing into the rafters until captains cart them out. This twice-nightly drama is hugely popular with bystanders but exhausting for Mardi Gras and especially for captains. When women and men run together, the group is often too large for D.I.'s cramped performance space, curtailing their ability to "cut up" freely. Renée Frugé Douget comments, "I feel that we have too many running during the week and for the space we have, the people aren't getting the real deal." Todd is reluctant to limit the number of maskers—he doesn't feel it's fair to turn volunteers away, his sister says—so Renée and some other seasoned Mardi Gras "dress out" only if they are needed.

Erika Frugé and Regina Myers, cousins and Mardi Gras partners, wearing burlap-covered masks they created, dance to a two-step during a house visit. At each visit, the Mardi Gras dance to two tunes—a fast two-step and a waltz. Sometimes the maskers dance with each other, as these two do, but often they pull women, men, or children from the audience to be dance partners.

Mardi Gras planning meetings, held on three consecutive Friday evenings, also bring men and women together to prepare for their runs. Tee Mamou planning meetings are far better attended than Basile's because they are compulsory. Rules state that all members must attend at least two of the three scheduled meetings, unless the head *capitaine* agrees to waive the requirement. Meetings combine business, socializing, and rehearsal. They build community among members (some of whom see each other only at Mardi Gras time), giving them a chance to reminisce about past Mardi Gras runs, critique the previous year's event, and voice their suggestions and complaints. In theory, at least, the association's rules may be changed at pre–Mardi Gras meetings. Perhaps most important, meetings ensure that maskers understand what is expected of them—especially crucial for new members.

The final gathering takes place outside D.I.'s Restaurant, immediately before the group's Friday night show. But the first two meetings are held at Tee Mamou's small Knights of Columbus Hall on Highway 97. On meeting nights, women and men trickle into the hall, find seats at long tables along the hall's two sides or buy a can of beer from the bar at the rear. Here, as in many rural Cajun get-togethers, women tend to cluster together on one side of the room and men on the other. Perhaps because their runs are separate, women and men engage in a friendly rivalry during meetings, bantering and criticizing each others' Mardi Gras skills.

Much of the secretarial work having to do with the run falls to Todd's girl-friend, Jennifer, whose responsibilities mirror those of Cassie LeBlue in Basile. On meeting nights, Jennifer and another young woman sit at a table at one end of the hall, registering members, collecting their dues (thirteen dollars for women, and fifteen for men because they drink more), and making sure they sign a release form. The two women also hand each member three photocopied sheets: a copy of the Mardi Gras association's rules, lyrics for Tee Mamou's Mardi Gras song (in French, with English translations), and a schedule of performances at D.I.'s Restaurant.

Shortly after seven o'clock, *capitaine* Todd Frugé calls members to attention by blowing his coaching whistle.[21] Asking for a show of hands by first-time runners, Todd then reads each of the association's rules aloud. Many listeners laugh when he reads "You are not to wrestle with captains," because this rule is broken more often than not, especially by women. Frugé takes the laughter in good humor but comments that the Mardi Gras run "has to be regulated." Captains also address problems and oversights in previous runs. A number of Todd's comments are directed specifically at the women's shortcomings—for example, a reminder that every rider must get down from the wagon at every stop. (One woman protests that they can't help it if they have to wait in line for the truck's bathroom.)

One meeting objective is to polish the group's performance of the Tee Mamou Mardi Gras song. All runners are expected to learn the song's sixteen verses in Cajun French, but few young women and men speak fluent French these days.[22] They memorize the lyrics phonetically, through repetition at planning meetings. Todd Frugé tells the singers: "Last year was a great year, but we had problems with the song last year. . . . Make an extra effort to learn the song." The women, in particular, he says, have trouble with some verses. Women's voices are not as strong as men's, and novices have trouble hearing the handful of women who know the song well.

After a couple of practice rounds by the entire group, Todd calls the women forward to circle him and sing the song on their own. Tee Mamou's song describes the progressive emptying of a bottle—and then a glass—of wine, and Todd prompts the singers by holding up a bottle of sweet wine. He passes the bottle around the room, and women take a swig before handing it on. The women sing the entire song twice, before Todd leads the men in singing it once. This prompts longtime Mardi Gras Suson Launey to call for equal rights; if the women had to sing twice, the men should too. Catcalls and teasing continue for a few minutes, until Todd calls the meeting to a close shortly after eight o'clock.

Tee Mamou meetings offer a good example of how local women have used Mardi Gras associations to gain access to the festival. Back in the early 1970s, a few determined women, who ran Mardi Gras more or less on their own, attended a meeting of the all-male association to recruit Gerald Frugé as their captain. He agreed, and the women's run grew steadily under his direction. Women became members of the Mardi Gras association and regularly attended its meetings.

The women's persistence paid off again a decade later in the mid-1980s. This time they protested their exclusion from pre–Mardi Gras outings and at other times of the year. The male Mardi Gras were being invited to perform at various public programs, as well as at local dance halls, and the women wanted in. Shirley Reed told me, "At first, they didn't want to mix us with the men, you know, for any activities or anything. And we'd *beg*, you know, like when they had the dances at the Lakeshore [Club] and stuff, we weren't going with the men. And Gerald wouldn't let us."[23] She explained, "We put up a fuss because the men were getting all the attention and we weren't getting anything." This changed, however, when the Mardi Gras association was asked to demonstrate their run in the French Quarter in New Orleans. Few men volunteered for the trip, but women did; for the first time, they performed alongside the men. Today, most of the association's performances at festivals, museums, and other public venues depend heavily on women's participation.

In the late 1980s, the Tee Mamou women once again brought up complaints of discrimination at Mardi Gras association meetings. The town of Iota, where the Tee Mamou men traditionally ended their Tuesday run with a parade, had

A Tee Mamou woman clowns by pretending to steal a rabbit from a host's coop. After singing and dancing for spectators, and begging coins ("tee cinq sous"), women "cut up" and make mischief in various ways. One of the most popular is trying to steal old tires, bicycles, green onions, chickens, and whatever else they discover in hosts' yards, gardens, and coops.

A Tee Mamou captain, burlap whip looped around his wrist, helps a female Mardi Gras down from a tree's branches. Climbing trees and refusing captains' demands to come down is another common form of "cutting up" for women Mardi Gras, who often boost each other up into the branches. The Mardi Gras in the foreground has a generous pouch sewn on the front of her Mardi Gras suit, to hide any contraband she picks up during the day. Here, a small dog (probably the host's) peeks out of the pocket. Courtesy of Carl Lindahl.

Captains use their burlap quoits to round up Tee Mamou women. When a Mardi Gras makes mischief—by stealing, leaving the front yard, or refusing to return to the Mardi Gras wagon—captains respond by chasing and whipping her. These comical and energetic contests are a popular form of entertainment for onlookers, captains, and maskers alike. Courtesy of Maida Owens.

created a new Mardi Gras Folklife Festival. As a result, the men found themselves performing for thousands of people on Iota's main street. Meanwhile, the women's Saturday visit to town was eliminated. Women, like men, enjoy town visits because they "can do a lot more" with so many spectators to beg from and clown for, and they resented their exclusion.[24] They pushed to join the men's Tuesday parade through Iota because, as Suson Launey comments, "We *are* part of the Tee Mamou Mardi Gras."[25] They prevailed (one cocaptain jokes that captains gave in "for the benefit of not hearing all their cackling"),[26] and "made the run" with the men for the 1988 festival. Captains had mixed feelings about continuing this precedent—later that year, the question remained under discussion, and one organizer called it "a hot issue."[27] The women must have made a compelling argument for their inclusion; every Mardi Gras since, they have joined the men on Iota's outskirts for the Main Street parade and performance.

Tee Mamou Mardi Gras Association meetings still offer women and men a stage for airing their policy concerns and opinions, although there is no guarantee of change. One recurring issue concerns the Mardi Gras dances, held at D.I.'s Restaurant for the last eight or nine years. The restaurant is usually so full of diners (many tourists) that the runners' families and friends can't squeeze in to watch them. Indeed, maskers and captains themselves usually sit outside where their Mardi Gras wagon is parked; the group has been asked not to come back inside between marches because the restaurant is too crowded. Some association members feel that their dance has become more a show for tourists than celebration for the group; captains, on the other hand, argue that there is no other available place for the dances. So far, this issue has not been resolved—or maybe it has, since there is no sign that the Tee Mamou Mardi Gras dances will leave D.I.'s any time soon.[28]

Women in Basile and Tee Mamou, then, have "inserted themselves into a holiday traditionally commanded by men," in part through involvement in local Mardi Gras associations.[29] As women assume various administrative pre–Mardi Gras duties, engage in educational outreach, speak out at planning meetings, and (in Basile) become officers, they make their marks on community *courirs de Mardi Gras.* The following two chapters show how women's Mardi Gras performances in Tee Mamou and Basile complement and expand women's roles in Mardi Gras associations.

4

All's Fair in Love and Mardi Gras: The Tee Mamou Women's Run

"Once you put on the mask, it's a different feel."
—Renée Frugé Douget

"I'm the first one to read the [Mardi Gras] rules. . . .
I read them backwards."
—Merline Bergeaux

Shortly after seven o'clock on the morning of *samedi gras* (the Saturday before Mardi Gras), cars and pickup trucks begin a slow, dusty progress along a rural Acadia Parish gravel driveway. Their destination, the Frugé family barn, sits half a mile off Highway 97 and serves as headquarters for the Tee Mamou Mardi Gras Association. Later this morning, the Tee Mamou women's run will start its countryside journey here, returning in the late afternoon to share a meal of gumbo and potato salad.

Women now run Mardi Gras in more than half a dozen Cajun communities, but Tee Mamou remains notable for several reasons. First, Tee Mamou is the only place to preserve a separate women's run, though all its captains are male. Elsewhere, women run Mardi Gras alongside men and sometimes children. After three decades, the Tee Mamou ladies' Saturday run is firmly entrenched in community life, and women's performances are squarely in the limelight.

A second remarkable feature is the women's playful wrestling matches against male captains. The Tee Mamou women's run, like the older and larger men's run it is modeled on, features horseplay aimed at the captains, but women are allowed far more leeway than men. Celebrants' descriptions of Mardi Gras runs reflect clear aesthetic standards: a well organized and skillfully performed run is "pretty." (Pretty can mean good or entertaining as well as beautiful.) Drawing on this shared aesthetic, a Tee Mamou captain comments that "It's pretty to see a woman act up" during the run. As women mutiny and scuffle with their captains, they play out the battle of the sexes in a very concrete way.

There are other elements worth examining in the Tee Mamou run: the women's flair for inventive costuming, for example, as they apply their own tastes to local disguise traditions. Women have also devised their own styles of clowning or "cutting up" that range from macho to maternal. And finally, Tee Mamou's female Mardi Gras are accomplished manipulators of the event's rules, as they both resist and exploit the sexual double standard that underlies the celebration. The Tee Mamou women's run, then, is an excellent example of how women, drawing on the same rules and conventions as men, nevertheless craft innovative Mardi Gras forms. Some of these inventions are then adopted by male Mardi Gras and become ingrained in local tradition.

The Tee Mamou women's run has more than tripled in size since its early days in the 1970s, when it included a dozen or so country women, all close friends, neighbors, and relatives. The present-day run typically has at least thirty runners, and often fifty or more. This growth has meant some loss of intimacy, and many members see each other only at Mardi Gras.[1] Still, the Mardi Gras run itself creates a strong sense of unity and community, or *communitas,* as anthropologist Victor Turner calls it.[2] The late Gerald Frugé, longtime *capitaine* for the group, and his wife, Linda, often remarked on the "instant bonding" that transforms strangers into Mardi Gras family.[3] Linda observed, "People that don't ordinarily associate with each other . . . [who] come from different areas of life and that, and all have their own friends and social life," can still get together for one day and "do their thing, and everybody gets along beautifully, in spite of being under the influence of alcohol."[4] Gerald once commented that this sense of community among "all these people from different walks of life" was part of what kept him involved. He said, "Everybody fends for each other. . . . And it's really something, a beautiful experience [from] my point of view, as being captain."[5]

Saturday Morning at the Frugé Barn

The Tee Mamou women's run is scheduled to take to the road by 8:30 in the morning, relatively late for a *courir de Mardi Gras.* The men's Tuesday run begins a bit earlier, because the riders must parade through Iota in midafternoon. The women's run, on the other hand, has few such time limits and can afford to start later. As the departure time draws nearer, the number of cars parked near the Frugé barn steadily grows. Sleepy-looking women mill around, chatting and sipping coffee from styrofoam cups. Some have been up all night, celebrating at local clubs or putting finishing touches on their costumes and masks.

A few women already wear their two-piece Mardi Gras suits, which look a bit like riotously colored pajamas, over jeans and sweatshirts. Under their arms, they carry masks and the pointed hats called *capuchons.* Other women, though, prefer to leave their disguises bundled in their cars until the last minute. Captains cluster near their pickup trucks, discussing logistics. Meanwhile, Suson Launey, an intrepid Mardi Gras for many years, mingles and passes out "magic" oranges that she injected with vodka the night before. Although participants are not supposed to bring their own liquor on the run, the oranges' alcoholic content is an open secret, and Suson shares them with runners, captains, and folklorists alike.

The Tee Mamou women's run is a favorite with ethnographers, journalists, and photographers, as it has always been for me. The number of cameras varies from year to year, but it is a rare run that does not include a few photographers or a video crew among its followers. Some photographers join the run in progress, but others begin the day here at the Frugé barn, snapping pictures of the waiting women. Most veteran Mardi Gras are accustomed to the ever-present cameras and have learned to ignore them during house visits. But as they wait for stragglers to arrive, the women obligingly answer questions, pull masks into place, and pose. Friends and relatives also circulate and take pictures; they, too, want to document the local tradition.

The truck-drawn Mardi Gras wagon that will carry the maskers along their route waits in the driveway. The wagon, a converted cattle trailer, has high wooden sides on three sides, each painted in slanting blocks of red, yellow, and green, with "Tee Mamou Mardi Gras" in black lettering. The countryside route means long drives between some stops, so the wagon has been adapted for comfort. Wooden benches line its sides and center, a toilet stall sits at the front, and a plank counter above the center bench has dozens of numbered holes, each big enough to hold a beer can or plastic cup without spilling. Men nail the wagon together each year, but women have done much of the decorating, including repainting the entire wagon recently.

Les Mardi Gras

Perhaps the most noticeable feature of the Tee Mamou women's run lies in gender: all its maskers are women, and all its captains men. As many as fifty or sixty women may turn up on Saturday morning, or as few as twenty. Turnout depends on women's work schedules, child care, and other factors, especially the weather. Very cold or wet days usually mean a low turnout. The best weather for running Mardi Gras, participants say, is brisk, somewhat cool but clear weather. Hot weather makes the riders sluggish and they don't feel like clowning as much.

Participants are drawn mostly from the local area, but this includes a lot of territory: the long wedge of countryside called Tee Mamou, as well as nearby towns such as Iota, Evangeline, and Jennings. A few women come from more distant Acadiana cities such as Crowley (perhaps twenty miles away) or even Lafayette, fifty miles from Tee Mamou. Occasionally, an out-of-state visitor receives the *capitaine's* permission to run, as I did in 1989. Tee Mamou's women Mardi Gras come from a variety of backgrounds. They range in age from seventeen (thirteen, if their mothers are longtime Mardi Gras) through middle age, and include school teachers, short-order cooks and waitresses, college students, health aides, and a flight attendant/folklorist, among others. Typically, women run Mardi Gras regularly with a cluster of close friends, age-mates, or relatives, and may know most of the other runners only casually. For women as well as men, Mardi Gras is often a family tradition passed from one generation to the next. Two generations of women frequently run together, as mothers bring their daughters into the tradition.

Participants include a mix of experienced Mardi Gras and novices. The distinction between *vieilles* (old) Mardi Gras and new members is important, because longtime runners expect a certain measure of privilege and respect from captains. In turn, old Mardi Gras coach and keep an eye on neophytes. For many years, a handful of core members of the pioneer women's run—Merline Reed Bergeaux, Linda Frugé, Patsy Simar, and Shirley Reed—continued to run each year. Now in their fifties, these *vieilles* Mardi Gras provide valuable continuity with the run's early history.

Over the last few years, some old Mardi Gras have retired or participate only sporadically. Some are sidelined by demanding work schedules, illnesses, or injuries, and others quit running as friends and contemporaries drop out. But as one generation retires, other women become the *vieilles* Mardi Gras. Experienced performers such as Suson Launey, Linda Gatte, and Becky Monceaux have all run Mardi Gras for about twenty years, and are among its current *grandes dames.* Linda Doucet's daughter Renée Frugé Douget began running when she was thirteen. She is now a veteran at twenty-nine and a role model for novices a decade younger. New members are constantly recruited by friends or boyfriends who run Mardi Gras themselves, and by husbands who "captain for" the women. A few are simply captivated by the show, as I was, and want to be part of it. Dana David, a folklorist originally from Vermilion Parish, joined the women's run in 1995 after a folklore class field trip, and she has been an adept regular ever since.

Despite its growth, the Tee Mamou run continues to be an expression of lasting female friendships. Most women have a regular partner they run with every year—a "partner in crime," as Suson Launey puts it.[6] A regular partner means having someone to sing, dance, and march to houses with. Women often stay with the same Mardi Gras partner for many years, and may quit running when their partner does. Men sometimes have longtime Mardi Gras partners as well, but these close friendships seem especially important in women's Mardi

Gras performances. Mardi Gras partners work collaboratively to overcome physical disadvantages in the run, boosting each other into trees, ganging up on captains, and planning pranks in advance, so "you'll know what to do," Patsy Simar says.[7]

Core members frequently go to great lengths to run Mardi Gras, taking risks with their health, jobs, and marriages. One or two women have even run in the early stages of pregnancy. Despite chronic knee pain, Linda Frugé Doucet limped on and off the truck for years, until she realized she had to quit, she says, "before I crippled myself."[8] Another young woman used to drive back to Tee Mamou from her home in Florida each year, just to run Mardi Gras with her mother and aunts.

Tee Mamou Disguise

Disguise is another noteworthy facet of the Tee Mamou women's run. Here, as in most runs, disguise defines the Mardi Gras role, because captains and spectators traditionally do not mask. Although anonymity may be fictive to some extent (the runners unmask frequently during the day, for example), costuming allows women to briefly assume a new identity and to act silly or outrageous. Renée Frugé Douget says, "Whenever you put the mask on, it's so different. You can act the fool, and [neighbors and friends] never know who it is."[9] Women's disguises are also artistic expressions reflecting their own tastes and needs as well as community expectations. Many women wear a new suit and mask each year, but others wear a favorite suit or mask for years, perhaps refurbishing it occasionally.

Tee Mamou has specific disguise guidelines that male and female members alike must follow. In the early 1980s, in an effort to revert to a more "traditional" style, captains decided to ban the plastic masks, painted faces, and hodgepodge costumes common in many Cajun runs. They created the current rule that "a traditional Mardi Gras costume is required to run Mardi Gras. A traditional costume must have a hand-made mask (no rubber or Halloween-type mask), a traditional suit and a *capuchon.*" This rule imposes some constraints on members, but most feel strongly about the importance of "holding true to our tradition," as several have commented to me. The strict requirement for disguise is a point of pride, one way their run differs from many others. And within the rule's limits, as Suson Launey says, "You still have room to do" and be creative.[10]

Tee Mamou suits and masks say much about the nature of the run. Most women either make their own or have a friend sew them to their specifications. Many Mardi Gras have two suits and masks each year: one for the daytime run, and one for the dance that night. Because day and night suits function differently, they are constructed differently. Nighttime suits can be a bit glitzier and flimsier, because they need to last only a few hours. A day suit, on the other hand, is simple and sturdy because during the run, in Suson Launey's words, "You're in a rice field, you're under a house," and climbing trees.[11] Daytime suits are two-piece cotton outfits, usually cut from a pajama or clown suit pattern, loose enough to fit over jeans and allow free movement. Necks and waists are usually closed with elastic, drawstrings, or Velcro, since buttons could pop off or gouge as the Mardi Gras climb trees and horse around. Suson Launey says that the suits she makes for herself have "no buttons, no zippers because I'm rough."[12] Suson also uses elastic at the ankle, so her pants won't pull off when she's wrestling with captains. Bells are popular additions to Mardi Gras disguises in most places, but Tee Mamou women rarely sew them directly onto their suits; to quote Suson again, "If you're wrestling and you land on a bell, that hurts."[13] Instead, they sew bells onto elastic to wear around wrists or legs, or onto their *capuchons.*

Pretending to steal from hosts (or perhaps *not* pretending) is a central part of Tee Mamou women's comic play, so many have added a pouch to the front of their suits. There they hide live chickens, green onions, and other contraband. Suson Launey comments that this outside pouch is the public one, intended for plunder they don't mind the captains discovering. Some Mardi Gras also have pockets inside their shirts for stolen goods (captains' burlap whips, for example) they really want to conceal.

Women make their suits distinctive by using eye-popping fabrics and trim. A few suits use the purple, green, and gold of New Orleans, but bright primary colors, even hot pink, are more common. Shirts and pants often have a solid color on one side and a contrasting print on the other. Fabrics with a Louisiana theme—crawfish or hot peppers—are popular, as are those with chickens or roosters, icons of the rural Mardi Gras celebration. Other familiar symbols, such as American flags, also show up from time to time, as does hunters' camouflage fabric. Makers trim their suits with hand-cut fringe along the seams, heightening the sense of movement as they run and dance. Some turn their suits into comic statements, like the two Mardi Gras partners with batwing sleeves. When they stood side by side and stretched out their arms, hand-cut letters spelled out "Double" on one woman's sleeve and "Trouble" on the other's. Mardi Gras also like to carry or wear comic props—a rubber chicken, for instance, or (one memorable year) a live, costumed rooster named Gumbo.

All Tee Mamou Mardi Gras wear *capuchons* resembling dunce caps or clown hats. Madeline Reed, who runs Mardi Gras in Tee Mamou most years, says, "You have to have a *capuchon.* Because that's the tradition. You don't have a *capuchon* . . . you don't get on the truck."[14] Tee Mamou riders usually make their own *capuchons* of twisted poster board covered with fabric and fringe matching their suit. Tee Mamou Mardi Gras like their capuchons tall, almost two feet high, with a fabric skirt to cover their neck and hair. The towering hats can be a liability, however, getting snarled in tree branches and ceiling fans during the run.

In addition to a Mardi Gras suit and *capuchon,* each rider must wear a hand-made mask, perhaps the single most important part of the Tee Mamou disguise. These one-of-a-kind masks, created to be as "ugly" or strange as possible, become displays of individuality and humor. Many women make or decorate their own masks, but others buy them, as I did when I ran. Usually, they buy from one of three local women—Suson Launey, Renée Frugé Douget, and Jackie Miller—who make and sell masks that appeal to Tee Mamou women. Conventions vary from one place to another. A screen mask made in Eunice or Basile, where mask makers simply paint stylized features on the screen, might look stark and out of place in Tee Mamou. The lavish decoration of a typical Tee Mamou mask, on the other hand, would seem over the top in Basile.

Preferences for mask materials vary among Tee Mamou women. Many choose wire screen masks because they are cool, easy to breathe through, and generally considered the most traditional style. Renée Frugé Douget says that for the "traditional and scary" effect, she still likes screen masks best.[15] However, women often find that stiff, galvanized wire screen scratches their faces. These days, women can choose various kinds of flexible screen to make more comfortable wire masks.

Another choice, equally popular among Tee Mamou women, is the needle-point mask, invented by Suson Launey almost twenty years ago. Suson first tried wire screen masks, but comments, "Our group is rough. To run with a screen mask, my face would look like hamburger."[16] Her solution, yarn masks stitched on plastic screen, quickly caught on with other Tee Mamou women and some men. Suson's needlepoint masks are an example of women's innovation within the local Mardi Gras tradition.

Whether wire screen or needlepoint, Tee Mamou masks are always richly and whimsically decorated. Many are covered with fur, feathers, or Spanish moss, and Renée Douget comments that wig hair makes "some of the scariest masks to me."[17] Facial features are grotesquely misshapen: noses are short and snout-like, or long and pointed, made of cotton-stuffed fabric to match Mardi Gras suits and *capuchons.* Oversized mouths sprout fangs, teeth, long tongues, or rubber snakes and lizards; ears are huge and Spock-like. Novelty items—a miniature plastic skeleton, eyeglasses, rubber insects and reptiles, and junk jewelry—stud the surface of many masks.

Sometimes masks convey inside jokes about the wearer. One of Suson Launey's unforgettable masks featured a monstrous rubber mouth and tongue (cut from a commercial mask) because, she joked, she is known for her big mouth. Tee Mamou women's masks are always odd—sometimes scary, but mostly comical. Tee Mamou women often hand their suits and masks on to husbands or sons, because disguise conventions are similar for men and women. But women make virtually all Mardi Gras suits and many of the masks, and therefore their talents, tastes, and senses of humor shape the local men's run as well as the women's.[18]

Once disguised, women with wiry builds are almost indistinguishable from men or boys. Their baggy Mardi Gras suits are androgynous, and masks and tall *capuchons* give their heads a larger-than-life look. Cocaptain Claude Durio remarks, "When they're dressed up, someone that's not . . . familiar with them, you can't tell the difference between a man and a woman."[19] Telling the difference is important, because captains tend to treat female Mardi Gras more leniently than men, and take care not to whip them too hard. In reality, there is little danger of mistaking the women's group as a whole for men. For one thing, masks and suits do little to hide the shapes of more voluptuous women, or the fact that most are shorter than men. Posture and gait betray others. And ultimately, captains and community members all know that this is a ladies' Mardi Gras run.

Mardi Gras Captains

In Tee Mamou, as in most Cajun runs, captains are traditionally men. Gerald Frugé acted as head *capitaine* for Tee Mamou's men for almost thirty years, and led the women for twenty-five years. Gerald's evenhanded style of "captaining" inspired tremendous respect and loyalty among both male and female Mardi Gras. On his death, Gerald's son Todd Frugé inherited leadership of both runs. Like his father, Todd is a strong leader without being a "temporary despot," as Mardi Gras captains have been called; he reminds me of an affable but determined sports coach, down to the coaching whistle around his neck.[20] His mother, Linda, who ran Mardi Gras for years when Todd was a cocaptain, remarks that he is "easygoing, he's respected, and he's even-tempered" and he "doesn't get bent out of shape easy," all important qualities for a Tee Mamou head *capitaine.*[21]

Six to eight cocaptains assist Todd, sharing various responsibilities before and during the run. Most, like Todd, are in their twenties or thirties, and many are Frugé relatives or friends. Many Cajun Mardi Gras captains wear satin capes, but Tee Mamou captains wear everyday work or hunting clothes: jeans and tee shirts, coveralls, or camouflage fatigues, with braided burlap whips dangling from their wrists. Todd Frugé also wears a red cotton vest, its back embossed with a photograph of his father as captain. Todd's vest, a gift from his fiancé, clearly marks him as the leader. At the same time, it is a visible reminder of Gerald, whose presence is still strongly felt.

Many of the same men "captain" for the men's and women's runs, although the women's run often has a few more. For one thing, several young cocaptains prefer to "dress out" and run Mardi Gras themselves on Tuesday. For another, the women suggest that they are hard to handle, and it takes more captains to control them. Shirley Reed once commented, "Yeah, I think we have extra ones because we are a little rowdier than the men are."[22] On the other hand, Suson Launey argues that some young captains refuse to captain for the women "because the women are too rough. They say the women gets away with more than the men."[23]

Captains (representing accountability and order) and Mardi Gras (as subversive mischief makers) are symbolic adversaries in the run. In reality, maskers and their leaders are a team working together to put on an entertaining show. Linda Frugé Doucet explains that captains and Mardi Gras often perform what she calls "setups," staged struggles to amuse their audience. Still, resentments can arise if the women feel that a captain is whipping too hard or being too strict. Tee Mamou's rules promise that "Captains will be regulated as fair as possible," and women have the power to vote out a cocaptain they judge unfair.

Tee Mamou women say they like having male captains for several reasons. Merline Bergeaux once suggested that she and other women Mardi Gras would be too unruly for a woman to control. Most of all, women enjoy their verbal and physical tussles with male captains. Mardi Gras relentlessly tease their captains, trying to embarrass and disconcert them. During house visits, women pile on top of the young captains and try to overpower them. Suson Launey says, "It's too much fun beating up on the male captains" to consider female leaders.[24] Spectators enjoy the battles of women versus men just as much as participants do. Linda Doucet comments, "I feel the audience really enjoys the women's performance due to the fact that it's women and the men captains. . . . They seem to get more a kick whenever the women are doing their monkeyshines than when the men perform."[25]

Mardi Gras Rules

Respect for the captains' authority is essential to a good Mardi Gras run. In Tee Mamou, twenty-two written rules, read aloud at planning meetings and just before the run, reinforce the captains' control. Some rules describe conditions for participating (age limits, the need to attend meetings, and disguise requirements). Others offer a blueprint for how to run Mardi Gras, step by step: get to the barn on time; hurry and get down at every stop; sing the song, dance, and then cut up. And some are prohibitions that (as one captain says) give riders an idea of what's okay and what's not: do not litter, don't go behind houses unless given permission by captains, do not stop traffic, and so on. Gerald Frugé explained in a 1989 interview, "If you want a place to go, you have to have restrictions, for more reasons than just having a place to go."[26] He once compared the group's rules to the Ten Commandments; both, he noted, are "rules that's used to control people. And [our rules] were made to control Mardi Gras."[27]

In practice, however, captains may selectively ignore or modify particular rules.[28] Gerald observed that captains are "more lax on some [rules] than others. We're strict on some for the well-being of the Mardi Gras. For example, don't stand in the road and try to stop a car."[29] Other rules, though, are "made to be broken," in one captain's words—though not all the rules at once. Much of the run's comedy derives from celebrants flaunting rules and captains reacting. To quote Gerald Frugé, "It's pretty to see [the Mardi Gras] be mischievous."[30]

Knowing which rules are inviolable is key to being a good Mardi Gras. Seasoned women maskers respect the spirit of the rules but are willing to toy with them. Founding members Merline Bergeaux, Shirley Reed, and Patsy Simar joked in 1988, "Gerald, he always tells us the rules. And we always break them. . . . We shake our heads 'Yeah' and we go along with whatever he says, and then [do what we want to]." Merline, whom captains view as one of the most talented Mardi Gras, expanded on this, saying, "I'm the first one to read the rules. . . . I read them backwards."[31] This kind of manipulation works only if the Mardi Gras understand both the performance and their audience very well. Veteran Mardi Gras and captains usually know which hosts will be amused by, or at least tolerate, pranks that would anger others.

One of the more interesting aspects of the Tee Mamou women's run is the implicit double standard governing women's and (especially) men's behavior. For instance, rules forbid the Mardi Gras to wrestle with captains. Male Mardi Gras occasionally test this rule, but women are *expected* to. Gerald Frugé remarked, "I don't mind when women tackle a captain. . . . I think [the captains] like the women to pick at them. I think the women picking at the men, it's just part of the excitement that goes on" during the women's run.[32]

Women are allowed more latitude than men for several reasons, according to captains and Mardi Gras. First, they suggest, most women are careful not to harm other people's property, even as they drink and cut up; men are not. Second, women tend to listen to captains and be more conscious of the rules. If captains are overly strict in enforcing rules, it squelches the women's performance. Gerald Frugé commented, "I notice when I try to be the same with the women and with the men, in other words being as strict with the rules, it takes away from the women. . . . And when you fuss them too much, then they drag. Because they're not having fun."[33] Women, he suggested, are generally "afraid to go out of line" because they might be unmasked and kicked out of the run—the ultimate punishment in a Mardi Gras run. Linda, herself a Mardi Gras for many years, agreed: "Some [women Mardi Gras] are so afraid of the rules that they don't do anything, you know. Naturally the men and women have the same set of rules, but it's really mainly for the men."[34]

The main reason women are given more slack, especially in tangling with the captains, is that they are not as strong as most men. Women are less likely to hurt anyone and can be brought back into line more easily, members suggest. As Gerald once put it, "It's pretty to see a woman act up. Because it's easier to control the women over a man."[35] And in fact women are unlikely to start fist-fights with captains, as men occasionally do.

Captains, backed up by the association's rules, hold most of the official authority. The runners, however, have their own powers. The group works together as a whole to monitor and police itself, as veteran Mardi Gras keep an eye on newer ones. Gerald Frugé commented that the women's run has occasionally had "women who kind of mess up the rest of the Mardi Gras," just as the men's run has its disruptive members.[36] Women who use too many obscenities, get too drunk, or smoke marijuana seldom last long in the run. Over the years, several Mardi Gras and captains have illustrated this point by telling me a story about the 1987 women's run, when two members offended other riders by cursing and acting "pretty raw" and "ugly and nasty." Merline Bergeaux explained, "We got rid of them fast, we passed a petition, and got them off the truck." The couple had run the year before without incident, but this time, according to Merline, "They had drank two fifths of whiskey before they got on that truck. . . . And then once they got on the truck they decided, you know, 'Well, we can do what we want now.'"[37] A few years later, Suson Launey described the same incident, saying, "They were kind of like just after the captains. They wanted to grab the captains. . . . And it was taking away from our run." The women responded quickly and effectively. Suson says, "The women Mardi Gras themselves have kicked them out. . . . We don't stand for this."[38] Women, then, cooperate with each other and with captains to maintain their run's standards.

Taking Off

As the run's start time approaches, captains make sure all riders have signed release forms and give the women their first beer of the day. Shortly after 8:30, *capitaine* Todd Frugé calls the women to order with a whistle blast and his frequent refrain, "Let's go! All Mardi Gras, let's go!" Standing on the Mardi Gras wagon's steps, he reminds the runners what he expects of them. The following speech is from the 2003 run, but it remains much the same from year to year: "Listen up! Listen up! Whenever we get to a stop, everybody hurry, get down, line up, in rows of eight or whatever. Stay in a tight group. When we start singing the song, everybody try to follow along, sing it. After we sing, we're going to dance two waltzes. If they have any people to dance with, dance with them. If not, dance with y'all selves." When the women laugh, he clarifies, "[with] each other." Dancing is part of each house visit, and female Mardi Gras pull men, women, and children into the dances, or dance with their partners. Todd continues, "After that, go cut up. When I blow the whistle to load up, load up. Do not throw any alcohol, and beer cans or anything out of the wagon. We have a trash can, or throw them behind [in the back of] one of the trucks."

His instruction, "Don't wrestle with the captains" is met by snorts and more laughter from the women, who respond, "You always tell us that!" He continues, "Don't tackle the captains from behind. You all know what you can do. At a few stops, we're going to have some chickens. Y'all *catch* the chickens—y'all are famous for losing them." The women disagree loudly and one jokingly demands Todd's recall as *capitaine*.

Todd reminds the group that they will sing the shorter version of their Mardi Gras song (a mere twelve verses) at most stops; the "long verse," at sixteen verses, is reserved for special visits, usually at the homes of retired Mardi Gras. He ends his speech with roll call, making sure that each has paid her dues before she climbs on the wagon. The women's family names—Gatte, Doucet, Fontenot, Reed, and Klumpp, among others—reflect the area's mixture of French, German, and English influences. But after generations of intermarriage, most Tee Mamou families simply consider themselves Cajun. And, of course, married Cajun women frequently take non-Cajun husbands' surnames.

One by one, the women position themselves on the wagon. Some sit on the benches; others stand in the aisles or hang over the sides. Experienced Mardi Gras claim the most dangerous spaces, perching on the trailer's steps. Their choice is part risk-taking, part privilege, and part insurance that novices don't fall off during the ride. Recorded Cajun music blares from the wagon's speakers, and excitement builds as riders pound on the wagon's sides and hoot. An Acadia Parish sheriff's car, headlights flashing, leads the way down the gravel drive. Second in line is the head captain's pickup truck, miniature American flags fluttering on its hood. The Mardi Gras wagon follows, trailed by the beer truck and a trailer carrying the run's musicians. After official vehicles have pulled out of the barn's driveway, cars filled with spectators claim their places in the queue. Some years, more than a dozen cars trail after the run, and drivers zealously guard their places in line.

The Mardi Gras procession is impressive as it turns south on Highway 97, passing flooded crawfish ponds (planted with rice the rest of the year), soybean fields, and oil pumping stations. It's exciting to be part of the convoy, whether you're riding on the crowded Mardi Gras wagon, buffeted by wind on the musicians' wagon (my usual choice), or driving behind in the "tail." Children stand

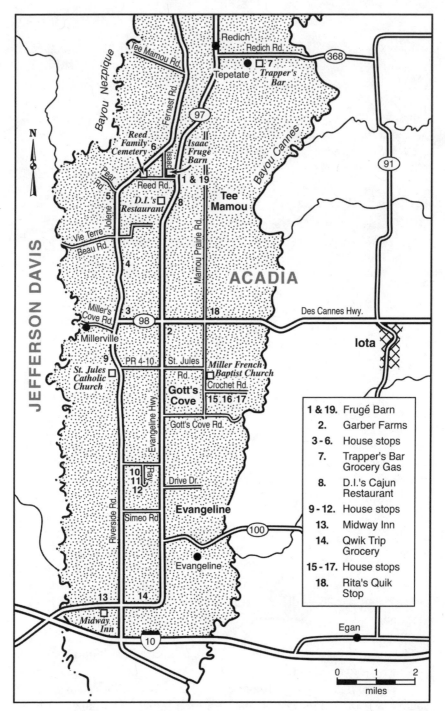

Map of Tee Mamou women's 2005 Mardi Gras route. The women's run (on Saturday) and the men's run (on Tuesday) share a number of stops, but the women's route takes them mainly west of Evangeline Highway (Highway 97). The men cover territory east of the highway.

outside their homes to wave at the passing Mardi Gras, who whoop and wave back. Horses, excited by all the noise and motion, run back and forth in nearby pastures.

The women's morning visits include rural neighborhoods such as Millerville and Vie Terre Beau, and the afternoon takes them through the town of Evangeline to the Gott's Cove neighborhood. The first stop of the day is always at the Garber sweet potato farm, a short drive down Highway 97. Cocaptain Claude Durio explains that this stop is timed for the Garbers' convenience; as farmers, they work on weekends and holidays but schedule a break for the group's visit. Walter Garber offered another explanation to a newspaper reporter: "I told them they had to come here first, before [the ladies] got all wound up. Later on, they'll tear up your place."[39] Clearly, not everyone sees the women as easier to control and more respectful of property than men. At any rate, the Garbers' large, shady yard gives the Mardi Gras plenty of room to run, climb trees, and jump over or slide into drainage ditches. This first stop is often a lengthy one and one of the day's liveliest.

Tee Mamou's Mardi Gras Song

As the Mardi Gras trucks pull up to the Garbers' neat brick home, the family waits under the carport with a small crowd of friends invited to share the performance. Head captain Todd Frugé formally asks permission to visit; when it is granted, he blows his whistle and calls, "Let's go, Mardi Gras!" As the musicians move into position near the hosts, the women, masks now in place, dismount from the trailer. Some horseback Cajun runs charge homes at full gallop, like brash raiders. The Tee Mamou Mardi Gras, on the other hand, approach slowly on foot as they sing their *chanson de Mardi Gras* or Mardi Gras song. Todd lines the maskers up in rows of eight abreast, arms linked, with pairs of *vieilles* Mardi Gras in front. As they wait, many of the maskers make the high-pitched whoops characteristic of Mardi Gras runners. On their captain's signal, the women walk slowly toward the house, singing in unison. The *capitaine* faces the group and helps lead the singing.

Several Cajun runs no longer sing their community *chanson de Mardi Gras* at house visits; instead, they broadcast a recording, or live musicians play an instrumental version. Singing the Tee Mamou song, however, is a central feature of the group's performance. Despite practice at pre–Mardi Gras meetings, captains find it hard to coax a tight, uniform performance from the bunch. The song's length makes it challenging to remember, and the tune is hard to carry. Even seasoned Mardi Gras admit that they "have to sing it along with someone." The song's tempo tends to drag out, and Gerald Frugé frequently used to remind the Mardi Gras to sing faster and "keep y'all's song together." Todd does the same today.

Tee Mamou women, in particular, have difficulty with the song, as their captains often remind them. Women's singing voices are not usually as loud as men's, and masks muffle their singing. Often, the most audible voice is their male *capitaine*'s. Renée Douget makes a point of singing loudly and lifting her mask slightly, but she suggests, "The captains, or people that know the song, need to be spread out through the crowd. Because whenever you're in the back, and you're not sure of yourself, you can't hear the front."[40]

Each Mardi Gras community has its own version of the Mardi Gras song. The Tee Mamou song belongs to a less common type, derived partly from old French and French Canadian drinking songs.[41] Most of the song describes the progressive emptying of a bottle and then a glass, with the last verse addressing the household's master and mistress, asking them for "la fille aînée" (the oldest girl) so they can "chauffer ses pieds," or warm her feet—presumably by dancing, although this is never made explicit. When I first ran Mardi Gras in Tee Mamou, three or four veteran women Mardi Gras, fluent in French, occasionally changed these lyrics and requested instead "le garçon aîné" or oldest boy. (In reality, women Mardi Gras dance with women and girls as well as with men and boys.) I haven't heard this version again, however, perhaps because it has too many syllables. A more likely explanation is that few young Cajuns speak French these days. In the past, older singers had different understandings of some phrases, but today there is little variation. Most people memorize the song, word for word, from the Tee Mamou Mardi Gras Association's printed song sheet. The French lyrics and English translation that follow are from this standardized sheet.

1. Les Mardi Gras et où viens tu?
   Tout à l'entour du fond d'hiver.
   Les Mardi Gras et ou viens tu?
   Tout à l'entour du fond d'hiver.

2. On vient de l'Angleterre
   O mon cher, o mon cher.
   On vient de l'Angleterre
   Tout à l'entour du fond d'hiver.

3. Les Mardi Gras quoi portes tu?
   Tout à l'entour du fond d'hiver.
   Les Mardi Gras quoi portes tu?
   Tout à l'entour du fond d'hiver.

4. On porte que la bouteille
   O mon cher, o mon cher.

On porte que la bouteille
Tout à l'entour du fond d'hiver.

5. Et la bouteille est bue
Tout à l'entour du fond d'hiver.
Et la bouteille est bue
Tout à l'entour du fond d'hiver.

6. Il reste que la demie
O mon cher, o mon cher.
Il reste que la demie
Tout à l'entour du fond d'hiver.

7. Et la demie est bue!
Tout à l'entour du fond d'hiver.
Et la demie est bue!
Tout à l'entour du fond d'hiver.

8. Il reste que la pleine verre
O mon cher, o mon cher.
Il reste que la pleine verre
Tout à l'entour du fond d'hiver.

9. Et la pleine verre est bue!
Tout à l'entour du fond d'hiver.
Et la pleine verre est bue!
Tout à l'entour du fond d'hiver.

10. Il reste que la demie verre
O mon cher, o mon cher.
Il reste que la demie verre
Tout à l'entour du fond d'hiver.

11. Et la demie verre est bue!
Tout à l'entour du fond d'hiver.
Et la demie verre est bue!
Tout à l'entour du fond d'hiver.

12. Il reste que le quart de verre
O mon cher, o mon cher.
Il reste que le quart de verre
Tout à l'entour du fond d'hiver.

13. Et le quart de verre est bue!
Tout à l'entour du fond d'hiver.
Et le quart de verre est bue!
Tout à l'entour du fond d'hiver.

14. Il reste que la rinçure
    O mon cher, o mon cher.
    Il reste que la rinçure
    Tout à l'entour du fond d'hiver.

15. Et la rinçure on la boit pas!
    Tout à l'entour du fond d'hiver.
    Et la rinçure on la bois pas!
    Tout à l'entour du fond d'hiver.

16. Bonjour le maître et la maîtresse.
    On vous demande un peu de chose.
    On vous demande la fille aînée.
    On va la faire faire une bonne chose.
    On va la faire chauffer ses pieds.

1. Mardi Gras, where do you come from?
   All around the end of winter.
   Mardi Gras, where do you come from?
   All around the end of winter.

2. We come from England
   Oh my dear, oh my dear.
   We come from England
   All around the end of winter.

3. Mardi Gras what do you bring with you?
   All around the end of winter.
   Mardi Gras what do you bring with you?
   All around the end of winter.

4. We bring only a bottle
   Oh my dear, oh my dear.
   We bring only a bottle
   All around the end of winter.

5. And the bottle is drunk
   All around the end of winter.
   And the bottle is drunk
   All around the end of winter.

6. Only a half bottle is left
   Oh my dear, oh my dear.
   Only a half bottle is left
   All around the end of winter.

7. And the half bottle is drunk.
   All around the end of winter.
   And the half bottle is drunk.
   All around the end of winter.

8. Only a full glass is left
   Oh my dear, oh my dear.
   Only a full glass is left
   All around the end of winter.

9. And the full glass is drunk
   All around the end of winter.
   And the full glass is drunk
   All around the end of winter.

10. Only a half glass is left
    Oh my dear, oh my dear.
    Only half a glass is left
    All around the end of winter.

11. And the half glass is drunk
    All around the end of winter.
    And the half glass is drunk
    All around the end of winter.

12. Only a quarter glass is left
    Oh my dear, oh my dear.
    Only a quarter glass is left
    All around the end of winter.

13. And the quarter glass is drunk
    All around the end of winter.
    And the quarter glass is drunk
    All around the end of winter.

14. Only the dregs are left
    Oh my dear, oh my dear.
    Only the dregs are left
    All around the end of winter.

15. And we don't drink the dregs!
    All around the end of winter.
    And we don't drink the dregs!
    All around the end of winter.

16. Greetings to the master and mistress.
   We ask you for a little something.
   We ask you for the oldest daughter.
   We'll make her do a good thing.
   We'll make her warm her feet.

Begging and Chasing Chickens

As the women end their song with a whoop, the musicians strike up a brisk two-step tune, followed by a short waltz. The Mardi Gras find men, other women, or children to dance with; as a last resort, they dance with each other. Women have more flexibility than men in their choices of dance partners; in everyday life, as in the run, no one thinks anything of women dancing together. (Male Mardi Gras, on the other hand, dance with other men only under strictly defined and festive circumstances—with a Mardi Gras partner. When men choose a partner from the audience, it is invariably a woman, usually a young, pretty woman.)

The sequence of the women's performance, like the men's, is spelled out in the rules: first they sing, then dance, then beg, and finally cut up. Begging, like singing, is traditionally an integral part of running Mardi Gras in Tee Mamou. As the music ends, the Mardi Gras approach hosts and guests, index fingers pointing to cupped palms. In falsetto voices, they make the customary request for "tee cinq sous" (five cents). Spectators place coins in their hands or toss fistfuls of change, which the Mardi Gras scramble on hands and knees to collect. Skilled maskers turn their begging into a comic performance, as—wordlessly, or in French—they admire a wristwatch or pen and entreat its owner to hand it over. Experienced targets laughingly refuse, though they may have to engage in a gentle tug-of-war for their property.

After canvassing homeowners and tourists, the Tee Mamou women are likely to turn to passers-by. A few Mardi Gras might surround a car and reach inside open windows in search of donations. In lieu of cash, most Mardi Gras will accept other goods, such as a six-pack of beer or a bottle of schnapps. One year, a Tee Mamou woman persuaded a passing hunter to donate two freshly dressed rabbits. Any money collected is handed over to the captains, but I don't know what happened to the rabbits.

In the past, hosts donated ingredients for the community gumbo that evening: live chickens, andouille sausage, bags of rice, oil, or green onions. Many households still hand out these food gifts, although they are largely symbolic today, since the Mardi Gras association buys most gumbo supplies in advance. Few people today raise chickens, but many buy one or two especially for the Mardi Gras. If the homeowner has a live chicken for the group, he throws it in the air for the maskers to chase. Often male hosts make the pursuit more difficult by standing on the roof to toss the chicken. Some throw a guinea hen, which is faster than a chicken. The riders scramble after the bird, climbing fences and trees, jumping drainage ditches, crawling under buildings, and running into each other. Through such traditional tricks, householders exert considerable control over the performance, making sure they get plenty of entertainment in exchange for their gifts. Sometimes, though, the Mardi Gras turn the joke back onto the host; in a recent run, they stole the homeowner's ladder, leaving him stranded on the roof until they decided to return it.

Occasionally chicken chases end with the bird's escape, and captain Todd Frugé teases the women: "Y'all are famous for losing chickens." Usually, though, the chicken is eventually captured and handed over to captains, who place it in a wire cage in the "chicken truck." Many female Mardi Gras handle captured chickens with casual ease, grasping them by their wings or legs and triumphantly holding up their trophies, as many men do. A few women cradle the chickens in their arms, petting and crooning to them.

Catching chickens has often been described as a rite of passage for teen-age boys, who are eager to prove their worth as providers.[42] Some women, too, are very competitive in chicken chases. Shirley Reed comments that "Some of the others might be afraid to be chasing [chickens] or to get dirty," but she and her partner Merline are "in the mud [and] the barbed wire fences" in the heat of the chase.[43] Others, though, say that chicken chases "aren't my thing," in Linda Doucet's words.[44] (They aren't my thing, either; my sympathies are with the chicken.) Linda says, "Now whenever I was running, I wasn't into chasing the chickens. And that wasn't my cup of tea, that was Merline and them."[45] She was happy to leave the chase to others while she found a bicycle, tire, or wheelbarrow to play with.

The Art of Clowning and Cutting Up

Tee Mamou Mardi Gras and their captains understand that their job is to "put on a show for the people," as many have told me. Suson Launey adds that their show is "kind of like earning what they're going to give us."[46] The better the show, the more donations they can expect to collect. Rules specify that Mardi Gras should "cut up" or (in Gerald Frugé's words) "horse around a bit" after dancing.[47] Cutting up is just as central to the show as begging or singing. Indeed, it is probably more important to some women.

The Tee Mamou women create their own clowning styles, ranging from macho to nurturing, by adapting conventional Mardi Gras practices. Pretending to steal from hosts, for example, is fundamental to any Mardi Gras run. Although they are officially confined to the house's front yard, pairs of Tee Mamou women furtively break away to explore backyards and outbuildings, looking for things to steal. Merline Bergeaux says that she and "two or three other Mardi Gras" are "going to cut up, a little too much sometimes. We get really down to it and . . . we'll make the round of [go around] the house, like we're not supposed to, and go and take a little bit of stuff, and take off for it."[48] In response, the captains chase down the miscreants and try to herd them back to the fold. Suson Launey says of these pursuits, "And that's when the captains come in and they are after us with whips . . . to keep us in line. . . . Those captains are kept awful busy."[49] At times, a young captain simply tosses a Mardi Gras over his shoulder and carries her back, something captains never do in the men's run.

Most often, the Mardi Gras steal obviously useless things—an old fishing net, a discarded mattress, a deer decoy—to make people laugh. Some feel their pranks fall flat if they go unnoticed by captains. Linda Doucet recalls one such incident, when "I was pretending to take something and none of the captains would see me, so I had to end up bringing it back on my own, you know. I made it all the way to the truck [without being discovered]."[50] Almost always, stolen goods are returned to the owners before the group leaves, but some women make off with green onions snatched from a garden, fresh eggs or an extra chicken from a henhouse, and other prizes. (Captains say that there is virtually no real theft today; if the women sometimes keep their loot, it is with the owners' permission. Some women tell a different story; this, presumably, is where the hidden pockets in their suits come in.)

Women, like men, perform classic Mardi Gras tricks such as clambering onto tree branches or, more rarely, scaling rooftops. However, many women have trouble hoisting themselves into a tree, so they work collectively. At almost every stop, a cluster of women surrounds a tree and boosts one or more Mardi Gras into the branches. Once treed, Mardi Gras ignore captains' commands and refuse to budge, agreeing to come down only after being swatted a few times, or when their wagon appears to be leaving. Some women scramble to the ground on their own power; otherwise, captains gallantly lift them down. (I like to think that I got down on my own after my one Mardi Gras tree adventure years ago, but I can't remember that part.) Male Mardi Gras in the Tuesday run, however, are left to their own devices in getting down. Captains' frequent gallantry toward the women, oddly juxtaposed with wrestling matches and whippings, is a reminder that this is, after all, only play. It also demonstrates deeply ingrained attitudes about women, who most often call themselves (and are called) *lady* Mardi Gras.

Male Mardi Gras often try to outdo each other with feats of daring, strength, and agility. In horseback runs, men sometimes dance on their horses' backs, or jump from one horse to another. Tee Mamou women's exploits are occasionally just as macho and physically demanding. Cocaptain Claude Durio recalls a woman Mardi Gras catching and riding a pony at one house, some years ago:

We stopped along the road there . . . and there was a little Shetland pony out there in the back. And she went out there and caught that little horse, and got on, and that little horse went to bucking, and finally threw her. . . . But that was . . . a real funny incident. Nobody thought she could have caught the horse, first of all, and then she caught the horse and said, "I'm going to ride it." And I was right there in the pasture with her, and I said, "Oh, you better not get on that horse, better not get on that horse." She jumped on that horse and he went to bucking. She stayed on for about four or five jumps and she fell off.[51]

Many women, however, suggest that they prefer "comical" or "mischievous" stunts to daredevilry. Because they are not usually as strong as men, women creatively use their wits instead of their muscles. Years ago, Gerald Frugé observed that women are often more "clever" and "witty" in their pranks, more skilled in subtle comedy. In a 1989 interview, he said, "You can do a lot of cute little things that [are] Mardi Gras, that doesn't require a lot of effort. Picking at a kid, or you might untie his shoe. Being mischievous. [You can] attempt to get a little toy, or if there's a little toy in the yard, you get on your knees and play with the toy. Try to dance with the people that are there if they care to dance with you. Climbing trees, just act[ing] witty in various ways."[52]

He especially admired Patsy Simar's interactive style of comedy. He said, "She'll do her little thing, she might get a person's pencil and really look at it, fool with it real close, dig at it. And if she sees an opportunity, she'll pull out the pen and try to stick it in her pocket. But she'll do it so the person will see and try to get it back. . . . It's not threatening, but it's real funny."[53] Linda Frugé Doucet was another one such mischievous clown. She says that when she ran Mardi Gras, "I always looked for a tire to roll or a bike to ride, or something that would entertain the kids, you know, and just do my little thing in that respect."[54] As her two daughters joined the run, they adopted her style and often beat her to the tire or bicycle she had her eye on.

Women's comical play illustrates a common tension in festivals, the tug-of-war between tradition's conservative forces and the dynamism of innovation. Much of their comedy is improvised around whatever they find in the yard; they hide in barrels, pretend to fish from a stationary boat, or try to drive a parked tractor. One year, a Tee Mamou woman chased spectators with a dead rat she discovered. Suson Launey says, "It's just when you see something and you think you can make a good show or cut up, you know, [you] go after it."[55] One recent inspired skit came about when two partners found a small canvas stretcher under their hosts' carport. The pair convinced a young girl to lie down on the stretcher, and instantly they became paramedics rushing their patient to a hospital, as one Mardi Gras made siren noises. In some cases, though, Mardi Gras partners know that regular stops have a promising feature—a trampoline or a pond full of crawfish traps—and plan tricks around it. Shirley Reed says, "Some of the things we do are spontaneous but we usually plan something, you know, to act up, so that we can put on a good show."[56]

Audience is an essential part of the country Mardi Gras performance, as it is in any folklore event. Moreover, a trained audience has certain expectations and exerts pressure to maintain traditional ways of doing things. Spectators become the comic performance's "straight men" as maskers pull them into a dance, beg or steal their caps, and mimic them. Photographers, fieldworkers, filmmakers, and their equipment are all fair game. Some years ago, for example, I set my jacket and field notebook down to take photographs. A few minutes later, I looked up to see a masked Tee Mamou woman dressed in my windbreaker and busily pretending to scribble in my notebook. Folklorist Karen Baldwin describes her encounter with a Tee Mamou beggar who wanted no part of the nickels Karen offered—she was after dollars. When Karen explained she had none, the woman replied, "Well, then, I guess I got me a nice, expensive camera!" and reached for it.[57] After a mock pulling contest, the Mardi Gras gave up and left without the nickels or camera, as she had always intended to.

Tee Mamou women especially pride themselves on involving children in their performance; they dance with toddlers and older children, engage them in games of chase and tug-of-war, and pretend to kidnap and carry them to their wagon. Even when their play is at its most subversive, women are careful not to genuinely frighten children, reflecting their everyday nurturing roles. Gerald Frugé once observed that women are naturally more skilled at playfully engaging children than male Mardi Gras. He commented, "Men want to do it, but they're so horsey [rough]." Women, on the other hand, know how to approach children; according to Gerald, "The way a woman's going to talk to a kid . . . [her] tone of voice, the kid realizes that it may not be afraid of this Mardi Gras."[58]

Years ago, Tee Mamou women began handing out candy to reassure children during house visits. Patsy Simar, who remembers being frightened of the male Mardi Gras herself as a child, started the custom. She recalls, "I would dress as a clown, and Gerald would hand me the candy and I'd give it to the kids, so they weren't scared of me."[59] The Mardi Gras association still provides candy, but younger runners sometimes forget to hand it out during the run. Maybe the original gesture is no longer needed, as a new generation of children has learned not to fear the lady Mardi Gras.

Captains versus Mardi Gras

After singing, dancing, begging, and cutting up a bit, some women immediately head back to their wagon for a cigarette break. Others unmask and linger a few minutes to visit with homeowners they know well. When the head *capitaine* decides the house visit has gone on long enough, he summons the scattered Mardi Gras by blowing his whistle and shouting, "Let's go, Mardi Gras!" Some women obey, but tradition demands that some hang back and refuse to leave, hiding or taking refuge in trees. The captains' attempts to herd stragglers back to the truck, and the women's efforts to evade or resist them, lead to some of the day's most intense whipping bouts.

Years ago, Mardi Gras discipline was harsh; *capitaines* in some communities carried leather buggy whips and used them with a heavy hand. Today, Tee Mamou captains say they use their burlap whips, or quoits, mainly as a "reminder." Whipping, according to Suson Launey, is "basically to keep us in line. And if we behave ourselves, we don't catch the whip. But to be a good Mardi Gras, you got to be bad. And I'm an excellent Mardi Gras. So from the time I get down from that trailer to the time I get back up, I'm catching the whip."[60]

Most Mardi Gras whipping is consensual play, part of the run's slapstick comedy. Captains swat the Mardi Gras on their rears and legs, popping their burlap quoits to make an impressive noise. They are especially careful not to whip women Mardi Gras too hard. To quote Suson again, "You're really playing with the captains. But we just clown around and it looks a lot worse than it is, except for that whip, you know. When you catch that whip, if you're on the receiving end, it's not too good."[61] Other women, too, point out that Mardi Gras whipping is not "fake"—the quoits can sting and bruise. Experienced women learn tricks to lessen their impact, such as padding their pants with a sponge or a wad of toilet paper, or wearing a girdle. Then, as Suson says, "Everything's packed so it's tight. And when they hit it, you hear the pop of the hitting, but it's hitting on that girdle, you're not feeling anything."[62]

Occasionally, though, the struggles between captains and female Mardi Gras lead to real anger. Captains may get exasperated and use too much force; many women have stories of being whipped too hard and reacting with protest or retaliation. Women have several resorts if they think a captain is being too rough or punitive. First, they can complain directly to the offender. Some years ago, Renée Douget sharply scolded her brother, then a cocaptain, because she thought he hit her too hard. Women can also report a heavy-handed cocaptain to the head *capitaine.* Recently, a young cocaptain mistook Renée for a man during the group's Tuesday parade through Iota, and whipped her for stopping to talk to a bystander. She says, "I got whipped so hard . . . literally the crowd turned around, it was so loud. And I had an instant bruise."[63] In that case, her brother, Todd, and other captains reprimanded the young man. Another option is for women to plan their own retaliation at the dance that evening.

Burlap whips, symbols of captains' authority, are natural targets for the Mardi Gras. Time after time during the run, women try to wrest captains' quoits away and turn them on the captains. Suson Launey says, "They whip us and then we'll sneak up behind a captain and just grab the whip and start flinging the captain, because he's going to keep ahold of his whip. Because if we get it, he's going to be whipped."[64] Tee Mamou's lady Mardi Gras also smuggle their own whips onto the truck, hiding them until they can challenge a captain to a whipping duel. Or they improvise whips from garden hoses, ropes, and other finds. Several years ago, one woman picked up a dead snake as a whip and held a disgusted captain at bay with it.

Despite the roughhousing, captains usually handle women Mardi Gras more gingerly than men. Suson Launey, like others, comments on captains' tendency to give women more rein in cutting up: "A woman's run is different than a man's run. Because even though we say we're rougher and [all] that, we get away with more than a man would, for the simple fact we're women."[65] Captains take care not to whip unruly women too vigorously for fear of hurting them. Because women pose less physical threat than men, Tee Mamou captains tolerate women's horseplay, even when it is aimed at them. Throughout the day, Mardi Gras collaborate to wrestle young captains to the ground and immobilize them by sitting on them, grabbing their whips, and even hogtieing them until fellow captains come to the rescue. These melees intensify and transform everyday gender struggles into comic theater, to the amusement of spectators and (usually) the participants. Gerald Frugé pointed out, "If the women . . . can succeed in knocking down a man captain, they've really done something there, boy. It kind of livens the crowd up, gets everyone excited."[66]

When things begin dragging, the *capitaine* himself may urge the women to stir things up. Gerald described one such house visit some years ago: "I told [the women] . . . 'Well, it's getting kind of boring,' at one of the places. And I said, 'Y'all go knock [cocaptain] Joe Todd down.' 'Oh, that big old thing, we can't.' I said, 'No . . . People will come help.' So I saw these two heads turn to each other, and after a while the whole Mardi Gras jumps on Joe Todd. They got him down and there were about five or six girls [on him.]."[67] Gerald's wife, Linda, noted that most of the mock battles are good-natured and consensual. She described one friendly standoff when she held a cocaptain nephew at bay, and accidentally pinched him, with automobile jumper cables. She recalled, "Poor little fella, I remember I got him with a piece of cable. We were at a house, and he was after me, beating me with the quoit, and they had some booster cables in the yard, so I pinched him, thinking I'd grab his shirt, and I caught [his skin]. He let out a holler good."[68] Captains and Mardi Gras often plan encounters ahead of time to ensure a good show; if captains really wanted to stop the Mardi Gras, Linda points out, they could.

Nevertheless, young male captains are often reluctant to let women publicly defeat them without a struggle. Many women, in turn, take pride in pinning a burly captain and making him call for backup. Suson Launey, always one of the most irrepressible female Mardi Gras (she calls herself one of the "extreme ones"), proudly describes tackling a burly captain: "That big one, did you see him roll over me? . . . He rolled over, and I mean my *capuchon,* the cardboard . . . was all torn up from him rolling over. . . . Well, you know I deserved being rolled over on. There's no question. I won't deny that. But he rolled over. And I had him in a scissors hold, and he couldn't hit me and he couldn't get loose. And you could hear him hollering, and calling to [other captains] and [they] just stood back and laughed . . . until he begged me to let him loose."[69] Ultimately, of course, captains always prevail, restoring authority and order to the game. But for women Mardi Gras, briefly bringing a male captain to his knees is victory enough. Suson Launey says when she manages to overwhelm a new young captain, she admonishes him for being defeated by "an old woman." She says (perhaps with some hyperbole), "This year, after I'd let them up, I'd tell them, 'Y'all should be ashamed of y'all selves, letting an old woman do that to you.' They hung their heads."[70] Suson's daughter Crystal, who began running at thirteen, boasts that it took four captains to subdue her that first year.

Women Mardi Gras, like all tricksters, use their wits to trick or evade stronger adversaries. Suson says, "You learn new tricks every year" to use against captains. A common tactic is to ambush and spray captains with garden hoses. Captains, of course, watch out for this trick and try to turn it against the instigator. One year, for example, a wet captain managed to lure the responsible Mardi Gras back to the hose and soaked her in retaliation.

Women and male captains alike agree that "captaining" for the women is different, and often harder, than leading the men—mainly because of men's assumptions about women. Don LeJeune, a women's captain for many years, called managing the women "a different game altogether."[71] For one thing, captains feel they must walk a fine line between controlling female Mardi Gras and inhibiting or offending them—or their husbands. Above all, many male captains are hobbled by their own courtly attitude toward women, whom they still expect (against all evidence) to act in "ladylike" ways.

Women, on the other hand, are happy to exploit male captains' chivalric images of them. Don LeJeune once remarked: "By noon you lose track of the thought that these are women. Because they are really rougher than you are expecting them to be. And you've been reserved all morning and they haven't been. So . . . of all the things that go on, that is probably the toughest job, is being a captain for the women. Because again, you are dealing with women, and what all that entails and you try to be courteous to them and all that. But yet they're still willing to drop you, and roll you, and get you dirty and all of that, and then you try to temper all of that and it's a tough job. It really is."[72] Suson Launey, one of the women most likely to drop and roll captains, agrees. She is not above fighting dirty when needed, and says of captains, "Everything's fair in love and Mardi Gras."[73] In fact, these wrestling matches sometimes blur the lines between love and war, as captains sit astride disorderly women to subdue them, or women pin men to the ground by straddling them. The intense play between male captains and women Mardi Gras is one of the Tee Mamou run's most arresting features. Over the years, much of the women's cutting up has been redirected from householders to captains. Some veterans feel that women now concentrate too much on picking at captains, neglecting singing, dancing, and begging. Linda Frugé Doucet once suggested of newer Mardi Gras, "I think they're more interested in cutting up with the captains and horsing around than putting on a performance for the people at the houses. They're trying to think up the next trick, which is fun, but you need to do your thing first for these people that have been waiting to see you all this time."[74]

Moving On

Eventually captains herd errant Mardi Gras back to their wagon, and the group moves on to the next stop. Periodically captains call a beer stop, a welcome chance for the women to unmask, smoke, and quench their thirst. Lite beer, wine, and bottles of flavored mixed drinks travel in the back of the beer truck, locked in a chest-style freezer until captains dole them out during breaks. Making sure that Mardi Gras don't drink too much is one of the captains' most important duties; intoxication makes the Mardi Gras unmanageable and disrupts their performance. Claude Durio, a senior cocaptain who managed the beer truck for many years, emphasized this: "The main thing is, don't let them get drunk. If they get drunk, all you're going to have is a mob."[75] Monitoring women's drinking is especially crucial, captains say. Most women are less experienced drinkers than men, and less likely to know their limits. Claude suggests, half-joking, that women are even worse than men when they drink: "A man that's drank [regularly], he knows . . . how long he can drink. Now that's a long time, yeah, from seven-thirty in the morning till eleven o'clock at night—you know, to drink. And stay pretty active, that's a hard day's work. . . . The men realize how long and how hard it is, and they know if they get drunk early . . . that's it. But the women don't realize that."[76] Captains try to control how much the Mardi Gras drink by strictly rationing beer stops. Women, on the other hand, resist captains' authority by lobbying for more frequent breaks, by coaxing or tricking captains into giving them extra drinks, and by smuggling their own bottles onto the wagon. Captains search the truck when they suspect contraband liquor, but often a bottle or two escapes detection. One memorable year (memorable because I drank from the bottle), the women hid a fifth of schnapps in the truck's wooden bathroom stall—or, as Claude Durio likes to say when he tells the story, "right around that old plop." In subverting captains' checks on their drinking, women determine how disorderly they will become. Claude Durio pointed out that their insubordination makes captains' jobs more difficult; he comments wryly, "A sober woman is hard to put up with. Now you take twenty or thirty drunk women, it's bad."[77]

In reality, though, some women Mardi Gras drink little or not at all during the run. Suson Launey comments, "I have run without drinking, but it's a lot easier to drink and run than not to drink and run. It hurts too much to run without drinking." Women, she comments, learn not to get too drunk after passing out once or twice. Linda Doucet points out that the performance itself keeps most women from getting seriously drunk. She says, "When you're running around, horsing around, it's hard to get a buzz sometimes." Linda also emphasizes that what looks like drunken horseplay is usually not: "A lot of people, seeing the Mardi Gras and knowing they're drinking . . . just take it [for granted] that that's why they're acting the way they are. But it's not true. You have to put out that effort to put on a show. It's not the alcohol that's doing it." Much of the cutting up, she says, is because "You know that you're there to put on a show, and so you do it."[78]

On the Road Again

Stops in the Tee Mamou countryside are sometimes miles apart, so the Mardi Gras spend long periods on their wagon. In motion, the wagon is female territory, shielded from the view of captains, husbands, children, and the public. Men drive the trailer but rarely ride on it. (In jest, women do sometimes invite them on board to prove their manhood.) As it negotiates narrow parish roads, the wagon becomes a truly liminal refuge, a betwixt-and-between place. It offers hiding places for liquor, whips stolen from captains, and, one year, a live chicken that captains searched for repeatedly but failed to find. Long rides build rapport, as women take off uncomfortable masks and *capuchons* to drink, joke, complain about captains, and compare bruises. Some women doze off, while others dance and call out to passing cars or animals in the fields.

The Tee Mamou run's stop-and-start pace can make it difficult for Mardi Gras to maintain their energy and momentum. One of the things that surprised me most the first time I ran Mardi Gras there was how quickly the routine becomes monotonous: get off the truck, sing, dance, climb a tree, get back on the truck. The repetitiveness can wear on participants as they tire. Linda Doucet says, "And it's really not that exciting [at times] . . . to try to get involved with a dance, carry a tune, a beat and there's really no one . . . for us to dance with. And it's hard, you've got to kind of just make yourself do it."[79]

The women's run makes anywhere from fifteen to two dozen stops during the day, fewer than the men's run most years. Their route has grown even shorter in the last few seasons. Many country people today work, go camping on weekends, or are otherwise busy. Linda Doucet notes, "A lot of our people that used to accept us are dying out. . . . They're just not there anymore."[80] Some Tee Mamou residents count on seeing the entire group perform at Tuesday's Tee Mamou–Iota Folklife Festival and no longer bother to receive the women's Saturday run.

One stop, added in 1999, was at the tiny Reed family cemetery. There, the group paid tribute to Gerald Frugé by singing their Mardi Gras song at his tomb. Afterward, veteran Mardi Gras and captains lingered to wipe away tears or stand quietly at his crypt. After three or four years, captains decided that the women's *courir* would no longer stop at the cemetery, as members found it too hard to recover momentum after the emotional visit.[81]

Tee Mamou's Gumbo and Dance

By late afternoon, the Tee Mamou cavalcade heads back to the Frugé barn, its last stop. Weary women dismount for a meal of chicken-and-sausage gumbo, their traditional reward for a long and hard day. The meal usually takes place inside the sheet-metal barn, where wooden picnic tables are set up, or down the road under a Frugé family carport. Three or four helpers hand out plastic bowls of gumbo and rice, saltine crackers, and potato salad (a frequent gumbo side dish in Acadia Parish) to Mardi Gras and captains. Tee Mamou's gumbo is still symbolically important to the run, but it is no longer really a community-wide event. The day's hosts are all invited, but few attend, and captains and Mardi Gras riders make up most of the feasters. Some women, eager to get home and cleaned up for the dance, skip the gumbo or hurry through their meal.

The run officially ends with the women's Mardi Gras dance, the high point of the day for some celebrants. (Claude Durio has told me several times that I've never *really* run Mardi Gras because I've never masked for the dance.) Many women change into new "nighttime" masks and Mardi Gras suits, more intricate than sturdy daytime disguises. Suson Launey observes, "Nighttime is more elaborate. You'll have feathers on your mask, your costumes will be pretty. It's for show at night."[82] One of Suson's nighttime masks featured plastic battery-powered eyes with blinking lights, for example.

Over the years, the Tee Mamou women's dance has been held in various clubs, then in Iota's Catholic church gymnasium, without ever finding a permanent home. In the mid-1990s, the women's dance and the men's Tuesday *bal* both moved to D.I.'s Cajun Restaurant, a popular business operated by the Frugé family. On Saturday night, the Tee Mamou women are scheduled to perform two "marches" at six-thirty and eight-thirty. By six o'clock, the restaurant is packed with tourists and locals waiting for the show. As a Cajun band plays, a few couples two-step on the small dance floor, and family groups feast on boiled crawfish and fried seafood platters. Others squeeze into the restaurant and find any available standing room to watch the march.

Meanwhile, captains and Mardi Gras gather around their Mardi Gras wagon in the gravel parking lot. Captains hand out beers from an ice chest, and a fire in a barrel provides some warmth on cold nights. Near the appointed time, members mask and line up in pairs, arms linked, outside the restaurant's front door. On a captain's signal, the band inside plays the "Hee-Haw Breakdown," the group's signature tune, and Todd Frugé leads the hooting revelers through the crowd. Reaching the now-empty dance floor, they "make their round" or dance around its periphery, still making as much noise as possible. Spectators ring the dance floor and try to peer past each others' heads; excited children kneel in front, risking being stepped on.

When the last notes of "Hee-Haw Breakdown" die down, the Tee Mamou women crowd around their head *capitaine,* kneel, and begin to pound their hands on the wooden floor. Experienced audience members recognize this as begging; they toss handfuls of coins into the circle, and Mardi Gras scramble on hands and knees to pick them up. Once the barrage of money slows down, the women sing their Mardi Gras song before picking dance partners from the crowd. Just as they have throughout the day, the women dance a waltz and two-step, and then their captain announces that it's time to leave.

What follows is a mutiny that spectators, captains, and especially Mardi Gras have all been waiting for. In a custom shared with the Tee Mamou men's run, the women scatter and hide underneath tables and chairs, between diners' legs, on the bandstand, and in the rafters, anywhere they can find a space. Captains, in turn, must find and eject them. A few women obediently leave once discovered. Most, though, vigorously fight being pulled over an imaginary line and having to unmask. Gerald Frugé, who called the resulting melee "the highlight of the whole Mardi Gras," explained: "They always refuse to leave, so you got a tug-of-war going on, and you got to wrestle up with the Mardi Gras. And these ladies, they are tough, let me tell you. They put up a good show and it's all in fun, [but] when you see them, you get concerned whether or not someone's going to get hurt sometimes."[83] In a show that makes the daytime contests seem mild, women jump on captains' backs or wrestle them to the floor. Merline Bergeaux offers a Mardi Gras's perspective on the tradition: "The captains have to find us and pull us out. That's the best. We get beat [whipped] there. But they get beat too."[84]

Women have various tactics to delay being pulled over the line. One is to wrap arms and legs tightly around a captain and refuse to let go. Often, fellow captains have to pull a young captain across the dance floor by his legs, a Mardi Gras still firmly attached to him. Another trick (perhaps borrowed from more peaceful protesters) is for two or three women to link arms and legs, making themselves difficult to move. A third is to grab something immovable. Janice Ashford, who ran Mardi Gras during the 1980s, describes hanging onto a support pole as captains dragged out other women around her. She recalls with pride that it took five captains to finally remove her: "When they'd get one arm undone and they'd work on the other leg, that arm would come back."[85] Other women tell similar tales of their own indomitability. Merline Bergeaux, for instance, once bloodied her nose when she "played horse" by jumping on a captain's back and hanging on as he tried to shake her off.

Some women also use this time to retaliate against captains who whipped too hard during the day. Suson Launey says, "We'll gang up on one, and if one captain has been extra mean to us, we'll just tell the other captains, 'You back off, I want this one,' you know. And you got a good wrestling match going on."[86] When the last straggler is finally rounded up, couples once again take over the dance floor, and sweaty Mardi Gras and captains head back to their wagon until it is time to do it all over again.[87]

For some women, the Saturday dance marks the end of their Mardi Gras performance. Others are far from done. There are still performances with the men at local nursing homes (on Sunday) and again at D.I.'s (on Monday night). On Mardi Gras afternoon, they join the men on Iota's outskirts for a parade and performance—the main event of the Tee Mamou–Iota Folklife Festival. Thousands of residents and visitors line Main Street to watch the men (in the colorful Mardi Gras wagon) and women (following on a flatbed trailer) make their way through town. The maskers, like float riders in more urban parades, wave to the crowds and toss candy to them. Dismounting, the men and women dance through the crowd to the main music stage, where their *capitaine* leads them through their Mardi Gras song. The group is rewarded by a shower of coins flung by onlookers. Being part of this performance is a hard-won victory for the women Mardi Gras, who (like the men) enjoy the chance to mingle with, "pick" at, and beg from the large crowd. That night, the men will hold their own dance at D.I.'s, but for women it is time to wash muddy Mardi Gras suits and put masks away until next year.

5

Letting It Fly: The Basile Run

"[Mardi Gras is] in my blood, and still to this day,
I always tell my husband, 'If I'm down in bed
in the hospital, put that French music on, I'll just
bounce right back up,' you know."
—Debbie Andrus

"Mardi Gras's not meant to be censored. It's like,
'Let it fly, Jack.'"
—Kim Moreau

The eight-mile drive from Tee Mamou's Frugé barn to Basile takes you north on Highway 97, then west onto Highway 190 into Evangeline Parish. Like many rural south Louisiana towns, Basile—with a population of perhaps eighteen hundred people—struggles economically, especially in the wake of periodic declines in the oil industry. Many of its younger citizens move elsewhere to find work. But the community prides itself on three things: its annual Louisiana Swine Festival, its reputation for superb Cajun or "French" music, and its Mardi Gras run. The late Vories Moreau liked to assure outsiders that the Basile Mardi Gras "may not be the biggest Mardi Gras, but I promise you it's the best." Other residents echo the sentiment. Longtime Mardi Gras Debbie Andrus recalls telling her son Nicholas, who wanted to try running in a nearby town, "If you want to try it, fine. . . . But you will never find another Mardi Gras like the one in Basile.'" As for herself, she says, "I never ran in different towns because [my] heart was in the Basile one."[1]

Basile women have been running Mardi Gras since the 1960s, a few years earlier than the Tee Mamou women. Women's performances in both places share many basic "conventions of performance,"[2] but there are significant differences as well. First and foremost, the Basile run is now coed. When membership in Basile's ladies' run and the long-established men's run dwindled in the mid-1980s, the two groups joined forces to cut expenses. The merger worked well, and Basile women and men still mask together. There are vestiges of the earlier single-sex runs, however; men and women each have their own *capitaine* and

Debbie Andrus, a veteran of the Basile run, and her son Nicholas pose during the 2005 Mardi Gras run. Many of Basile's seasoned female Mardi Gras have brought their sons and daughters into the run, ensuring survival of the celebration that many say is "in our blood."

cocaptains and travel on separate wagons or trailers. These days, the women's head *capitaine* and cocaptain are female, just as the men's captains are male. Basile's inclusion of female captains is a significant departure from other Cajun runs and offers a rare view of women wielding festive authority.

The Tee Mamou ladies' run spotlights and celebrates gender differences, as women and their male captains tease, banter with, and wrestle with each other. Gender influences the Basile Mardi Gras run in more subtle ways; women and men mask, beg, clown, and dance alongside each other in mostly similar ways. They regularly "pick at" and test both male and female captains, but these encounters rarely reach the intensity of Tee Mamou women's onslaughts. Within local conventions, however, Basile's women Mardi Gras devise their own idioms for disguise, begging, singing, and playing pranks. Women captains, in turn, have their own leadership styles. Basile women's performances diverge not only from local men's but also those of Tee Mamou women. Women Mardi Gras in Basile, then, offer insights on localization of tradition, as well as on gendered nuances of Mardi Gras performances.

Getting Started: The Pig Barn

Mardi Gras day begins early in Basile. By five o'clock that morning, key organizers are already at work. Although it's still dark outside, the lights are on at the Town Park Barn, known locally as the Pig Barn because it was built to house the annual Louisiana Swine Festival. The barn, a metal-roofed pavilion, has served as the Mardi Gras association's hub since 1996. Other members begin trickling into the pavilion by six o'clock; they know that the group is serious about its seven o'clock departure time. (This is something I learned early on about Basile, where I've spent every Mardi Gras since 1992: if you arrive even a few minutes after seven, the group is likely gone.) Two converted rice trailers, borrowed from a local Mardi Gras family, are already parked in front of the barn. The men will ride on the larger wagon, the women will follow on the smaller one, and various Mardi Gras helpers will bring up the rear in pickup trucks.

Inside the pavilion, captains and Mardi Gras association officers are busy registering participants and making sure they sign release forms. Cassie LeBlue, the women's head captain, sits at one picnic table collecting dues from female participants; her counterpart, Leander Comeaux, the men's head captain, sits at another doing the same for the men.[3] The hour or so before departure is a busy one for organizers. Captains never know exactly how many riders to expect, because many Basile women and men make the final decision about whether they'll run at the last minute, depending on work schedules, weather, and (for women) child care.

Basile's Captains

Slightly built, barely five feet tall, and wearing thick glasses, women's head captain Cassie LeBlue seems an unlikely authority figure. Cassie masked and ran Mardi Gras herself for several years when she was younger, before becoming a cocaptain for her older sister Ella Ruth Young. When illness forced Ella Ruth to retire as women's *capitaine* in 1996, she asked Cassie to take over. Despite two heart attacks, Cassie remains the women's head captain; like Ella Ruth before her, she has inspired other women in her family to "captain," as it is called. Cassie's cocaptains have included her daughter Laura, sister Ramona, and sister-in-law Rebecca. Women's captains and cocaptains, like the men's captains, wear red capes over jeans, sweatshirts, and other work clothes. (Laura LeBlue, in a tribute to her late aunt's leadership, wears Ella Ruth's old cape.) All carry either leather whips—Ella Ruth Young called them "real whips"—or braided cloth quoits.

Until Ella Ruth's twelve-year tenure, female captains and cocaptains were mostly older women, retired Mardi Gras who captained for only two or three years. Then as now, few women were willing to exchange the fun of masking for the headaches of captaining. Debbie Andrus, who once commented that she might consider captaining when she got too old to clown and dance, observed, "When you're captain, you really don't get to have as much fun as we're having, you know."[4] While the maskers "cut up and have fun and dance and all that," captains must stay sober and maintain a work frame of mind. The LeBlue women, however, seem to have found their niche. Cassie says of Mardi Gras, "I love it, you know. And I'm going to do it as long as I can."[5] Her daughter Laura, at twenty-two, has been a captain for three or four years and says she would now rather captain than run. Cassie's younger daughter Jenny, now fourteen, runs Mardi Gras every year and says she would consider becoming a cocaptain, too, in time.

In theory, the women's captain rides with the female Mardi Gras on their truck and keeps them in line during house visits, while the men's captain travels with and manages the men. But the separation between men and women often breaks down during the day; Ella Ruth Young once commented that "the women tend to go [on the truck] with the men and the men tend to come with us"[6] much of the time. In practice, captains' roles overlap and they work cooperatively. Cassie says of her own role and of Leander Comeaux's, "We work together. We watch out for each other."

Basile's female *capitaine* must be an effective disciplinarian, but she also has more maternal caretaking duties. For example, Ella Ruth Young once told me that she always came prepared with safety pins, needle, and thread for emergency repairs on torn costumes during the day. Cassie and her assistants do the same today. As Snookie LeJeune, a seasoned female Mardi Gras, remarked, "We've had split seams up the back, we've had to sew somebody's thing on the trailer. . . . Those men, they don't care [if] they're torn, but the women got to have that draft in the back fixed."[7]

Basile, unlike Tee Mamou, has two parallel leadership structures: elected Mardi Gras association officers who oversee the planning and production of the run, and captains who (nominally, at least) take charge during the *courir* itself. Potic Rider, Mardi Gras association president for twenty years, explained the different roles to young, mostly male riders at a recent organizational meeting: "You listen to your president, you listen to your captain, because they're the bosses. The *capitaine* is stud duck, the boss on Mardi Gras day. Go talk to him if you have a problem; if he can't handle it, he'll come to me."[8]

Potic's announcement, however, hints at two unspoken aspects of the run's power dynamics: first, that in practice the male *capitaine* is more of a "head honcho" than the women's captain ("go talk to him"), and second, that the ultimate authority lies with Potic, even during the run.[9] Captains appeal to Potic when they have difficulty disciplining riders, and he makes many decisions during the run. This is fine with Cassie, who sees her own position as subordinate to Potic's. Her heart disease also makes her careful about getting too stressed by rough Mardi Gras play. When she can't handle an unruly Mardi Gras, she says, "I don't get mad, me. When I give up, I just go get Potic. . . . And he takes over."

Basile has eight or ten regular "helpers," men and women who work alongside captains and officers to ensure an orderly run. They drive trucks that pull the Mardi Gras trailers, dole out beer and whiskey, run errands, direct traffic, and keep an eye out for trouble. (Geneva Comeaux and her husband, Pat, two such helpers, usually let me ride along in the back of their truck, saving me the stop-and-start bother of driving in the procession's wake.) Sometimes at the last minute, veteran women Mardi Gras sacrifice their own plans to run because they are needed as helpers instead. Helena Putnam, for example, remembers not running one year because she had to ferry food and drink back and forth between the runners and gumbo cooks.

The Mardi Gras

The size of the Basile run fluctuates from one year to the next, but typically women make up almost half of the maskers. In especially cold years, as few as twelve women have run; in nicer weather, women sometimes outnumber men. The Basile run generally draws from a smaller area than Tee Mamou, and most women runners live in Basile or the nearby countryside. Helena Putnam commented a decade ago that "most of [the women] are from this area, and a lot of them . . . have a long history of involvement with Mardi Gras in their family."[10] Expatriates or those with family ties to the area often come home each year to run Mardi Gras. Berline Boone, for instance, has several nieces from Lake Charles (less than an hour's drive away) who travel to Basile each year to run Mardi Gras with Berline. In recent years, though, the *courir* has attracted as many as two dozen young men and women from other communities, some veterans of other Mardi Gras runs that have disbanded or become too crowded for their tastes.

Twenty years ago, membership was so low that Basile's run faced extinction. In an ironic reversal, organizers now are concerned that the run is becoming too large and unwieldy. The 2004 run, despite the threat of rain, had over 120 runners: more than fifty women and about seventy men. Although this was not a record turnout, the run did overflow its usual two Mardi Gras wagons. Many women were seated on an auxiliary flatbed trailer, and both men and women perched in the backs of helpers' pickup trucks.[11]

Not every girl or woman is cut out to run Mardi Gras; many try it once and decide that's enough. Longtime Mardi Gras Berline Boone once suggested that to enjoy running, "You've got to be somebody that . . . don't mind being stepped on, pushed at, and [so on]."[12] (Berline should know; she once had her foot broken when another Mardi Gras fell on it, but she finished the run anyway.) Regular "lady" Mardi Gras include politicians, a couple of nurses and pharmacy employees, bank workers, school teachers, bartenders, students, and homemakers. Here, as in Tee Mamou, women often have a regular Mardi Gras partner near their own age, someone to dance and clown with. These partnerships can last decades.

Girls can join the adult run at thirteen, and many—graduates of the local children's run—are already skilled Mardi Gras at that age.[13] The run's backbone, though, is seven or eight women, now in their late forties and early fifties, who have run Mardi Gras for three decades. These veterans or *vieilles* Mardi Gras are the ones I always look for first—maybe because they're my contemporaries, but partly because they are inspired and dynamic Mardi Gras. They speak Cajun French, dance well, and learned to run Mardi Gras from older Basile ladies in the 1960s and 1970s. Their masterful performances today are an important link to the earlier women's run and a model for younger Mardi Gras.

Berline Boone, now in her second term as Basile's mayor, is one of these old Mardi Gras. (The term "old Mardi Gras" is a positive term used by maskers and captains to refer to festive experience and skill, not age.) She first ran Mardi Gras at fifteen in the early 1960s with a group of older country women. Debbie Fontenot Andrus, who works in the Basile bank, is another Mardi Gras matriarch. Debbie has a distinguished Mardi Gras heritage: her father took part in the men's run, and several older female relatives and neighbors masked for the early women's run. All were, in her friend Susie Lopez's words, "big-time Mardi Gras people."[14] Debbie joined the ladies' run in the late 1960s, when she was twelve or thirteen, and today she is one of the run's best singers, dancers, and clowns. Her son Nicholas is now also a pillar of the coed run.

Snookie LeJeune, Susie Lopez, Janell Ashford, and Gloria Miller were junior high classmates when they began running Mardi Gras not long after Debbie did. Susie, a registered nurse, comments that they have "tended to kind of stick together since then" and still run Mardi Gras most years. Susie's longtime Mardi Gras partner is Janell Ashford, a former schoolmate who now works in a pharmacy. Helena Putnam, who teaches junior high school French, joined Basile's Mardi Gras Association in the early 1970s, and has been intensely involved with the tradition in various ways over the years. Determined to teach her students about their heritage, Helena sometimes documents other Cajun and Creole runs in the region, and at other times joins one or both of her daughters in the Basile run. Like one or two other *vieilles* Mardi Gras, she now has grandchildren who mask in the children's run.

Running Mardi Gras for thirty years is demanding, a true test of devotion for middle-aged women with careers and families. Debbie Andrus says, "And every year, I keep saying I'm not going to run and then when you hear the little kids in town, or my kids [say], 'Oh Miss Debbie, you gotta run Mardi Gras.' And then you start feeling kind of guilty. It's like, 'Okay, one more year, I'll try.'"[15] Berline Boone told me in a 1994 interview, "I don't know how many more years I can run.... [But] every year that they give me off [work], I will run. I'll do it until I can't no more, you know."[16] A decade later, she's still at it.

Women have many of the same obstacles to running Mardi Gras as men do, such as work schedules. Mardi Gras is a state holiday, but many have jobs that require them to work anyway. Susie Lopez comments, "With work and everything, you tend to see some stay out a year and then some jump back in." Women also face complications men do not. Pregnancy and child rearing often sideline even the most dedicated women for a few years. Debbie Andrus recalls that she sat out a few years to adjust to married life; she says, "I kind of slowed down some, you know, until I got used to that other life, besides running Mardi Gras, becoming a mama and a housewife."

Mothers of young children frequently have trouble finding babysitters willing to care for their children all day on Mardi Gras, when so many entertainments are available. Debbie says: "You know, most people want to go and see the Mardi Gras also. But you have to have a sitter from six-thirty in the morning until late at night, you know, and so it's hard to find you a babysitter for all day long, while Mom runs Mardi Gras. So that we found hard to do.... Sometimes you can get the little high school girls to come, but they don't want to come at six-thirty in the morning. They might come at nine-thirty or ten o'clock."[17] Women sometimes meet the truck along its route and join the run later in the day, because they have had to wait for babysitters to arrive.

Basile, like most runs, recognizes unofficial differences in rank among the Mardi Gras. Old Mardi Gras are often given more leeway, and in turn, they help guide and instruct novices. The group works together to regulate itself, with experienced women Mardi Gras (the "old mamas," as Debbie Andrus once referred to herself and her friends) monitoring initiates on their truck. Younger maskers, who may view the Mardi Gras run as an opportunity for public drunkenness, need particular supervision. Debbie says, "And sometimes those little young ones, they think, 'Well, oh, we're going to go run Mardi Gras just so we can drink.'... But then they forget they've got old mamas watching them."[18] Berline Boone suggests that the run takes on a different meaning for participants over the years: "The older you get ... the more you realize what it really is. You know."[19] For Berline and other old Mardi Gras, the run's importance lies in its sense of tradition and ties to community, family, and friends, not the chance to drink too much.

Basile Disguises

Basile has no specific rules on costuming, and revelers wear a greater variety of masks and suits than in Tee Mamou. Leaders recommend a fringed Mardi Gras suit, *capuchon,* and wire screen mask, but do not require them for fear of discouraging participation. Potic Rider says, "If you would stipulate [a specific disguise], you wouldn't have that many Mardi Gras. And we want the people to run. Dress—get the mask you can and come on. If you can't put on a mask, paint your face—that's it."[20] Thirty years ago, there was even more variety in both the women's and the men's (then separate) runs. Debbie Andrus, for example, comments that many women found wire screen masks uncomfortable, and rarely wore them. Instead, she says, "we did up our faces [with paint] or we went [to] buy rubber masks or whatever."[21]

Today, the majority of women and men do wear brightly colored Mardi Gras suits, *capuchons,* and wire screen masks in a conscious effort to be more traditional or "original." Basile screen masks are usually constructed of stiff screen bent and shaped to the wearer's face. Women often wear a more comfortable, cutoff version of the traditional wire mask, leaving their mouths and sometimes their noses uncovered.

Few Basile women make their own screen masks, but they frequently decorate them. The Basile aesthetic for masks is spare compared to Tee Mamou's: decoration typically consists of stylized features painted or drawn on with markers—or in recent years, with glitter. Some women's masks have distinctly feminine features and themes; I've noticed butterflies and flowers on several recent masks, for example, and long eyelashes painted on others. Mask designs are not usually topical, but occasionally they reflect current events or enthusiasms. In the 2004 run, not long after Louisiana State University (LSU) won its first national football championship in fifty years, Selena Young wore a screen mask painted with tiger stripes (in honor of the university's mascot) atop a suit covered with LSU emblems.

Although many women do wear screen masks these days, some prefer homemade fabric masks. Still others choose dominos (cloth eye masks), often with an added fringe or fabric skirt—a style that male Mardi Gras rarely wear. Rubber or transparent plastic masks, still seen on a few holdouts, are also more prevalent among women than men. (Of six rubber or plastic masks in the 2004 Basile run, four were worn by women.) Berline Boone says of the traditional screen mask, "I think it's beautiful, but that's not my kind of thing." Instead, "I usually wear a rubber mask, one that covers my whole face. Because everybody knows me, they'll recognize me [otherwise]."[22] Berline's rubber mask is invariably the run's strangest and goriest.

Women also wear a wider variety of Mardi Gras hats than men. Most men today favor *capuchons,* but some women find them too awkward. Berline Boone says, "There's a lot of people over here [who] don't like that tied around their neck. It gets caught. It's so pointed, it's so long . . . I very seldom wear that."[23] Instead, women may wear sombreros, glittery plastic derbies, or flat-topped mortarboards that resemble gaily printed graduation hats. Mortarboards were the favored hat for many ladies in the early Basile women's run. (Years ago, older men sometimes preferred mortarboards as well.) Indeed, some women still consider the *capuchon* "a man's headdress" and the mortarboard a woman's.[24] From time to time, Susie Lopez and one or two other veterans wear mortarboards, preserving what they see as a primarily female custom.

A final kind of disguise, prized by a few Basile women, is thematic or character costumes. Early lady Mardi Gras masqueraded as such exotic figures as Charlie Chaplin, circus clowns, old men, gypsies, wizened crones, gorillas, and Indians.[25] These days, a handful of local women (and less commonly, one or two men) are still fond of theme costumes and masks. For one thing, these disguises allow women's imaginations and creativity more rein. In a 1998 interview, Helena Putnam (who has masked in both traditional suits and less conventional costumes) explained that she appreciates a disguise that is "unique, and that took some creativity to put together."[26]

Creating character disguises frees women's imaginations, and wearing them offers new possibilities for comic role-playing. Running Mardi Gras is theater, "just like acting on stage," Potic Rider points out.[27] A role such as an exotic gypsy fortuneteller, a querulous old woman, or an Indian maiden in beads and buckskin inspires different ways of begging and clowning. Women's greater variety of imaginative disguises, then, creates a wider range of Mardi Gras roles for them. Debbie comments, "If you're all dressed in the same costume, you pretty much all kind of do the same thing. Whereas if you have your own personality, [and are] dressed as someone different . . . [you can] pick at people"—and skillful picking is highly valued by Basile's experienced Mardi Gras.

Taking Off

Shortly before the Basile Mardi Gras group leaves the Pig Barn at seven o'clock, Kim Moreau, a former Mardi Gras association vice-president, climbs onto the wooden stage to recite rules for the day. Basile's guidelines are not printed like Tee Mamou's but are "just understood rules" that are transmitted orally, Helena Putnam says.[28] Most focus on respecting property, not becoming excessively drunk, and obeying captains. Debbie Andrus says, "We're well warned and told, that whenever you go to someone's home, you do not mess with their flowers, you do not mess with their things, [or do anything] that will make it destructive, you watch where you're walking."[29] Although the rules are a useful reminder for young runners, especially, experience is more important than the rules themselves. New Mardi Gras learn how to act by watching and listening to more seasoned members.

Once members have been reminded of the day's rules, Potic Rider leads them through their *chanson de Mardi Gras,* the first of many performances that day. Organizers then call out each rider's name from sign-up sheets. Still unmasked, the Mardi Gras come forward one by one to be frisked perfunctorily for alcohol or weapons—men by their captain, and women by Cassie LeBlue. After being searched, women and men head for their separate wagons and climb aboard. Wagons are borrowed trailers with wooden posts supporting wire fencing on three sides, less intricately decorated than Tee Mamou's Mardi Gras wagon. A rented portable toilet (essential for women Mardi Gras) sits at the front of the women's truck. Cassie LeBlue and her cocaptain ride in the women's wagon to maintain discipline and ensure the riders' safety, just as Leander Comeaux and his assistant do with the men. Usually captains position themselves at the back of the trailer, holding a rope across its open end as a barrier.

Potic Rider's blue-and-silver pickup truck leads the procession, followed by the men's and women's Mardi Gras trailers and various helpers' trucks carrying drinks, musicians, and a chicken cage. Because the town sits on the border of Acadia and Evangeline parishes, sheriffs' deputies from both parishes join the procession in marked cars, lights flashing. They are closely followed by a train of cars carrying relatives and friends, three or four folklorists, and a scattering of other visitors. Basile does not publicize its run much, and it generally receives less media and tourist attention than Tee Mamou. But following the Mardi Gras is a popular sport for local families, many of whom have a friend or relative running. Debbie Andrus says, "I guess the best entertainment for a lot of the people in our community is that they follow the Mardi Gras."[30]

Years ago, when Basile women and men ran Mardi Gras separately, their routes lay mainly in the countryside. The two groups alternated territories each year: one year women traveled north toward Duralde, the next south into Acadia Parish. Today, the focus of the combined run is largely the town itself, with only a few stops in the countryside. Urbanization has gradually emptied the countryside, and many older, rural homesteaders who once welcomed the Mardi Gras have died or moved to town. Because stops in town are close together, the Basile run goes at a faster pace than Tee Mamou's countryside run. The revelers sometimes walk from one house to the next, reboarding their wagons only to travel several blocks.

The group's early morning route covers the heart of town, north of Highway 190, and late morning finds them heading into the Acadia Parish countryside. The Basile run traditionally goes as far south as the rural area known as Tepetate, the northernmost boundary of the Tee Mamou men's run. According to Potic Rider, a two-lane parish road forms a mutually agreed-on border between the two runs. He says, "They couldn't come on this side and we couldn't go on the other side. . . . It's always been understood. 'This is our territory, that's yours.'"[31] Today the two groups are still careful to avoid meeting, although both visit a local bar about an hour apart. After a lunch stop, the run heads back to Basile to visit a string of service stations, bars, and other highway businesses.[32]

Some women and men call their visit to the Basile nursing home, scheduled for ten o'clock in the morning, their most important stop. Here, they sing and dance in tribute to the elderly residents, many former Mardi Gras runners, cooks, and supporters. During a recent run, Potic Rider reminded the Mardi Gras in his booming voice, "These people are the reason we're doing what we do now. We learned it from them." As the group performs its *chanson de Mardi Gras,* a few patients sing along softly. When it is time to leave, many maskers are teary eyed; they linger to greet patients, kiss their cheeks, shake hands, or gently drape Mardi Gras beads around their necks.

Les Quémandeurs: House Visits

Women's performances during house visits follow generally the same pattern as men's—they all dance, sing, beg, and cut up—but some stylistic differences emerge. Both groups stay on their separate trailers until homeowners have agreed to receive them and a captain signals the go-ahead by waving a white flag. Riders then walk, run, or scramble to the front yard, jumping the drainage ditch that separates most houses from the road. Often women lag behind the men in their approach, because their truck follows the men's in the procession. Once everyone is assembled, Mardi Gras partners dance a two-step and waltz. Basile women and men both learn traditional dance gestures; to fast tunes, they stomp their feet, pump their right arms in the air, and whoop in what Potic Rider calls their "Indian war dance."[33]

The highlight of each house visit is the group's performance of their *chanson de Mardi Gras.* The song, members say, is their way of explaining what their run is about and thanking hosts in advance for what they will donate. One member, encircled by kneeling maskers, leads the singing, and the others join in enthusiastically on its two choruses. Five or six singers take turns leading during the day, but Debbie Andrus is the only woman to do so regularly these days. The scarcity of lead singers in general reflects dwindling fluency in French among younger members, a problem virtually every modern Mardi Gras run

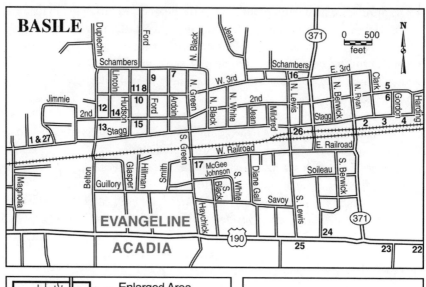

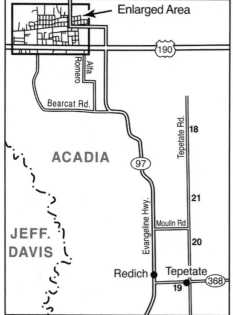

Basile Mardi Gras Route

1 & 27.	Basile Town Park
2 - 16.	House stops
17.	Basile Care Center
18.	House stop
19.	Trapper's Bar
20 - 21.	House stops
22.	Betty's Lounge
23.	Basile Exxon Station
24.	The Roadhouse
25.	E-Z Mart
26.	Street Dance

Map of the Basile Mardi Gras route in 2005. Today's run makes most of its visits in town, and often stops are so close together that the maskers walk from one house to the next. Part of the group's route still lies in the Acadia Parish countryside, where Basile's captains are careful not to cross paths with the Tee Mamou men's run.

shares. Susie Lopez observed in 1991, "There's only a handful [of us] that know it, maybe three women that know it [all]. I know bits of it, but I can't say it all the way through." One reason women song leaders are so few may be that their voices are not loud enough for dozens of runners to hear and follow.

Because the song is orally transmitted, its lyrics vary a bit from one lead singer to the next. It has two refrains that the song leader can insert at his or her discretion: "C'est hip, c'est hip, c'est hop, et mon cher de camarade"(always repeated twice), which Helena Putnam describes as a "rallying cry for the band of runners where they reinforce their sense of camaraderie,"[34] and "tout le tour autour du moyeu," or "all around the hub." Basile's modern-day maskers today are most familiar with Potic Rider's version, which follows here. Potic's interpretation of a few key phrases differs from that of older singers, and more common wordings are included in brackets.[35]

1. Capitaine, capitaine, voyage ton flag et hale ton camp.
   La route est grande, la nuit est longue et les belles sont pas invitées.

2. Les Mardi Gras, ça vient une fois par an demander la charité.
   Une fois par an, c'est pas trop souvent pour vous quand-même.
   C'est hip, c'est hip, c'est hop, et mon cher de camarade.
   C'est hip, c'est hip, c'est hop, et mon cher de camarade.

3. C'est les Mardi Gras, ça vient de loin
   Ça devient de les langues de terre [l'Angleterre].[36]
   Tout le tour autour du moyeu.

4. C'est les Mardi Gras, c'est des tous des bons jeunes gens
   Des bons jeunes gens qui vient des bonnes familles.
   Tout le tour autour du moyeu.
   C'est pas des malfacteurs, c'est les queues d'en bonheur [des
        quémandeurs].[37]
   C'est hip, c'est hip, c'est hop, et mon cher de camarade.
   C'est hip, c'est hip, c'est hop, et mon cher de camarade.

5. C'est les Mardi Gras ça demande pour une petite poule grasse, du riz,
        ou de la graisse.
   Tout le tour autour du moyeu.
   Pour faire leur grand gumbo ce soir à Grand Basile.
   C'est hip, c'est hip, c'est hop, et mon cher de camarade.
   C'est hip, c'est hip, c'est hop, et mon cher de camarade.

6. Tu me promettrais ci, tu me promettrais ça, mais tu m'en donneras pas.
   C'est hip, c'est hip, c'est hop, et mon cher de camarade.
   C'est hip, c'est hip, c'est hop, et mon cher de camarade.

7. Capitaine, capitaine, tes sauvages ça peut plus chanter à force que leurs
   gorges est secs.
   Une bonne petite bière froide les ferait chanter meilleur.
   C'est hip, c'est hip, c'est hop, et mon cher de camarade.
   C'est hip, c'est hip, c'est hop, et mon cher de camarade.

1. Captain, captain, wave your flag and move your group along.
   The route is long, the night is long, and the pretty girls aren't invited
   yet.

2. The Mardi Gras come but once a year to ask for charity.
   Once a year is not too often for you.
   It's hip, it's hip, it's hop, oh my dear friend.
   It's hip, it's hip, it's hop, oh my dear friend.

3. The Mardi Gras come from far away.
   They come from the peninsulas [England].
   All around, around the hub.

4. The Mardi Gras are good young people, good young people from good
   families.
   They're not troublemakers, just some good-timers/early risers
   [beggars].
   It's hip, it's hip, it's hop, oh my dear friend.
   It's hip, it's hip, it's hop, oh my dear friend.

5. The Mardi Gras ask for a little fat chicken, some rice, or some oil
   To make their big gumbo this evening in Big Basile.
   It's hip, it's hip, it's hop, oh my dear friend.
   It's hip, it's hip, it's hop, oh my dear friend.

6. You'll promise me this, you'll promise me that.
   But you won't give me anything.
   It's hip, it's hip, it's hop, oh my dear friend.
   It's hip, it's hip, it's hop, oh my dear friend.

7. Captain, captain, your Indians can't sing any more because their throats
   are dry.
   A little cold beer would make them sing better.
   It's hip, it's hip, it's hop, oh my dear friend.
   It's hip, it's hip, it's hop, oh my dear friend.

As the singing ends, the singers disperse, some returning to the trailers but
others remaining to beg. Skillful begging is a valued art for men and women in
Basile. Hosts are targeted, of course, but so are any followers and photographers.
(I always find that I'm approached for money much more often here than in

Tee Mamou, and have learned to bring a pocketful of change and a few backup dollar bills.) Maskers not only point to their empty palms in supplication but also kiss onlookers' hands, kneel, crawl on all fours, and shine shoes with their sleeves in hopes of a few coins—or preferably, a few dollars. The group as a whole picks up several hundred dollars during the day, all of which must be turned over to captains. If leaders suspect a Mardi Gras of holding back money, as occasionally happens, they confront the person and may bar him or her from running Mardi Gras again.

One common begging tactic is surrounding and immobilizing a target, by hanging onto her or his leg if necessary. Helena Putnam says: "Sometimes they'll gang up on one person. Several Mardi Gras will surround one person and just beg him to death. . . . It's usually someone that they're very familiar with. And they'll just surround him and get on their knees and beg, and so everywhere he turns, there's a beggar there. . . . Especially someone that's reluctant to give. And that they know can give, or will eventually give, and they kind of pressure him that way."[38] Helena bore out this statement during the 2005 run, when she recognized a well-known Cajun record producer in the audience. She vowed to get a generous donation from him at the next stop, but he disappeared. Later in the day, at Trapper's Bar, she cornered a retired Tee Mamou cocaptain whom she knew well. Helena refused to accept the quarter he offered, insisting in French that she wanted a dollar, but he refused to yield, even when Debbie Andrus joined her in her efforts. As the Basile group sang their begging song, Helena stood near him and shook her finger accusingly at him as she sang the lines, "You'll promise me this, you'll promise me that, but you won't give me anything."

Basile women and men are both clever and determined *quémandeurs,* but they approach begging differently. For women (especially *vieilles* Mardi Gras like Debbie Andrus, Susie Lopez, Janell Ashford, and other core members), begging is largely a comic verbal art. It becomes a contest of wits between Mardi Gras and givers; the women joke and plead with their hosts, often in Cajun French, trying to convince them to give more money or food than they intended. Disguises can offer a "theme" or personality around which to clown and plead one's case. Susie Lopez and her partner were costumed as a pair of playing cards one year, and gambling became their theme for comic begging. Susie explained to one man—known for his fondness for gaming—that she had lost all her money playing cards and needed enough to get back in the game. These exchanges frequently develop into improvised skits, as hosts spur the women on to even more inspired comedy. (The gambler, for example, asked Susie a series of questions about what kind of card game she lost.) Debbie Andrus, dressed as an elderly Cajun lady, told hosts that they should give generously because, old as she was, this might be her last gumbo. A good gumbo, she argued, might make her ancient bones feel better.

Longtime Mardi Gras Kim Moreau comments that female spectators are par-ticularly amused by thematic begging, and often conspire to get their husbands to give generously.[39] When Debbie Andrus, in her wrinkled crone disguise, had difficulty talking a local man into donating, his wife urged him to give because obviously the old lady needed a facelift. Debbie then hoisted her sagging breasts (part of her outfit) and petitioned for cash for a breast lift, then pressed for money for a buttocks tuck.

Women's comic begging performances, then, are interactive and reciprocal. Homeowners, many former Mardi Gras or captains themselves, cue beggars with questions ("Did you get any rice yet?") and egg them on to ever more ludicrous entreaties. Some enjoy turning the tables on the maskers by playing pranks on them under the guise of *la charité*. Debbie Andrus tells the story of a long-ago run that visited a small country store owned by Morris Young, a man they all knew well. Pretending he had a gumbo donation in a sack, he summoned Deb-bie, who recalls: "I remember they made me go and [Mr. Young] had something in the bag, and he wanted to say it was rice or whatever. And when I pulled that thing out of there, it was an old armadillo. . . . He was alive. I went to reach in there—and they had put that in the sack. [And I was] thinking that was our chicken or our hen, you know. And they thought that was fun."[40] Male Mardi Gras also use verbal comedy to beg, but they are more likely than women to use aggressive and persistent tactics. Men may fish in a spectator's pockets in search of wallets or cash, if they know him well, or playfully try to slip a ring off a woman's finger. Helena Putnam commented in a 1992 interview, "I think the men are more apt to try to dig in someone's pocket, to try to get money. The women would not [usually] approach anyone that way. They would be more apt to continue with the begging and the pleading rather than becoming that aggressive."[41]

Women—including Helena—do sometimes beg very persistently, but their aggressiveness may be seen as more offensive than men's. Helena ran Mardi Gras in Basile in 1994 after sitting out the celebration for some time—and was named best all-around Mardi Gras among the women. During one house visit, she tried to reach into a male acquaintance's pocket for his wallet. Later at the downtown street dance, she was punched by the man's wife, who accused Hel-ena of "feeling up" her husband. (Other participants later suggested that the wife mistook Helena for another, similarly dressed female Mardi Gras who had groped the man.) Whatever the explanation, this incident illustrates that women Mardi Gras who play as hard as men can face unexpected repercussions from other women as well as men.

Chicken chases remain a symbolically important part of the Basile run (as they are in Tee Mamou), although live chickens are no longer needed for the gumbo. Many households still make a point of having a live chicken or two for the Mardi Gras to chase, and sometimes they release the same chicken several times to make a better show. The Basile Mardi Gras Association even comes prepared with ten or so of its own chickens, to ensure that maskers have something to chase when things slow down too much—a mark of the tradition's significance.

Some women throw themselves wholeheartedly into these chases, ignoring or failing to notice fences and other obstacles. Helena Putnam, a determined chicken chaser and catcher, recalls a pursuit many years ago when she went flying after tripping over a wire: "I remember that year I had an intimate contact with a guy wire, a telephone guy wire. . . . I had dressed as an old man, and I had worn a pair of my father-in-law's shoes, and was running. . . . I never saw the guy wire, and it hit me across the thigh. I'll never forget that. I was airborne for quite some time."[42]

Men, however, tend to dominate chicken chases in the coed Basile run; they are bigger, usually stronger, and more aggressive in their pursuit. Debbie Andrus notes, "When we go to some of the houses, sometimes the men knock us over . . . [and] we don't have a chance." As a solution, the group occasionally holds separate men's and women's chases. Debbie explains, "They'll let the men run after the chicken and then they'll have a chicken for the ladies, and just the ladies will chase the chicken."[43] Chasing chickens is mainly a young person's game, longtime Mardi Gras say. Debbie commented in a 1991 interview: "Shoot, you know, I'm not that old, but . . . I don't use all those muscles I used to any more, and then when you get out there and start dancing and acting crazy and all that, it's a long day, you know. I can't hardly run those chickens like I used to run. Because we don't do it as much."[44]

Being Canaille

Skillful mischief making, like good begging, is a prized Mardi Gras talent among Basile's women and men; indeed, begging and mischief are often inseparable. A good Mardi Gras, women say, is supposed to be *canaille,* or naughty in a crafty way. Debbie Andrus says, "I was taught, when you run Mardi Gras, that . . . you weren't a mean Mardi Gras but you were a clever, or as we would say, [a] *canaille* . . . Mardi Gras."[45] Snookie LeJeune agrees: "That's part of [being] a Mardi Gras. . . . You go sing and everything, but you've got to be mischievous."[46]

One way of acting *canaille* is to tease or "pick at" audience members, trying to disconcert them. Debbie Andrus says that in the early women's run, as now, "There was always someone who was trying to beg, or goose the woman or the man [of the house]. If you knew somebody was scared of the Mardi Gras, well that was too tempting, I mean you had to go around them to pick at their feet or their legs or whatever."[47]

Gender shapes "picking" styles as well as begging. Young men are more likely to be very persistent or aggressive pickers; they often steal visitors' caps and throw them on the roof, tie their shoelaces together, or run off with a victim's shoe, for example. Some get carried away and persevere even as a victim's amusement turns into annoyance. Women, on the other hand, generally take a milder approach and are quicker to back off—hardly surprising, because women are rewarded for politeness and deference in everyday life. Teen-age girls and very young women, however, seem to be more persistent "pickers" than *vieilles* women Mardi Gras, perhaps because they have grown up in the mixed-sex children's run.

Mock thievery is a favorite form of mischievous clowning, here as elsewhere, and both women and men indulge in it. Comic stealing usually involves two kinds of objects: food (especially live chickens) and absurdly useless things. Susie Lopez recalls one such chicken theft: "At one house in particular I remember, the man said it was okay, we could catch one chicken. We caught the chicken, we got back in the truck, one of the ladies had got a guinea, so that was two that was taken from the house. Not by mistake. . . . Of course they understand when you have the Mardi Gras come to your house, something like that could happen. But I don't know if it was ever returned or not." Most Mardi Gras theft, though, is aimed at things with little value or use: a discarded bathroom sink, a bucket of water, or a yard ornament. Helena Putnam once tried to abscond with a ladder taller than she was, and got as far as the women's trailer before being stopped by captains. Being discovered misbehaving, of course, is the point. Susie Lopez remembers snatching a host's ceramic duck and "running away with the duck down the road and getting beat all the way back and stuff, because I had left with her duck. . . . [We do] just anything, you know, just anything to make people laugh and [that] you get beat for."

Women, like men, also play classic tricks such as wheeling one another in a wheelbarrow, or riding a child's bicycle in circles; when captains notice them, the Mardi Gras drop their borrowed vehicle and take off running. Frequently, though, male Mardi Gras get to wheelbarrows and bikes first, leaving women to find other ways of cutting up. Women generally agree that the men are simply more mischievous, more aggressive in their clowning styles, and more likely to take the initiative.

One factor, of course, is physical strength. Helena Putnam suggests, "I've seen some of our men Mardi Gras pick someone up and carry them around on their shoulder or something like that, and the women of course, you know, don't do that."[48] Helena herself was scooped up by a male Mardi Gras while she was photographing the 1992 Basile run. He teasingly held her over a hill of stinging red ants and threatened to drop her.

The majority of very physical or dangerous stunts are reserved for men. A few women climb trees; Helena Putnam held captains at bay from a tree fort one year, for example, taunting them and refusing to come down. But women rarely engage in (or are allowed to try) the most daredevil pranks: lying in the path of oncoming cars on Highway 190, trying to drive off on an unguarded backhoe loader, or scaling roofs, as men have done. Former women's captain Ella Ruth Young said, "The women are not going to do it, it's the men that does it. . . . Women, I don't believe they take too much of a chance doing that." Nor are most women likely to be given a chance, because leaders pick the three or four Mardi Gras veterans allowed to stop cars and trucks on the highway. These are usually men, but there are exceptions; Helena Putnam has joined male maskers in their highway raids.

There are exceptions to most of these generalizations about women's Mardi Gras play, in fact. More than a decade ago, Potic Rider commented, "[We've] got some women, they'll try anything, you know. They're not scared."[49] Ella Ruth Young observed that women give a more intense and daring performance at particular stops where they know the hosts well. She said, "It depends where you go. If . . . it's relatives of theirs, yeah, then they're going to make a good show. They'll really act up." On the whole, however, women have preferred to show their Mardi Gras prowess by dancing, singing well, begging cleverly, playing *canaille* tricks, and engaging children in their play.

Women's talents for Mardi Gras clowning are most evident in their performances of "themed" roles, suggested by a particular disguise, to the hilt. According to Debbie Andrus, a good disguise makes its wearer "figure out what you can do" as a clever beggar and trickster. She says, "Whatever I wore, it's like I had something up my sleeve that day. . . . I have a goal, you know, if it's to act crazy or a certain way to act crazy. Or if it's an old lady [then] you can be teasing old men or old women." One year Susie Lopez and her Mardi Gras partner, Janell Ashford, dressed as "Cajun chefs" and carried kitchen utensils. Both women hid huge fabric-and-yarn phalluses and testicles (made by one of Susie's patients) under their aprons, and periodically lifted the aprons to flash adults they knew would enjoy the joke.

Some gender differences in clowning derive from the nature of a coed Mardi Gras run. Lady Mardi Gras, several women and men comment, used to be rowdier and "let loose" more in their single-sex run, where they did not have to compete with men. For one thing, men simply beat women to certain pranks, because they are faster or because their truck leads the procession. Snookie LeJeune remarked in 1991 that during the run, the women are "always behind, they get there last, and since the men are doing all this, [women Mardi Gras] tend to be a little reserved." For another, a sexual double standard can constrain women running Mardi Gras alongside husbands and boyfriends. As one woman observes, it may be fine for men to drink and act "wild" in public, but they often frown on such displays by their spouses.

Mardi Gras and Their Captains

One notable characteristic of the Basile run is that it has both male and female captains, a rarity among Cajun *courirs* de Mardi Gras. Gender also molds captaining styles, as well as how Mardi Gras respond to captains. In Basile, as elsewhere, Mardi Gras' playful challenges of captains and the whippings they receive provide much of the event's entertainment. Helena Putnam has read extensively about Mardi Gras, documented other Cajun and Creole runs, and performed in her hometown run, the Basile *courir*. The first time I talked with Helena, she pointed out, "A lot of the trickery that was practiced [in the past] was done towards the homeowner, or towards the people who were receiving the Mardi Gras." Much of the most persistent mischief is now aimed at captains instead, perhaps because it is safer and less likely to anger householders. Helena said: "Now there seems to be a tendency for the Mardi Gras to try to undermine the captains. It's more directed at the captains. . . . A lot of people do things in hopes that they do get caught, you know, so that they can antagonize the captain. . . . Anything to get at a captain, anything to upset that, that order, you know, change things around. 'I'm the boss now, I've got the whip.'"[50] However, playful conflicts between Basile captains and Mardi Gras rarely even approach the intensity of Tee Mamou women's battles with their male captains.

One mild form of subversion is resisting male and female captains' efforts to keep their charges on different trucks. Susie Lopez says, "A lot of times, you know, the men will cross over and jump on our truck and get beat, and we'll do the same, and that type of thing." More direct contests include chasing, picking at, and "aggravating" captains. Like Tee Mamou Mardi Gras, Basile's women and men target the captains' authority symbols, particularly capes and whips. A favorite trick is flipping captains' capes over their heads and momentarily blinding them. Women's captain Cassie LeBlue comments, "They do that all the time. A thousand times a day." Cassie continues, "Or they're going to steal your whip. Or they're going to steal your cape. Like one year . . . I lost one of my good whips."[51] A Mardi Gras stole it, and Cassie never saw it again. (This went beyond a joke for Cassie, because the whip had belonged to her sister Ella Ruth and had sentimental value.)

Although Basile Mardi Gras seldom wrestle as vigorously with captains as Tee Mamou women do, their play can still get rough. Mardi Gras don't hesitate to drag captains through the drainage ditches that line most rural roads, leaving the captains wet and smelly. Ella Ruth Young commented of her charges in

1992, "They do aggravate you sometimes.... Oh, they'll throw you down, they'll throw you in the ditch or whatever." These tricks are aimed at both male and female captains, although women (especially the small, slight LeBlues) seem more vulnerable to being overpowered. Ella Ruth's niece Laura LeBlue was nineteen the first time she helped her mother out as a cocaptain, and had been running Mardi Gras since she was small. She recalls what seems to be an initiation rite for captains: "My first day that I was captain, [the Mardi Gras] drug me in sewage ditches, rice fields, crawfish farms. I got it all."[52] Men were the ones dragging her into ditches, she says—"The women would just tackle me."

Before her heart attacks, Cassie used to get the same treatment, and even now some Mardi Gras forget to be careful with her: "They don't ease [up] on me," she says. The women, Cassie reports, can be just as bad about roughhousing with her as the men are. She remembers that soon after her first heart attack, a young female Mardi Gras "caught me by my cape and drug me on the blacktop. . . . And they kept on doing it." Potic reminds the Mardi Gras each year not to rough Cassie up, but she says, "It don't do no good. They forget when they get a little beer in them." Despite this, Cassie keeps captaining because "I liked it—*me*—you know. But I do it right back to them."

Female and male captains may be subjected to many of the same pranks and trials, but women may also find their authority is not taken as seriously as men's. Laura LeBlue, who looks far younger than her twenty-two years, says of being a disciplinarian, "It *is* hard." The hardest part of captaining, she suggests, is "getting people to take you serious." Even middle-aged women sometimes find it hard to be taken seriously as leaders. Years ago, Ella Ruth Young commented that the Mardi Gras, especially the men, sometimes respected her authority less than president Potic Rider's. She explained that when riders became too unruly, "That's when we put a couple of them together, the ones that are real bad, you know, and Potic comes and he talks to them." According to Ella Ruth, "Yeah, they listen to Potic. Me, if I tell them something, they don't listen to me, because I guess I'm a woman, so, you know, that don't go too far." She added, "Now the women does [listen], but not the men."

Ella Ruth's successor, Cassie LeBlue, also turns to Potic when she has trouble managing unruly Mardi Gras. She refuses to let herself get too aggravated, and says, "You know, when I can't handle them, I just go and let Potic know. And he takes over." Ironically, she finds that women, especially the veterans she once ran Mardi Gras with, are most likely to ignore her commands.[53] Cassie and her cocaptain, Laura, both say that men "listen more" than women. Cassie observes that Basile's most seasoned female Mardi Gras—those responsible for watching over and teaching new revelers—can themselves be hard to manage. They know the rules but (like longtime male Mardi Gras) often see themselves as exempt. Cassie says women sometimes refuse to take her reprimands seriously, and "it don't pay" to scold them because "they'll do it anyway. And they laugh at me."

Part of the difficulty may be that they are her peers; they went to school together and later ran Mardi Gras together. Cassie says, "I guess the women, we all know each other, you know. And we all hang around together." Another factor may be that although Cassie did run for a few years, and has captained for many more, she is still newer to the tradition than those who have participated for thirty years or more.

In some ways, then, things have changed very little over the years. Women captains now hold positions of power, but are not always at home in them. Leadership still implies traditionally masculine qualities such as aggressiveness, and men's authority still commands more respect than women's, at times even among other women.

Beer Breaks

Basile women's *capitaine* Ella Ruth Young once made essentially the same observation as Tee Mamou captains: women are generally easier to manage than men, but they can quickly become very unruly when they drink. Ella Ruth suggested, "They are more rowdy than the men, when they get to the country" in the afternoon. She explained, "Well, you see they drink. . . . I guess the women are not used to drinking as much as the men. So when they do start drinking good . . . they get wild fast. It don't take them long . . . to get riled up." Making sure that women don't drink too much too fast, then, is essential to a "pretty" run.

Cases of beer, sweet wine, and premixed drinks travel in the back of a pickup, ready to be handed out whenever captains call a beer stop (usually every three house visits or so.) However, old Mardi Gras have been known to raid the bottles when captains aren't watching, and have even tried to drive off in the beer truck itself. In a recent run, several women Mardi Gras managed to steal the captains' secret stash of Mudslides, a chocolate-flavored bottled liquor that Cassie and her cocaptains were saving for themselves.

Debbie Andrus, who drinks very moderately, says that experienced women Mardi Gras learn to pace their own drinking throughout the day. This is necessary not only to keep them from being "ugly" and "too rude," in Debbie's words (things women are taught to avoid being), but also because running Mardi Gras demands physical endurance. Drinking excessively is taxing. She says, "You can't possibly have fun, dance like that if you're drunk to where you have to be laid out on the bottom of the truck or you're [just] sitting there, or if you're getting mean or wild."[54]

Berline Boone says that with experience, "you learn to pace yourself" during the run.[55] *Vieilles* Mardi Gras and captains together supervise how much young riders can drink. Debbie Andrus remarks: "You don't want to make it to where they're so drunk that they're throwing up or getting wild or rude because then you get a bad reputation. You know, and people don't want you." However, as she notes, "Sometimes you can't control everybody, you can't watch everybody."[56] One goal of the children's run is to teach young people to enjoy "acting the Mardi Gras" without having to drink a lot.

Beer breaks often stretch on for twenty minutes or more, allowing runners to rest, regroup, and line up for the Portolet. Although these breaks are officially offstage, many seasoned women Mardi Gras continue to dance with each other to the taped Cajun music blaring from their truck. Debbie says, "I was taught that you dance a lot as a Mardi Gras," even in down times.[57] (Susie Lopez likewise calls dancing "the old Mardi Gras tradition.") Debbie and Helena Putnam sometimes pick up a *tee fer* (triangle) and provide percussion for the music. Part of being a good Mardi Gras is being an "all-around fun" person and motivating fellow maskers; the best performers help keep flagging energy levels high until everyone catches his or her second wind.[58] To those of us watching, it looks like the *vieilles* Mardi Gras (many of them classmates more than three decades ago) are having the best time of anyone there. Running Mardi Gras, then, is an expression of strong and lasting female friendships. Basile women, it seems, feel freer to "let loose" among other female Mardi Gras, away from competition with men.

The Mardi Gras' final, midafternoon visit is to downtown Basile. Maskers and captains traditionally perform a spirited "march," or parade, along Main Street (officially Stagg Avenue) on their return to town. Since the Mardi Gras association began sponsoring a Cajun street dance on Main Street in the mid-1980s, the crowd awaiting the riders has grown, but it is nowhere near Iota's festival audience. Basile's street dance and march is still largely a community event, with a smattering of out-of-town visitors and folklorists. After putting on a show by dancing, singing their *chanson de Mardi Gras,* and "picking" at onlookers, most Mardi Gras unmask and take off increasingly hot and uncomfortable *capuchons.* Their performance is over for the moment, but many women continue to dance with each other, their spouses, and their children. Distinctions between Mardi Gras and captains are set aside for now, and captains Cassie and Laura LeBlue are pulled into two-steps and waltzes with their male and female charges. Although the game requires captains and Mardi Gras to be at playful odds for much of the day, all recognize that in fact they are a team, working together to produce a good performance and a community feast. As Potic Rider told folklorist Carl Lindahl, "The Mardi Gras's not doing this for them, now. It's for the town. So they can eat one last good meal before Lent starts. *That's what it's all about.*"[59]

The late-afternoon gumbo at the Pig Barn is not only the maskers' reward for their hard work but also a thank-you to hosts and other supporters. By 4:30, the group loads back onto their wagons for the short ride back to the barn; they have come full circle after more than nine hours en route. Gumbo cooks have been working since morning to prepare two huge pots of chicken gumbo and several electric steamer pots of rice. Here, as elsewhere, Mardi Gras etiquette demands that the Mardi Gras and captains be fed first. They file past folding tables where servers spoon rice, meat, and juice into plastic bowls, and then sit at the pavilion's picnic tables to eat. Once all celebrants are served, everyone else is invited to come eat their fill at no charge.

After their meal, many revelers return home to clean up, change clothes, and rest briefly before returning to the Pig Barn for their *bal de Mardi Gras.* Others, especially younger riders, go to nearby bars to drink, dance, and maintain their energy level. Captains, however, usually remain at the barn, as community members begin arriving early for the seven o'clock dance.

The Grand March

For Tee Mamou Mardi Gras maskers, the focal point of their Mardi Gras dance is the intense hide-and-seek game with captains. The highlight of the Basile dance, though, is the group's "grand march," the day's most joyous and prolonged procession. Community members pay a three-dollar entrance fee (five dollars per couple) for the dance, but Mardi Gras and their spouses enter free. Women and men, once again masked, begin lining up behind the pavilion's stage shortly before seven o'clock. Some (like Tee Mamou Mardi Gras) are in new nighttime suits, designed to shimmer beneath overhead lights as the maskers dance.

Basile Mardi Gras, especially women, have long been fond of rich fabrics such as satin, lamé, or velvet for night costumes. In Debbie Andrus's words, "A march is kind of like a parade, you know, you just want that pretty [effect] with the lights and all that shine." Basile has always been known for its beautiful costumes; Mardi Gras take pride in having striking suits, and their audience expects "a beautiful show," according to Debbie.

Twenty years ago, women sometimes wore extravagant ensembles that rivaled urban masquerade ball outfits. Now, most women and men wear more "traditional" Mardi Gras suits and *capuchons* for the dance, but usually two or three are made of lamé and other luxurious, sparkly materials. (These suits usually win prizes for "prettiest suit.") Some veteran Mardi Gras, however, no longer bother with elaborate nighttime suits. They've won enough prizes, they say, and are content to let younger people compete for them. Debbie Andrus says, "I haven't had a new costume in a long time. You know. I used to have a new costume all the time. But I've been there, done that. Gotten Best Mardi Gras so many times, won it, it's like, it's just fun now."

When the Cajun band on stage sounds the first notes of the Mardi Gras song, spectators stand on tables and chairs for a better view of the grand march. Led by captains, the Mardi Gras dance in, two by two, and circle the empty dance floor. Now, as throughout the day, men enter first, with seasoned men in front, followed by the women. Despite their weariness, the Mardi Gras put everything into this final march of the day, stomping their feet, whooping, and pumping their arms. Years ago, the *bal* was held in Basile's tiny Woodmen of the World Hall (now burned down), where the wooden floor reverberated with the dancers' energy. This, for many, is the most important performance of the day, and it never fails to move me, even on the Pig Barn's concrete floor.

After their march, women and men maskers dance two dances with their Mardi Gras partners, as they have many times throughout the day. Meanwhile, captains and Mardi Gras association officials confer; they will choose one male and one female winner in each of four categories: prettiest, ugliest, and most original costumes, and best all-around Mardi Gras (selected on the basis of their performances throughout the day).[60] Jurying is often a drawn-out process, but eventually winners all receive their trophies and are photographed for the next issue of the *Basile Weekly*. Each year since 1987, the Mardi Gras association has also used the dance to induct two or more people (usually former captains or officers) into its Mardi Gras Hall of Fame, and to award appreciation plaques to notable Mardi Gras helpers.

The awards ceremony ends the Mardi Gras' performance, and the public is invited to join them on the dance floor. A few Mardi Gras remain disguised and continue to "act the Mardi Gras." Most, though, unmask to drink, dance, and visit with spouses and friends, and perhaps rehash the day's events with captains and other Mardi Gras. Although the dance officially lasts until eleven o'clock, the march is the main attraction, and the pavilion is almost empty by nine o'clock. The revelers have been up since six (or all night on Monday), captains even earlier, and most have to work the next day. Cassie LeBlue, as a captain and Mardi Gras association officer, is one of the last to leave the Town Park Barn: it is her job to clean the gumbo pots and pack up all of the cooking equipment.

The next day is Ash Wednesday, a day many Cajuns observe by attending Mass, avoiding eating meat, and giving up beer, tobacco, or other pleasures. It is also the middle of the work or school week for many people. Returning to the everyday world can be hard as adrenaline wanes and bruises and sore muscles make themselves known. Debbie Andrus, who works at the Basile bank, remarks, "It is rough, you know, as you get older, it is rough. And you're not tired when you get up that morning, because you're still like trying to go. But it's about noon time, or two o'clock the next day, when you [feel it] . . . or [even] the Thursday."[61] Mardi Gras is over for the year, until planning starts again the next January.

* * *

Basile women have twice refashioned the traditional role of Mardi Gras masker: first in their early ladies' run, and again in the current mixed-sex run. Their disguises and actions, often very different from those of Tee Mamou women, offer another perspective on gendered differences. Performances by present-day *bonnes* (good) Mardi Gras are shaped by those of their Mardi Gras "mothers," the older women they learned from, but are creatively adapted to new circumstances. Within local conventions, women craft inventive disguises, including some that allow them to create new comic personas. Many women choose to focus on artful begging, clever "themed" clowning (especially improvised character sketches), dancing, and singing rather than competing with men's more aggressive, physical pranks. Women captains, too, are constantly reinterpreting leadership styles. "Captaining" has traditionally been based on male ideals, but women are gradually creating their own methods. Basile women, then, have created their own performance conventions that lend the local run much of its distinctiveness.

6

Festive Reversals:
Inversion, Intensification, and Coding

> "We're the chicken chasers . . .
> in the mud and the barbed wire."
> —Patsy Reed Simar

Cajun women's Mardi Gras performances, like other festive performances, enact deeply ingrained social values and hierarchies. Most of the time, Mardi Gras play exaggerates and turns these norms inside out, creating a temporary "reversible world" that in many ways "inverts, contradicts, [and] abrogates" everyday ideals.[1] Through these playful reversals, cultural assumptions usually taken for granted become transparent and susceptible to challenge. Cajun women, like men, draw on a variety of traditional symbolic inversions in their Mardi Gras disguises—reversing gender, age, and ethnicity, for example—and in their comic role-playing. At other times, women choose not to invert but to exaggerate these characteristics. Women, then, reinvent Mardi Gras conventions to highlight their own female concerns and points of view, creating a continuum of alternatives that sometimes topple cultural stereotypes of femininity, sometimes affirm them, but always broaden our view of womanhood.

This chapter examines how women in Basile and Tee Mamou use traditional Mardi Gras disguise and actions to redefine the celebration in their own terms. Three overlapping threads run throughout the chapter. The first is the powerful motif of unruly women who rebel against male authority—"women on top," in historian Natalie Zemon Davis's term. Writing about early modern France, Davis explains that woman was traditionally considered "the disorderly [sex] par excellence," because her womb, which tended to wander around her body, controlled her.[2] Given her own way, woman would try to upset the natural order by "rul[ing] over those above her outside" just as the "lower ruled the higher within [her]."[3] Most often, women's disorderliness took the form of trying to dominate men. The image of women on top was used to suggest disorder and revolt in many different contexts, including political protests. Although parallels between sixteenth-century France and modern-day Louisiana have limits, this notion of undisciplined "women on top" underlies much of Cajun women's Mardi Gras play, as they beg and steal, make mischief, and rebel against their captains. Now, as then, the unruly woman in all her "sexual power and energy" is a disconcerting and multivalent image that can be used to challenge male dominance and the everyday social order.[4]

A second thread is the notion that women's often-ambiguous Mardi Gras performances are coded acts. Folklorists Jo Radner and Susan Lanser, in their groundbreaking essay "Strategies of Coding in Women's Cultures," show us that women's traditional performances often convey subversive messages to other women within their culture, but these covert meanings may be inaccessible to men. Women's coding is "a set of signals-words, forms, behaviors, signifiers of some kind" that protect the performer from the consequences of more direct messages.[5] Coded messages, according to Radner and Lanser, sometimes help to empower women and bring about change.

I argue that women's Mardi Gras disguises and role-playing incorporate various forms of implicit coding, which need not be deliberate or intentional. Appropriation is one key tactic, as women coopt and adapt forms "normally associated with male culture or with androcentric images of the feminine" to their own purposes.[6] Impersonation, another kind of coding, is equally central to Mardi Gras performances. By replacing their own voices with new personas, female maskers distance themselves from their often-subversive messages. Women Mardi Gras also use artful juxtaposition (which Radner and Lanser define as "the ironic arrangement of texts, artifacts, or performances") to create new, ambiguous meanings for Mardi Gras masks and clowning.[7]

A final strand is the concept of the grotesque body as an essential principle of carnival and its festive laughter. Literary critic Mikhail Bakhtin, whose ideas have transformed the study of festival, asserts in *Rabelais and His World* that carnival (a broad term that includes a range of folk festivities) is essentially ambivalent; it both degrades and exalts, destroys and gives new life to whatever it touches. The grotesque body, a central carnivalesque image, revels in acts such as having sex and giving birth, eating, and defecating, often in excess. Bakhtin writes: "In grotesque realism ... the bodily element is deeply positive. It is presented not in a private, egoistic form ... but as something universal, representing all the people. As such it is opposed to severance from the material and bodily roots of the world; it makes no pretense to renunciation of the earthy, or independence of the earth and the body."[8] The "unfinished" grotesque body constantly "outgrows itself, transgresses its own limits."[9] The body's boundaries with the outside world, its openings, are exaggerated and elevated in comic play, which particularly focuses on what Bakhtin calls the "material bodily lower stratum"—the belly, reproductive organs, and buttocks.[10]

Throughout this chapter, I explore how women's symbolic inversions and intensifications work to resist male dominance and rebel against their own subordination. Most important, women's festive play resists and transforms constraining female stereotypes. Through their Mardi Gras performances, women present their own, often contradictory images of themselves as comical and "crazy," maternal and nurturing, boisterous and bawdy, polite, insubordinate, rule-abiding, clever, and complex human beings.

Inversive Disguise

Mardi Gras disguise is a "self-constructed façade" that allows women to transform themselves at will.[11] Under the cover of new and easily discarded identities, female Mardi Gras are free to act in unconventional ways. Certain kinds of festive reversals are traditional to Cajun Mardi Gras runs: men and women alike invert gender, ethnicity, age, social class, and species in their costuming. Men have customarily been the stars of Cajun Mardi Gras runs, and until recently their symbolic reversals received the most attention.[12] But as women adopt and amend these inversions, they bring their own gender-specific meanings to Mardi Gras disguise.

Gender is among society's most basic organizing categories, and inverting everyday gender roles is one of the most widespread types of festive and ritual play. Crossdressing, the most obvious form of sexual reversal, is a traditional part of many all-male Mardi Gras runs. Unlike the New Orleans Carnival's often convincing transvestism, Cajun men's female impersonations are purposely broad caricatures. Men—usually very large and brawny men—stuff pillows or balloons under dresses, pull on cheap wigs, and slather lipstick on their mouths to play the *vieille femme*, or old woman, a classic comic figure.[13] The *vieille femme*, sometimes performed in blackface as *la négresse*, exudes overripe sexuality as she chases, flirts with, and tries to kiss spectators. Sometimes a much smaller man plays her browbeaten and cuckolded husband. The couple, then, offers a masculine perspective on the "women-on-top" theme of wives trying to dominate their husbands and, by implication, upsetting the natural social order.

Female Mardi Gras also use gender crossover in their disguises, although less commonly than men. Photographs of pioneering women's runs in the 1940s and 1950s show women masking as bridegrooms, old men, and pirates. Basile women often dressed as men in their separate ladies' run during the 1960s and 1970s, and once in a while they still do in the current blended run. For the most part, women's male disguises are simple: masculine clothing (a suit jacket with tie or denim overalls, for example, and a hat), a painted-on beard or moustache, or a rubber mask with a man's face. On rare occasions, though, women's crossovers emphasize male sexual features. One woman in the early Basile ladies' run, for instance, is remembered for wearing an oversized cloth penis under men's denim coveralls. More recently, in the coed 1994 Basile run, two women masking as "Cajun chefs" hid fabric phalluses and testicles (an echo of the earlier Basile precedent) beneath white aprons. Periodically, they "flashed" friends by lifting their aprons and pulling the penises erect with a ribbon.

Most of the time, however, women's male costumes are sexually innocuous. The most common male disguise in Basile's early ladies' run was an old man, presumably past his sexual prime—unlike men's *vieilles femmes,* who sometimes mimic pregnancy and childbirth during the run. Helena Putnam remembers that when she masked as an old man (wearing her father-in-law's shoes), she played a fairly restrained role rather than an "aggressive type of character."[14] Her restraint was appropriate to her character's advanced age, but mainly she was reluctant to offend other female Mardi Gras and onlookers. Now and then Basile women still run Mardi Gras in male-identified clothing such as overalls or a tuxedo, but they generally still downplay aggressive male sexuality—perhaps even more than in the past, now that men and women run together. Even the risqué Cajun chefs confined themselves to briefly flaunting their false endowments to certain onlookers, in what could be read as mockery of male exhibitionism.

Women, then, sometimes use the implicit coding strategy of impersonation to indirectly comment on and subvert culturally determined gender roles. Their male parodies, however, are usually more polite and restrained than men's performances of womanhood. Cajun women do not act out machismo in the exaggerated (and unflattering) way that men portray femininity, perhaps because—like Helena Putnam—they don't want to upset anyone, especially in a mixed-sex run. Carol Mitchell, in her 1985 study of gender differences in joke telling, points out that women tend to use humor less aggressively than men, and are less willing to tell jokes they perceive as hostile, especially in mixed-sex groups.[15] Similarly, women Mardi Gras may be reluctant to antagonize others by mimicking men, and they may view these impersonations as more hostile than men do.

Gender-inversive disguise also takes other forms, such as gender neutrality or androgyny. Tee Mamou women, for example, tend to emphasize the genderless nature of the clown-like Mardi Gras suit, pointed *capuchons,* and handmade masks that all Tee Mamou guisers wear. "We're just Mardi Gras," one explained to me in a 1988 interview.[16] Deemphasizing gender, in this case, seems to empower Tee Mamou women and give them greater comic range.

Often women's Mardi Gras masks and costumes blend male and female signifiers in ambiguous ways, in a more subtle form of gender inversion. Tee Mamou women's masks may mix beards and moustaches with long, feminine eyelashes or dangling earrings, for example. Basile women have even more room to create enigmatic hybrids in their thematic disguises. One of Basile's anatomically enhanced Cajun chefs, for instance, also had apron pockets marked "His" and "Hers"; when she lifted the flaps, tiny male and female genitalia were revealed. The wearer's femininity, imperfectly concealed behind screen mask and apron, was central to the joke, emphasizing what Deloria names the "doubled identity produced by costumed mimicry."[17] Five years later, another Basile woman based an even more androgynous disguise on the same practical joke. Dressed as a grotesquely ugly hag with wild black hair, long red fingernails, and a shapeless dress, she periodically displayed an oversized penis made of cotton-stuffed pantyhose.

These sexually indeterminate disguises are more fundamentally inversive and disturbing, I think, than women's straightforward male disguises. They are very much in the spirit of Bakhtin's notion of carnivalesque grotesqueness and its celebration of the "material bodily lower stratum" of bellies, genitals, and buttocks. Through enigmatic juxtapositions of male and female attributes, these composites provoke laughter (which is the point), but they also nudge the bounds of local social convention. The Cajun chef and old hag ambisexual disguises were a little shocking—all the more so because they were worn by women not usually associated with public performances of bawdy humor.[18] On an abstract level, ambiguous costumes like this undermine binary definitions of gender. As Hotchkiss argues, women's crossdressing suggests that "gender inscription and the sexual code are, most emphatically, not absolute codes."[19] The main target, though, seems to be cultural expectations, not biological difference. By raising questions about where one sex ends and the other begins, women suggest wider possibilities for female behavior.[20]

Women Mardi Gras, then, sometimes play with traditional notions of gender by crossdressing, by wearing gender-neutral costumes, or by provocatively mixing feminine and masculine features. On the whole, though, Cajun men seem to favor Mardi Gras crossdressing more than women do. There are many likely reasons for this, including the fact that the sight of women in male clothes— once associated with prostitutes and "rude" women in the New Orleans Carnival—has lost much of its dramatic punch. Masculinity lacks much of the "artifactuality of the 'feminine,'" especially now that many women wear trousers regularly.[21] Too, most women are smaller and slighter than men, and in male drag they tend to resemble young boys or grandfathers, somewhat diminutive or infirm (and therefore feminized) figures. Perhaps this is one reason that women often choose elderly men for their male impersonations.

Much of the answer to the asymmetry of crossdressing, though, may lie in what crossdressing is really about for each gender.[22] When men dress as women, they reaffirm masculinity and male power by ridiculing the feminine, and therefore ratify the existing social order. As Michael Taft (writing about similar role-playing in Canadian mock weddings) notes, crossdressing men make clear the fact that they are not playing women but "playing with the roles of women."[23] When women mask as men, on the other hand, they are masking upward in the social hierarchy. Women's mimicry rarely reaches the same level of ridicule as men's, but it is ultimately more transgressive, revealing the malleability of gender codes and posing a symbolic challenge to the sexual status quo. Women may once have found that sex role switching gave them access to male liberties, but today dressing as men seems neither creative nor comical enough for many female Mardi Gras.[24] They find more comic freedom and power in gender-neutral and androgynous costumes, as well as in other kinds of innovative disguises.

Some of women's most imaginative disguises emphasize rather than invert their gender. Both Tee Mamou and Basile women sometimes feminize their disguises through small touches: they add bowed satin mouths or earrings to their masks, or cover them with silk flowers and painted butterflies, for example. Over the years, I've seen a few young women in Basile (and one or two in Tee Mamou) add trailing scarves or ribbon streamers to their *capuchons,* or allow long hair to show underneath their hats.

Basile women draw attention to their gender even more explicitly in their representational costumes. Rarely are these disguises based on glamorous sex symbols like Marilyn Monroe or idealized women, although some early women Mardi Gras did dress as brides. (Perhaps these figures are too close to everyday ideals of how women should look and act.) Nor do women dress as prostitutes, a common theme in the New Orleans Mardi Gras and, according to Da Matta, the Brazilian Carnival.[25] Instead, Cajun women often adopt exotic and symbolically powerful female identities such as voodoo queens, fortunetellers, and Indian maidens. At times, they also dress in floor-length, full skirts, petticoats, and *gardes de soleil,* or sunbonnets, evoking a nostalgic image of old-fashioned and superrespectable Cajun ladies, made exotic by time. Women Mardi Gras, then, have a wide range of disguise options, and their preference for powerful female characters suggests that women see more options in female roles than men do.[26]

When women mask as female figures, they often choose characters decades younger or older than themselves. Inverting age but not gender, these costumes offer both anonymity and countless comic possibilities. In one example, a pair of Basile Mardi Gras partners dressed in pigtailed wigs, bucktoothed masks, pinafores, and striped stockings. When I asked, they explained that their "theme" was Raggedy Ann dolls, but the effect was decidedly little-girlish.

A far more popular choice is masking as wizened old women. Basile women create their own interpretations of the *vieille femme,* discovering a wealth of comic possibilities in the role. Old women, after all, are often seen as marginal and desexualized figures, and their very marginality allows them license to act and speak frankly. One of the most successful versions of the *vieille femme* was Debbie Andrus's memorable and cranky crone in the 1996 Mardi Gras run. A heavily wrinkled mask, drooping breasts made of balloons, padded hips, and rolled-down support hose transformed Debbie into a matronly figure whom even her close friends and fellow Mardi Gras could not identify. Debbie says of her disguise that year, "There were so many people that did not recognize me. . . . My walk was different, and the whole way. And I was dancing different. You know when you've got a big butt and big boobs and all this other stuff [you move differently]."[27] The effectiveness of Debbie's disguise was a form of power in itself, as friends had to guess at her identity while she "picked at" and teased them. She comments, "You don't want them to know who you are. And they try to guess, and you keep telling them, 'No, no.' . . . In fact, that's been the main thing, is not to let somebody know who you are."[28]

Debbie took advantage of her anonymity and used her old lady persona to pick at the run's leaders, including president Potic Rider, an old friend who failed to recognize her. She recalls, "And he [Potic Rider] was getting mad at me because I had gotten a dozen eggs. Somebody gave us some eggs. . . . And he kept saying, 'Bring me the dozen eggs.' No, I didn't want to bring him the dozen eggs. But he was getting kind of aggravated, so I took one out . . . like I was getting ready to throw it at him. He told Marshall [a Mardi Gras helper], 'I don't know who that damn old lady is . . . but I'm going to kick her ass out [of the run].' . . . I was laughing at him. . . . So when he found out it was me, he could not believe."[29] The next year Debbie planned to skip the run because of an injured leg, but she eventually agreed to re-create the old woman character with some changes. She added a beauty pageant–style sash announcing the title "Madame Basile" on one side, and *"la vieille femme"* on the other. Later she explained, "My theme was, I got [named] queen of the nursing home" for Basile's annual Louisiana Swine Festival.[30] The second time around, everyone knew who she was, but her disguise was no less effective as comic age inversion. Her skillful mimicry of a cantankerous old woman allowed her to act in a variety of licensed ways, as she teased old men and women, swatted at other Mardi Gras, and played her role to the hilt.

Women's portrayals of the *vieille femme* and other female figures differ sharply from men's. Women's female disguises are generally more matronly than voluptuous, and tend to deemphasize sexuality and reproduction. Their old ladies look and act elderly, and are affectionately referred to as *mamère* (grandmother) and *tante* (aunt).

However, broad generalizations about Mardi Gras inversions are dangerous, and inevitably there are exceptions. In the 2001 and 2003 runs, a couple of Basile women wore plastic, flesh-colored breasts over their *suits de Mardi Gras,* a joke more common among male Mardi Gras. These breasts reflect the influence of the New Orleans Carnival, where encouraging women to flash their breasts is common in some quarters. In wearing false breasts themselves, Cajun women reappropriate a male burlesque of femininity and symbolically reclaim their own sexuality—and perhaps mock the New Orleans custom of trading glimpses of bare breasts for beads. The breasts, like any good Mardi Gras prop, provided new opportunities for clowning. In one memorable instance, a Basile woman encouraged an elderly man, a nursing home resident confined to a wheelchair, to touch her plastic bosom. He did, to everyone's amusement, and then seemed both abashed and proud of his own audacity.

Racial or ethnic masquerade is another common feature of men's Mardi Gras runs that, like crossdressing, assumes less importance in women's runs. Cajun men sometimes paint their faces black to play the burlesque roles of the *nègre* (black man) and *négresse* (black woman), who act as both lead clowns and comic foils.[31] These roles are usually associated with particular men who perform them year after year, and this may be one reason that women rarely mask as African Americans.

Descriptions of early Cajun women's runs contain a few references to black-white reversals. Frozine Thibodeaux mentioned to folklorist Donna Onebane that the Richard ladies' run in the post–World War II years did feature a woman dressed as a *"négresse* or Indian" (terms she seems to use interchangeably).[32] Debbie Andrus likewise mentions that in Basile's women-only run of the 1960s and 1970s, women sometimes masked as an "old black mama."[33]

Indeed, celebrants in early Cajun women's runs may have found that the *négresse* role gave them greater comic range than other disguises. M. Alison Kibler, writing about white women who donned blackface in vaudeville shows at the turn of the century, notes that the "privilege of playing with blackness" allowed them to enact "less physically inhibited, more sexual selves" through "uninhibited dancing and slapstick comedy."[34] Women's appropriation of the (white) male blackface tradition, she suggests, constituted a challenge to vaudeville's ideal of refined femininity as they "overstepped the boundaries of vaudeville propriety."[35] In symbolically crossing racial lines, female vaudeville performers imitated the "exuberance and wild activity"[36] of black performers, along with what they perceived as a carefree sexuality. Likewise, Cajun women in the postwar years may have found compelling possibilities in blackface masquerade.

On the whole, though, blackface characters have never really taken firm hold as a regular feature in women's runs, or at least they have died out in recent years. Perhaps women fear offending spectators in the post–civil rights movement era (and indeed, these figures in men's runs are attracting controversy) or find other kinds of reversals more entertaining. The only time I've seen a Cajun woman wear Mardi Gras blackface was in 1993, when Helena Putnam briefly assumed the role of Basile's *nègre* for the *bal de Mardi Gras*. Tony Johnson, a relatively short and slight man who regularly played the *nègre* for a number of years, agreed to trade places with Helena that night. In heavy black greasepaint and curly wig, wearing Johnson's signature suit jacket and swinging his cane, Helena joined the men to lead the group's grand march into the hall. As intended, only half of this double crossover was convincing; she—like Tony—was clearly a white Cajun wearing black paint. On the other hand, Helena's mimicry of Tony as *nègre* was impeccable, so convincing that most people there never spotted the switch. Indeed, Helena confounded some spectators when, still disguised, she danced with her husband, Mike; they wondered why two men were dancing together, an unusual event even on Mardi Gras.

Although women rarely dress in blackface today, they sometimes assume other ethnic identities. Basile women, for example, have masked as Asians, as vaguely Roma-like gypsies, and particularly as American Indians. Their Indian disguises, reflecting popular stereotypes of Plains Indian culture, range from simple and stylized (a headband, feather, and face paint) to meticulously detailed, as was the Indian maiden costume Debbie Andrus wore years ago. Debbie recalls, "I had the [braided] wig, I had the actual costume that was like an Indian—the skirt, and a top with the fringes, the moccasins. And we had . . . the big bells all around [my] wrist and then around the ankles. And at that time I had painted my face brown [with theatrical makeup] . . . and I fixed my face up like an Indian."[37]

Some Cajun Mardi Gras celebrants identify strongly with Native Americans on several levels, and this lends extra meaning to Indian disguises. In Basile and some other prairie communities, Mardi Gras were traditionally called *les sauvages,* the term used locally for Indians. In the past, Lindahl suggests, masked Mardi Gras "played the roles of tribes beyond the borders of civilization, bent on unraveling the fabric of society."[38] To perform the Mardi Gras role itself, then, is to play Indian. Dressing as an Indian, even a female Indian, lets Cajun women draw on the multilayered (and mostly male) connotations of Indianness: they can be brave warriors and fearless raiders, noble savages, and wild women who stomp, whoop, and make trouble. Several years ago, a pair of Basile women wore shirts that spelled out *chauvage* (a phonetic spelling of *sauvage*) in handmade letters on the back, a reference to their role as rowdy Mardi Gras.

In addition to gender, age, and racial inversions, women's Mardi Gras disguises symbolically erase other kinds of hierarchies. Basile women, like men, often dress as other-than-human creatures such as animals or monsters. One of Berline Boone's favorite costumes was a gorilla suit, and Debbie Andrus and her partner once played dragons. Several years ago, Berline's nieces wore pink long johns, curly tails, teats made from baby-bottle nipples, and plastic snouts as the Three Little Pigs. (Evidently the Three Little Pigs are female, at least in Basile.)[39]

Similarly, Tee Mamou women integrate animalistic features into their home-made masks. Many women wear masks covered in fur, hair, or feathers, augmenting the feral look by adding plastic beaks, snouts, whiskers, and fangs. Renée Frugé Douget, whose masks are especially hairy, commented jokingly: "I always made them kind of resemble an animal, and I didn't know why, but I just did. . . . I always just liked a wild look."[40] Tee Mamou women also decorate their masks with miniature animals such as plastic alligators, chickens, roaches, snakes, ants, and rats.

Other disguises suggest human-animal or vegetable hybrids, monsters, or wild men—figures commonly associated with "nature without controls," in Roger Abrahams's words.[41] A shaggy yarn mask in Tee Mamou features a nose pierced by a chicken bone, for example. Other suits and masks are entirely covered with grasses or Spanish moss, creating a "Swamp Thing" persona. Basile's Berline Boone is a master of shaggy "wild man" or creature suits; for the 1999 run, she wore a shapeless costume covered with long, ropy strands of gray-green wool, topped with a grimacing mask.

These half-human, half-animal disguises blur the borders of tamed civilization and wild, unruly nature. Although male Mardi Gras wear similar masks and costumes, women's wild Mardi Gras metamorphoses are especially interesting because, across centuries and cultures, women have been symbolically aligned with nature. Carol Adams, for example, suggests that women and animals are often symbolically linked.[42] Anthropologist Sherry Ortner argues that men universally represent culture, while women's reproductive and childbearing roles keep them closer (physically, socially, and psychically) to nature.[43] Women's Indian and blackface costumes can be read as more subtle variants on the wild man or beast-human image; like other indigenous figures (and like women), they are imagined as untamed savages and "primitives . . . in close contact with nature."[44]

Women's animalistic disguises are one example of what Cajuns generally call "ugly" disguises. In this context, ugly can mean weird, unique, or one-of-a-kind rather than unattractive. But many masks in both communities are intended to be misshapen, grotesque, and even repellent. Cajun men's and women's Mardi Gras disguises often reflect Bakhtin's principle of the grotesque body: masks feature gaping mouths, crooked teeth and distended tongues (sometimes frozen in the act of devouring a rat or roach), silicone snot hanging from enormous warty noses, and eyes popping or crossing. Renée Frugé says that in decorating her masks, she looks for touches that make her think "Oh, that's ugly, gross, or scary."[45] In Basile, comical character disguises often depend on hunched backs, gargantuan bosoms, hips (and occasionally genitals), and various other deformities.

Women in Basile, and to some extent in Tee Mamou, have access to both ugly and "pretty" disguises such as shimmery lamé suits, and masks with feminine features. Ultimately, both have the same practical purpose—to attract as much attention and generosity as possible. But often ugly just seems to be more fun and offer better comic possibilities. Debbie Andrus has won awards for prettiest and ugliest costumes, and says that she likes "anything that you can act crazy in."[46] Often this means an outlandish costume. Tee Mamou's Suson Launey suggests that part of an ugly mask's attraction is "the novelty, that no one has one like you. And besides, it's crazy."[47] Berline Boone, especially drawn to horrific masks, says, "I always love the ugly masks. . . . They have some beautiful costumes at [Basile's Mardi Gras dance]. But I'm not into that."[48]

The idea of making oneself as ugly or strange as possible is, of course, common in festive traditions, where ugliness represents another type of exotic Otherness. The grotesque ideal becomes especially interesting when women mask, because it stands in sharp contrast to everyday life, where female beauty remains important. Debbie Andrus's portrayal of the wizened old lady wearing a pageant queen's sash, for instance, derives comedy from this disparity (and the local importance of beauty pageants). On Mardi Gras, then, ordinary aesthetics are upended and blurred, as masks become "so ugly that they're beautiful, or so beautiful that it's ugly," in Junior LeBlue's words.[49] Ugly disguises represent a final kind of inversion involving cultural ideals of feminine beauty, as ugly becomes just as desirable as pretty for women—but only in terms of disguise. When masks and *capuchons* come off, many women try to fluff sweaty, dusty, and flattened hair. (I know I did, with little success. Running Mardi Gras is hard on the hair.)

At the same time, ugly disguises offer coded critiques of the notion that the female body is inherently grotesque. Kate Chedgzoy, along with other feminist scholars, points out that although Bakhtin usually speaks of the body in general, non-gender-specific terms, his descriptions are in fact "replete with characteristics that have traditionally been coded as feminine—pregnancy, childbirth, menstruation," and transformation itself.[50] Woman, Bakhtin says, is "the incarnation of this [lower bodily stratum] that degrades and regenerates simultaneously. . . . but first of all, she is the principle that gives birth. She is the womb."[51] In Bakhtin's description, women are (once again) inextricably associated with, and ultimately reduced to, their reproductive abilities.

Women's ugly disguises, it seems to me, are playful responses to opposing male ideas of womanhood as earthy, fecund, and essentially grotesque, or idealized as dainty, polished. and feminine. Women's Mardi Gras transformations embody the ambivalence many women feel about impossible beauty ideals and are a form of momentary resistance to them.

Role-Playing as Inversion

Mardi Gras disguise offers women a variety of ways to symbolically invert or affirm cultural codes. Festive role-playing offers still other means of coded reversal and intensification, especially in terms of gender. Much of women's Mardi Gras play involves gender inversion, which can consist of "simply taking on certain roles or forms of behavior characteristic of the opposite sex."[52] Just by masking and running Mardi Gras, a traditionally male activity, Cajun women engage in sex role reversal and appropriation.

Moreover, women's specific Mardi Gras actions frequently sabotage cultural codes for feminine conduct, as they climb trees, drink publicly, stir up trouble, and oppose their captains—or, in Basile, crack the whip themselves as captains. Tee Mamou Mardi Gras Merline Bergeaux takes pride in the fact that she and her partner are rambunctious and fearless "chicken stealers," and she says, "We're the ones that always manage to get the chicken." Her partner, Shirley Reed, comments, "Some of the others I think might be afraid, you know, to be chasing them or to get dirty.... [But] Merline and I are in the mud [and] the barbed wire fences."[53]

In other ways, women's performances conform to female norms and values. For example, women's Mardi Gras play often revolves around collaboration, a frequently mentioned female value. Women work as teams, helping each other climb trees or gang up on a male captain, for instance. Many women prize creative or witty clowning over competitive chicken chases, daredevilry, and the physical prowess associated with male Mardi Gras. They distance themselves from comic aggression, preferring to make people laugh by playing a nonthreatening clown role. Even the most disorderly women act maternally toward children, taking care not to frighten them and engaging them in play. Women, then, have created a greater range of Mardi Gras role-playing than men—from very macho and assertive mischief making and "cutting up" to more traditionally feminine roles and comical clowning.

Women with Whips

Women's Mardi Gras runs, like men's, have usually reproduced the gendered hierarchies of everyday life: men are largely in charge, and male leadership is more or less taken for granted. Indeed, leadership in general is often defined in terms of "masculine" attributes such as competitiveness and aggression.[54] Women, on the other hand, historically had little access to public positions of power, and powerful women are often seen as unnatural beings. Given this male model of authority, it is not surprising that in most places Mardi Gras captains are men, strong figures who wield "irrevocable authority" and command obedience from the maskers.[55] Even women's Mardi Gras runs have usually followed this example and had male *capitaines*.

For Cajun women, then, "captaining" is as fundamental a role reversal as Mardi Gras clowning. Basile is one of the few communities that includes women *capitaines* and cocaptains serving alongside male captains. Basile's female captains have not always found their duties comfortable, and sometimes maskers—especially male Mardi Gras, but women, too, at times—trivialize women's authority. However, longtime Basile captains like Ella Ruth Young and Cassie LeBlue have refashioned and feminized the captain's role, making it more cooperative and using a number of "maternal strategies," as Elaine Lawless calls them.[56] Younger women, including Cassie's daughters and sister-in-law, seem more amenable to becoming captains, although they may decide to wait until they're too old to "cut up" and dance as Mardi Gras.

Indeed, I've been struck by women's explanations of why they would rather mask and run Mardi Gras than to be captains; they prefer the chance to "let loose" and "act like a little kid" to being saddled with the headaches of leadership. Ironically, perhaps the captain's caretaking responsibilities are too close to the everyday oversight required of mothers. On Mardi Gras, many women don't want to be a parental figure in charge, they want to play, create mischief, and be carefree.

Women on Top: Female Assertion

Even in communities with no female captains, women seldom seem to resent men's hold on the highest Mardi Gras positions. Instead, they enjoy undercutting captains' authority in various ways: by sneaking extra alcohol during the run, verbally teasing captains and disobeying their commands, spraying them with hoses, and other horseplay. Runners and captains perform a stylized battle between order and disorder, as the Mardi Gras try to turn the tables by stealing their captains' whips, flipping their capes over their heads, dragging them through ditches, and wrestling with them.

Men and women use similar tricks to defeat captains, but the battle takes on new meanings when women are pitted against male captains. The contest becomes a struggle between male authority and female insubordination—the illicit power of the disorderly woman who refuses to recognize her proper place. As Mardi Gras, women (usually associated with passivity and submissiveness) invert traditional gender roles by acting in assertive and aggressive ways. Tee Mamou women in particular wrestle with, topple, straddle, and ride the backs of young male captains, becoming "women on top" in a very literal sense. Captains may ultimately prevail, but the Mardi Gras are often temporary victors, and this is triumph in itself.

Captains, especially male captains, bear the brunt of women's aggressive Mardi Gras play, but female maskers also use various ruses on other men. Many male folklorists, for example, have stories of their first encounters with masked women. Nick Spitzer recalls that in the mid-1970s, he was photographing moss pickers near Evangeline on the weekend before Mardi Gras. A group of female Mardi Gras, led by a male captain and riding on a flatbed truck, passed him on the road and pelted him with tomatoes.[57]

Nick got off lightly with a drive-by tomato attack. Women in Tee Mamou, and occasionally in Basile, will sometimes tackle a male onlooker, upending or sitting on him until he begs for mercy or buys his freedom. Other times, a man might be pulled through mud puddles, or abducted and dragged toward the Mardi Gras wagon. Often these ambushes are reserved for men the Mardi Gras know well, or for visitors pointed out by captains and other followers, targets who can be expected to take the joke in good humor.

Over the last five years or so, fellow folklorist John Laudun and I have engaged in an annual bidding war during the Tee Mamou women's run, when each of us bribes Suson Launey to tackle or kidnap the other. Suson, of course, takes our money and then does whatever she wants. So far, I've escaped attack, but John is usually pounced on and pinned to the ground—it's more fun for the women to pick on him. He in turn initiated a male graduate student by paying Suson to tackle him during the 2004 run. Women, then, can use the role of Mardi Gras mischief maker to subdue men and challenge male power, and sometimes they can make a profit for the Mardi Gras association while doing it.

Perhaps women's most unsettling form of inversive play is taking the sexual initiative. Customarily, women are on the receiving end of flirtatious or aggressive overtures during men's Mardi Gras runs; they may be chased, thrown over a young man's shoulder, or pulled into a dance. When women run Mardi Gras, they in turn try to confound men with playful sexual advances. Tee Mamou women, in particular, taunt, goose, and wrestle with their male captains, inviting them into the women's Mardi Gras wagon to prove their manhood. (This kind of overt play is rare in Basile's coed run.)

When folklorist Barry Ancelet began photographing the Tee Mamou women's run in 1988, he became a favorite (and mostly willing) target of provocative play. Initially, he recalls, he was just "roughed up a little" by a few women, although it was "nothing out of the ordinary" for Mardi Gras.[58] As he became friendly with male captains and with some of the bolder women Mardi Gras, the picking escalated. In 1989, he naively accepted a ride on the women's wagon. There, several women surrounded him and subjected him to what he called a "group grope," briefly unzipping his jeans to (they explained) check the color of his underwear.

As it happens, I first ran Mardi Gras with the Tee Mamou women that year, although despite Barry's suspicions, I was not one of the gropers. However, I did mention to one of the women that he would make a good victim. Initially, captains also were complicit in Barry's kidnapping; in an interview later that year, then captain Gerald Frugé commented that one reason the women picked on Barry was that a cocaptain jokingly pointed him out and said, "That's the one you've got to get."[59]

The women's assault on Barry became an annual tradition, one he played along with, and each year the stakes got higher. In 1990, Ancelet says, "I was passed around the wagon and felt up. I had anticipated another underwear check and was wearing briefs tie-dyed in the traditional Mardi Gras colors of purple, green, red and gold." The clowning progressed to the point that the women tried pulling his pants off to "wave them down the road as a victory flag" the next year, he says; they were foiled only by his boots.

Eventually, perhaps inevitably, the game "crossed a social barrier," in Barry's words, and captains brought the abductions to a halt. In an essay describing his Tee Mamou experiences, Ancelet writes that the following year (1992) the women "took him down" early in their run, and then assured him he was safe. To avoid being left behind after one house visit, he jumped onto the women's wagon—a liminal and female-dominated space if ever there was one—as it pulled onto the highway. He recalls: "I was again attacked by two of the most notorious outlaws of the bunch. With only a bare toehold on the back of the wagon and only one hand available at a time (the other being necessary to avoid falling off the wagon) I was unable to fend them off effectively (though by now I was genuinely trying) and they succeeded in mooning the countryside with my buttocks until the captain bringing up the rear (so to speak) radioed ahead that the wagon driver should stop to let me jump off."

The Mardi Gras were scolded by captains, and Barry was "asked to keep a distance for a while, a request I was delighted to oblige," he writes. Some of the other female Mardi Gras and their captains worried that these antics might give the group a bad reputation, making households reluctant to receive them. Ancelet sums up his experience: "A symbolically aggressive, subversive and openly sexual game had gotten out of hand and blurred some of the other important functions of the Mardi Gras involving a reaffirmation of community through ceremonial begging, visiting, dancing and eating. We were all called to refocus and the game checked itself so that it could continue."

These risqué pranks are certainly attention-grabbing, and only after several years did I realize that such openly sexual play is in fact rare and limited to a handful of women. It is, however, in its own way very empowering for female maskers, who claim the right to assert their sexuality—or to question a particular man's. On some level, these antics may parody men's aggressiveness, but they are not intended as real invitations. Instead, they are meant to embarrass and disconcert men by coopting a male prerogative. Gerald Frugé observed that if men "pay them no mind," female Mardi Gras will leave them alone. However, he added, "If they see it's going to disturb a man, [if] they can intimidate [him]," they inevitably pick at him.[60] In fact, many men have absolutely no idea how to respond when women turn the sexual tables, and are virtually immobilized by the women's teasing. Gerald Frugé noted that male Mardi Gras likewise enjoy picking on women, but said, "I haven't seen it as much in the men, or it hasn't been brought to my attention as much in the men."[61] Men are unlikely to be granted the same license as unruly women, who are less of a physical menace than men, but whose strategic uses of humor, aggression, and sexual intimidation create more cultural anxiety in many cases.

Women as Clowns

Women's rowdy, assertive Mardi Gras play is a striking example of festive role reversal, but their performances also transform gender roles in more subtle ways. Running Mardi Gras offers women the freedom to clown and be funny in public, for example; indeed, one of the event's main attractions is the chance to act "silly" or "crazy." It seems to me that public clowning—even nonaggressive clowning—is itself a departure from stereotypical feminine behavior. Although many Cajun women love jests and practical jokes, women's humor (as several feminist scholars observe) is usually performed in private settings, often away from male audiences. Humor is often perceived as aggressive, a trait more acceptable for men than women, and cultural expectations dictate that "men should be the initiators of humor, while women should be responders."[62] Moreover, performing humor is a kind of power.

Women's public Mardi Gras clowning, then, coopts traditionally male liberties, but women find their own comedic styles. Women's clowning is often less aggressive and less competitive than men's, and it reflects their own views and experiences. At times, women create comedy from their own roles as mothers and caretakers. In one instance of improvised comedy, for example, a Tee Mamou woman fumbled with a (clean, I think) disposable diaper she discovered during a house visit, clumsily trying to tape it onto her partner's back.

Women as Outlaws and Raiders

Much of women's "cutting up," like men's, revolves around begging and pretending to steal from their hosts. Although the maskers and their captains approach homeowners as supplicants, their visits are in effect mock raids. An implied threat (once real, now mainly pretend) that the visitors will take what they want underlies their performance. These invasions are particularly subversive when women perform them, because they target specifically female territory and possessions.

The home itself, of course, is usually women's domain and has always been a refuge for women and children frightened by the maskers. Although Mardi Gras runners never enter the house itself without permission, they do play with its façade, peering in windows or doors, climbing onto porches and porch swings, clambering up support poles and even onto roofs. The maskers also beg for, and if necessary snatch, goods traditionally controlled by Cajun farm wives: chickens, eggs, and garden produce. Spitzer, in fact, suggests that in rural French Louisiana, the chicken "stands for women, their work and their respectability."[63] Women's pranks also test family stability, as female maskers pretend to abscond with other women's children and husbands. Women Mardi Gras, then, symbolically threaten their own traditional domain and by extension their identification with everyday norms of home, order, and respectability. (In reality, though, women's actions usually avoid any real threat of damage, as they are generally more careful than men not to trample flowers, cause property damage, or terrify children.) At the same time, running Mardi Gras opens up other, more public spaces to women—country roads and town streets, dance halls, clubs, and other places usually associated with men.

*   *   *

Cajun women use their imaginations and skills to reconstruct male traditions of Mardi Gras disguise and play, adapting them to their own aesthetics, senses of humor, and viewpoints. Using symbolic coding strategies such as appropriation, indirection, and juxtaposition, women present their own, wide-ranging interpretations of contemporary womanhood. Often their actions and masks demolish traditional gender roles and assumptions of male dominance; at other times they seem to affirm, but perhaps revalue, certain aspects of the status quo.

Are women Mardi Gras really rowdier and more unmanageable than men? It depends on whom you ask. Participants describe the event in very different terms and emphasize different aspects. Some women and captains agree that female maskers are naturally more rule-abiding and obedient than men, less likely to go over the line. Others stress the unpredictable and "rough" nature of women's actions, especially when they drink too much.

In fact, women's Mardi Gras performances encompass a spectrum of behaviors, from polite and respectful to raucous and unrestrained. Mardi Gras runs, Carl Lindahl points out, include many overlapping roles, and different communities elevate certain roles over others.[64] Similarly, individual women adopt particular roles at different times. The most "extreme" women who push the boundaries of the performance can in fact be pretty rowdy. But often these women are just as daring and outspoken in everyday life. As Abrahams and Bauman contend, disorderly festive play is not really the opposite of what goes on in everyday life, and some community members regularly engage in "disorderly and indecorous behavior."[65] Women do drink, dance, clown, flirt, and get boisterous in real life, but it is allowed, even rewarded, in the licensed time of Mardi Gras.

In reality, though, I think that most women are *not* rougher and rowdier than male Mardi Gras. The threat of fistfights (among Mardi Gras, with captains, and even with spectators) is always present in men's runs, though fights are rare in Tee Mamou and Basile, where captains constantly guard against violence. The potential for injury is much smaller in women's runs. Women may tackle and wrestle with captains, but drunken male Mardi Gras must sometimes be restrained from assaulting them. Women who have been swallowed up in a crowd of male Mardi Gras often describe the experience as scary. Linda Frugé Doucet and a female friend once masked to crash the Tee Mamou men's Mardi Gras dance, and Linda describes it as "just [a] whole different atmosphere. . . . You could just feel it around you, the roughness. Kind of like when you go into a bar and there's a fight getting ready to start and they have that atmosphere."[66] Similarly, men are more likely to cause property damage and to frighten children, and are less adept at curbing and contouring their rowdy performances in different contexts.

Why, then, are women so often described as "hard to handle" and disorderly? Women's performances, though generally less physically threatening than men's, evoke powerful images of the unruly woman, out of (male) control. Women's playful attempts to resist male authority and temporarily rule over men make people laugh, but they are also a bit disquieting. Cultural stereotypes and a double standard play a big part in perceptions of women's Mardi Gras unruliness. Male captains describe women as harder to lead, in part because they still expect lady Mardi Gras to *behave* like ladies. Women frequently take advantage of these assumptions and confound their captains by acting in very unladylike ways. At the same time, women who run Mardi Gras open themselves up to more criticism than men, and their transgressions are judged more harshly. The Tee Mamou women were stung several years ago when a female visitor wrote a letter to the editor of the local paper, criticizing the women Mardi Gras for being drunks and bad mothers; but men's misbehavior evokes little comment. Normative Mardi Gras behavior diverges sharply from the feminine ideal; men are expected to drink, act rowdy, and fight on occasion, but women (especially mothers, it seems) are not.

Perhaps one reason women's Mardi Gras performances are symbolically subversive is that there is power in numbers. One unruly woman is bad enough; thirty or forty can be downright scary. Women—usually in charge of putting other people at ease—sometimes make them uncomfortable on Mardi Gras. They use humor (usually associated with men) and playful insubordination to create coded messages of female power and resistance, as they "demand a more active role than the one scripted for [them]."[67] Today, as in medieval Europe, the image of the "woman on top" provokes both laughter and disquiet.

Women's Everyday Lives and Mardi Gras

"A woman [today] isn't expected just to go to school,
get out of school or quit school, get married, and have kids.
We can go to school. We can go to college. We can still get married
and have kids, but we can be a person, not just a housewife."
—Suson Launey

"[Mardi Gras is] part of our heritage, too, and we have a lot to
show how we feel inside."
—Berline Boone

On January 12, 2004, Kathleen Babineaux Blanco, a Cajun originally from Iberia Parish, became Louisiana's first woman governor. In her inaugural speech, Governor Blanco described herself as the "first daughter, wife, mother, and grandmother" in Louisiana to serve in this office. This event, almost unimaginable twenty years ago, reveals much about the status of Cajun women today. For one thing, it demonstrates how some aspects of women's lives remain much the same: Family remains central, and women still define themselves in part by their maternal and filial roles. At the same time, there have been dramatic changes, as women enter and excel in male-dominated fields once denied them. Another remarkable feature of the ceremony is Governor Blanco's decision to recite the official oath first in English and then in (sometimes stumbling) French.[1] Cajun women, like men, are taking renewed pride in their once-stigmatized traditional culture, its language, and other customs such as Mardi Gras runs.

Kathleen Blanco, as far as I know, has never run Mardi Gras. But just as politics offers one lens on changing gender dynamics in Cajun society, the country Mardi Gras offers another.[2] Women's Mardi Gras performances are best understood within the context of their daily lives, especially family and work. A number of events and social trends—World War II, urbanization, technology, and the women's movement, for example—have altered the ways Cajun women see themselves and their place in the world. Changes in the last thirty years have been especially profound.

Often, shifting Mardi Gras roles have followed on the heels of broader trends. But on occasion, women's Mardi Gras inroads have anticipated and set precedents for other cultural changes. Mardi Gras allows women to try on different roles and ways of behaving, and inspires a new awareness of women's capacities. This awareness can extend beyond the privileged space of Mardi Gras and suggest more egalitarian social structures. As Natalie Zemon Davis notes of medieval France, the "topsy turvy play" of Carnival "had much spillover into everyday 'serious' life. . . . Inversion could prompt new ways of thinking about the system and reacting to it."[3] Licensed Mardi Gras performances may open up "an alternative way of conceiving family structure," as well as new ideas about women's work.[4]

One thing that remains constant is women's pivotal role in conserving and perpetuating the country Mardi Gras tradition. Many traditional practices and values are learned in the course of daily life, and Cajun mothers have always been important transmitters.[5] Some scholars contend that modern Cajun women are largely abandoning their conservator roles as they prepare their children for a fast-changing and Americanized world.[6] However, the country Mardi Gras celebration is one example of women's still-active role in cultural transmission. Women often describe their Mardi Gras involvement—whether they cook the gumbo, sew disguises for their husbands and sons, teach their children about the celebration, or run or "captain" themselves—in terms of their maternal roles.

Women who run Mardi Gras view their own performances as a form of cultural continuity, not change. They want, they say, to maintain their community Mardi Gras tradition for their children's sake. Many comment that their decision to run Mardi Gras was sparked, in part at least, by a desire to pass the custom on to the next generation. As Snookie LeJeune says of the Basile run, "Whenever I first ran, it just made such an impression on me. . . . It seems like we're obligated to keep it going, so that our kids can see [their heritage]."[7] Women in Tee Mamou and Basile have succeeded in their efforts to revitalize and sustain their local runs for their children; pioneering members brought their daughters and sons (and, in some cases, their grandchildren) into community *courirs*, ensuring their survival. Don LeJeune, a longtime cocaptain for Tee Mamou, says of several seasoned women runners there, "What really makes them so special is that they've got all their daughters involved and nieces and what have you, and nephews as well, on the men's side. And they're passing the tradition down very well, they're doing a very proper job of it."[8]

This epilogue explores the connections between women's everyday lives and Mardi Gras roles, focusing on four women born between 1918 and 1975. Their narratives provide a far more detailed and compelling view of Cajun women's lives than more generalized descriptions, revealing how gender roles have changed in both public and private realms. Throughout the years, women have creatively used their traditional Mardi Gras support roles and newer public performances to gain access to a male-dominated celebration; in Samuel Kinser's words, they "convert[ed] a barrier into a crossing point."[9]

One of the most significant trends in women's lives has been in employment. Two generations ago, most Cajun women were rural farm wives who labored in the fields alongside their husbands. Poverty, tradition, and lack of transportation kept them closely tethered to families and homes, although some took on outside work such as cleaning, cooking, and sewing to make ends meet. Today, agriculture has largely given way to working in the oilfield or service industries, although many people farm part-time. As husbands work seven-and-seven (one week on, one week off) or fourteen-and-fourteen schedules on offshore rigs, wives have learned to make important decisions on their own.[10]

Many Cajun women now work outside the home, both before and after marriage. In 1977, Simon observed that the number of working women in Louisiana rose particularly sharply between 1960 and 1970. The increase in employed married women is particularly striking; more than a third of French Louisiana wives now belong to the workforce.[11] Many women in the countryside and small towns have little choice but to work full-time, sometimes at two or more low-wage jobs. A number of women who run Mardi Gras in Tee Mamou and Basile work full-time—as nurses or other health care providers, short-order cooks, teachers, casino employees, convenience store clerks, and waitresses.

Women's employment outside the home has had a considerable impact on their domestic lives, as women marry later and have smaller families than their mothers did. Traditional Cajun culture still shapes family life; many older men, and some women, still consider child rearing and other domestic duties "women's work." But, as one Cajun historian argues, "life experiences outside of the domestic realm armed women with a sense of independence that altered relations between husband and wife . . . bolstering the self-image of Cajun women."[12] Women have learned—by choice or necessity—to be more independent and to provide for themselves and their families. Wives who contribute to the family's income are likely to insist on being equal partners with their husbands.

Young women in particular hold different expectations of marriage from those of their parents. Many no longer accept the idea that keeping a marriage intact is worth any sacrifice, and divorce is common today; so is living together outside of marriage. Modern couples are likely to view marriage as a partnership and agree to share responsibilities. Young women who work full-time expect their husbands to help with child care and housework—often to the amazement of their mothers.

Notions of gender equity have transformed women's participation in Mardi Gras in similar ways. Fifty years ago, Cajun women took part mainly through domestic support—sewing their men's Mardi Gras suits, cooking their gumbo, teaching their children about the tradition—and perhaps by masking for a masquerade dance at a local club. Essential though their activities were, not all women were satisfied. As women loosened their ties to the domestic world in their daily lives, they also made inroads in the community's festive life. At first, when the notion of women and men masking, drinking, and cavorting together was still shocking, women created their own Mardi Gras runs. Eventually, as mores continued to change (and maintaining parallel runs proved too costly), runs became coed in some places. Cajun women today are finding their own styles of Mardi Gras participation, and demanding equal privileges and a public voice. They mold the tradition to their own aesthetics, integrate it into their daily lives, and pass it on to new generations.

Agnes Miller

Agnes Miller's life—though hardly ordinary—is in many ways typical of prairie Cajun women's daily experiences and Mardi Gras roles during the early twentieth century. When I met her in 1991, Miss Agnes was in her seventies, long widowed, and living in a small house on the same piece of land where she was born. A true matriarch, Miss Agnes presided over a constant stream of family members and friends who stopped by for coffee (and, if they were lucky, gumbo) at her kitchen table. Like other women of her generation, she described a life shaped by strong family ties, hard work in the house and in the fields, economic hardship, and an enduring sense of humor. Although she never ran Mardi Gras herself, Miss Agnes delighted in her contributions as a longtime gumbo cook for the Basile Mardi Gras Association.

· Born in 1918, Agnes Langley Miller was one of three children born to Basile cotton farmer Joseph Langley and his third wife, Emma. Miss Agnes recalled years later that "all you did was work";[13] she and her siblings helped milk the cows and pick and hoe cotton before heading to school.[14] Like other girls of her generation, she was closely chaperoned by her family as she grew up, allowed to socialize with young men only under supervision. As Mrs. Miller said, "My daddy was strict on us." Even at dances, girls were always accompanied by parents or an older relative. Agnes Miller says, "I never went to a dance by myself . . . [or] with my friends. . . . You went when Mama went with you. . . . You didn't let them [daughters] go with a boy . . . That wasn't done." If a young man offered to walk Agnes part of the way home, she says, her mother would "walk in the back, and we would follow in the front, you know."

At fifteen, she married Adam Miller, a native of the countryside near Evangeline. Rural Cajun women often married as early as thirteen, and Mrs. Miller explained, "Well, after you'd be twenty-one you was considered an old maid then, you know." Adam, whom she met at a Basile dance hall, traveled on horseback to visit her family on Sunday afternoons. The young couple's courtship took place at Agnes's home, in front of her parents.

Soon after their marriage, the Millers moved to rural Tepetate in Acadia Parish, where Adam Miller worked as a tenant farmer. Poverty and constant work around the house, garden, and farm kept Agnes close to home. She remembered, "When you got married about my age, you had to have a few chickens to have a few eggs, you know. And you had to work. Do farming. Not many of them [women] would . . . have the opportunity to be well off enough so they could do anything else [but] work." Early in her marriage, before she had children, Agnes Miller took on occasional chores for wealthier people. She explains, "The man and woman we was . . . renting from, well, I would help her out if she had somebody sick or something. I'd scrub her house." Payment was a duck or other foodstuffs; Miss Agnes recalls, "[She] didn't give me no money, but something to eat." When the Millers moved to another farm, according to Agnes, "I would do washing for an old lady and an old man" in exchange for "some material to make me a dress or something."

After they left tenant farming, the Millers moved back to Basile, where Adam Miller worked for a construction company. When he became disabled by illness, it fell to Mrs. Miller, by then the mother of two sons and two daughters, to help support the family through various jobs. Often, she held several jobs at once. For years, she worked as a short-order cook; at various times she also provided child care and did housework, laundry, and ironing. She also held occasional nondomestic jobs, such as managing Basile's Bearcat Lounge, famous for its live Cajun music.

Like many women of her generation, Miss Agnes never ran Mardi Gras. When she was a girl, masking was reserved for men and young boys. The Langley family did receive the local run, but her father did not want his daughters associating too closely with the masqueraders. The girls watched from the safety of their porch and did not "go mix with the Mardi Gras," in Agnes's words. Many years later, in the 1960s and 1970s, some of her contemporaries took part in the Basile ladies' run; Agnes, however, was always too busy working.

Despite all the hard work, Mrs. Miller had an active sense of fun and loved to tell jokes. She took particular pleasure in fooling friends and neighbors one year when she joined her friend Thia LeBleu for a Mardi Gras dance at Quincy's Club. Dressed in her husband's overalls, a straw hat, and a silk stocking over her face, she escaped recognition, even when her brother-in-law asked her to dance. She remembered with delight, "He said, 'Well, I'd like to find out if you're a man or a woman.'. . . But we had fun that night."[15]

Mrs. Miller, though never a Mardi Gras herself, was an important member of Basile's Mardi Gras family. For many years, she turned her cooking talents to feeding the hungry Mardi Gras runners. Miss Agnes and two contemporaries, like generations of women before them, made and served forty gallons of gumbo each year. When a Sunday children's run was founded, Agnes Miller cooked for that, too. Eventually, her daughter Helena, a niece or two, and several grand-daughters all become mainstays of the Basile run, an unimaginable prospect in Miss Agnes's youth. In her own way, though, Miss Agnes was just as much a pillar; so important was her maternal presence that she was honored twice by the Mardi Gras association (once posthumously). More important, she enjoyed her behind-the-scenes role as much as any masker, taking great pride in her contributions to its survival.

Berline Boone

Berline Boone, who has run Mardi Gras in Basile for more than thirty years, was born in 1945, a generation later than Agnes Miller. The daughter of a share-cropper and his wife, she was one of ten children. The family lived north of Eunice, "way in the country," in her words. Although they were poor, she says, "We had wonderful parents. . . . I don't have any bad memories . . . of my child-hood, none at all."[16] Her mother, Violet Godot, was from a relatively wealthy family in Church Point, and therefore had some education. Berline's father, on the other hand, was "a poor guy" from rural Swords who never learned to read or write.

As a sharecropper's wife, Berline's mother worked in the fields as well as cooking, cleaning, and taking care of the children. Berline says, "She worked every day from sunup to sundown, and when she got off, got out of the fields, she had to go cook supper." Still, Berline remembers her childhood as almost idyllic: "Well, it was hard work but that's all we knew. Working in the cotton fields and digging sweet potatoes, because that was our way of life." The family was close-knit, and parents and children spent most of their time together. Its structure was patriarchal, with clearly defined gender roles, and her father was unquestionably the boss. Berline recalls, "My mama was a very happy woman because she loved my daddy dearly, but what he said went. . . . There was no discussion, there was no 'I'm not going to do it' or 'We're not going.' That's how it was, cut and dried."

Berline grew up immersed in traditional Cajun music, language, and culture. The family spoke French at home, and Berline knew no English when she started school. Some teachers understood French, but others did not; Berline says of her experience, "It wasn't very funny." Other children made fun of her, and as a result, she says, she taught her children not to make fun of others' differences. She says, "I do know by the time I was in the eighth grade . . . it was better. The situation was better. And I guess maybe they understood." Still, like many parents of her generation, she did not teach her own daughters to speak French.

The Boone family also took part in Mardi Gras, and Berline comments, "My interest in Mardi Gras all stem[s] from my early childhood." Her two oldest brothers, Thomas and Leroy, ran Mardi Gras on horseback in the Eunice run in the 1950s. Her two oldest sisters "dressed out" and walked five or six miles (the family had no car) to attend the Mardi Gras masquerade dance. Berline remembers, "They'd dress as Mardi Gras and they'd walk to town. And they won [the costume contest], too." As a young child, Berline was terrified of the maskers and hid under the bed to avoid them. She recalls, "I used to be scared to death. . . . It is scary if you don't know [who they are]. . . . And even if you know that person, and that person is acting like a real Mardi Gras, it is scary." Gradually she overcame her fear, and she observes, "As I grew older, I would watch my brothers and two older sisters get ready on that special day and I would wish it was me."[17]

Berline's Mardi Gras turning point came at the age of fifteen or so, when her family moved to the countryside between Basile and Duralde. Here, the maskers seemed less strange and frightening to her. She says, "I guess [as a child] I didn't know who was behind the masks, and over here I did." She first ran Mardi Gras as a teenager in the countryside between Duralde and Basile, an experience she described for me in 2003: "And Lord and behold, that wonderful day finally came. I was between the age of fifteen or sixteen years old and my first time I ran with the Duralde Mardi Gras and continued to run and I still get all excited when the time gets nearer to Mardi Gras."[18] The Duralde-Basile group consisted mainly of older women, and Berline was one of the youngest members.

Berline was twenty when she got married in 1965. Her husband worked in the oilfield on a typical schedule of seven days on followed by seven off. Although Berline had worked before marriage, she stayed home as a wife and young mother because in her experience, that was how marriage worked. Now she marvels at how marriage erased her sense of autonomy. She comments, "When I got married, I wouldn't even write a check. Can you imagine?" The young family lived in Basile, where they charged their clothes at a local store and had groceries delivered to their house, because Berline's husband worked a seven-and-seven schedule. She says, "And we didn't go anywhere. And I wouldn't say nothing. Because I thought that's how it had to be."

Her circumscribed life as a young wife and mother resulted from her own gender role expectations as much as from her husband's. Berline recalls, "It's just because I thought it was his duty to see about everything and not mine. . . . Because [of] the way my mama and daddy lived. . . . I thought that was how it had to be with me. Really." She continues, "You lose your independence in a sense when you get married. . . . I did. I'm saying about myself, I don't know about anybody else. But to me, I was more independent [before marriage]; then when I got married, it seemed like it faded away."

She and her husband eventually divorced. Berline had two daughters to raise, and she says, "I had to go to work." She held a variety of jobs over the years, working for a nursing home in Eunice, and then as a certified welder for Dresser Industries. She says proudly, "I can weld. They trained you there. And I can do upholstery work and I can refinish antique furniture." It was only after her divorce, she comments, that "I got on my own and I regained my independence, and stood on my own two feet, [and] it's a wholly different world." Berline had to rediscover her self-confidence after marriage and motherhood; she says, "I really didn't think you were supposed to [be self-sufficient] until I got divorced and I had to, because of my two girls. It's weird, how things happen."

It is indeed weird. Today Berline, like Kathleen Blanco, is breaking new political ground and becoming a role model for other women in public life. Berline, who once had no idea where to go to pay her phone bill, is Basile's first elected woman mayor. Her political career began when she ran for, and won, the position of alderman-at-large on the city council in 1994. Today she writes, "I dreamed of being on the council but never thought I could actually make this dream come alive. But, only with the help of the Good Lord and my people of this wonderful community, I did it."[19] She went on to serve two terms on the council and said, "I loved every minute of it." When the mayor resigned before his term was up, the town held a special election and elected Berline. She's now serving her second term as mayor, and she says her political life is "of great importance to me." Being mayor, she says, is "not an easy job, but it's so rewarding to me." The office of mayor is ostensibly a part-time position, and Berline also continues to work full-time behind the counter at the local Exxon service station, as she has for many years.

Ironically, Berline attributes her election partly to her traditional Cajun culture—just as Governor Blanco's ties to the Cajun community helped her campaign in southwest Louisiana parishes. Many Basile voters are elderly and feel most comfortable speaking Cajun French, the language they (like Berline) grew up with. However, few young people are fluent; only one of Basile's five council members can speak French. Berline says, "To me, my speaking French has been a big advantage overall."

Her success doubtless owes something to timing, too. Berline's election is part of a larger wave of women running for and winning political office—a trend that seemed almost impossible even a decade ago. These days, the nearby cities of Opelousas and Eunice also have women mayors. Berline says, "And there's a lot of women [holding office]. And they'll stand up and speak out now." She says of women leaders, "We can do it just as well as [the men]. Just because they're men, who says we can't do it better? And we do."

French Louisiana women have rarely held public positions of authority until recently, and some men were reluctant to take her seriously at first. She says,

"It seemed like they always put me off. . . . With some of them we sat down and talked about it. I am an elected mayor, and I do have the power to do this or that, or see what's fit for the town." Now, she says, "They have accepted me and I think they respect me for it. And they know I have to do what I got to do. Not only for myself but for the betterment of the people of Basile."

Despite a demanding work schedule, Berline has run Mardi Gras for more than forty years and continues to be one of the run's core members. She writes, "I'm fifty-eight years old and I've been running Mardi Gras more than half my life and I still love it just like when I was that little girl. And as long as the good Lord allows me to run Mardi Gras, I will keep running. The age doesn't mean anything to me, it's what's in our heart that counts."

Her reasons for running Mardi Gras, however, have changed over the years. She says, "When you start running you really don't know, you really don't care what the meaning of Mardi Gras is. The more you mature . . . the more you realize what it is, you know." Mardi Gras for Berline is part of a cultural whole, a traditional way of life that includes the French language. However, she comments that younger generations of girls "don't even know how to speak French. So it's hard" for them to sing the Mardi Gras song. She laments, "Nowadays, the parents don't talk to the kids in French. Makes a big difference. But they'll try to hum [the Mardi Gras song] or, you know, they'll holler."

As far as I know, Berline has never suggested a direct connection between her Mardi Gras role and her public service. But long before she entered local politics, Berline was an officer in the Basile Mardi Gras Association. She served as president of the (then separate) Ladies' Mardi Gras Association in 1975, and as vice-president for the entire group (the only woman to do so) a few years later. However, she disliked the burden of leadership at a time when she should have been cutting up and enjoying herself—it was too much like work, which she had plenty of. She says of being an officer, "It was okay, but you have so much responsibility. I didn't like that. . . . You worry about if things is going to go right that night, and, you know, if they have enough food or if you have to go get some more. I like to run. . . . To me it's a lot of headache [organizing the run], when you're supposed to be having a good time."[20] She has little time for going to Mardi Gras meetings or suppers because, she says, "I work all the time so, you know, I can't. I don't have time on my schedule." Her Mardi Gras duties—brief as they were, and despite her rejection of their "headaches"—can be seen as a sort of training ground for her future job as mayor. As Natalie Davis suggests, shifts in one domain can lead to new possibilities in others.

Certainly Berline has played an important part in conserving Basile's Mardi Gras custom. She introduced her two daughters to running Mardi Gras, and eventually her grandchildren. Her oldest daughter, who lives in Opelousas, loves Mardi Gras, according to Berline, but "her husband don't like that too much.

So she don't run." Tracy, the younger daughter, tried running, but "she don't like to be smashed [in the truck]. And it is kind of crowded sometimes." Berline has five grandchildren, three girls and two boys, some of whom run Mardi Gras. The Opelousas-based granddaughters, however, "don't like that. They're some little ladies." Six of Berline's nieces travel from Lake Charles each year to run Mardi Gras with her, and she comments, "The more young people that participate, the better off it is. Because sooner or later, myself and the rest of us, the older ones, [will have to retire]. But I'll do it as long as I possibly can."

Gender roles have changed dramatically since Berline was a girl. Her mother, she says with a laugh, would never have considered running Mardi Gras: "My mother, she didn't drink, she didn't smoke, she was a lady. Oh no. Not my mom." She did, however, proudly watch Berline run "quite a few times," although Berline says "she wanted me to behave, like a charming lady." Although Berline may have sometimes stepped out of the "charming lady" mold in her Mardi Gras performances and in her political career, her mother was very proud of her accomplishments.

Linda Frugé Doucet and Renée Frugé Douget

Linda Doucet has been involved in the Tee Mamou Mardi Gras tradition for more than thirty years—first as *capitaine*'s wife and gumbo cook, later as one of the pioneers of the Tee Mamou's women's Mardi Gras, and today as parent of two adult daughters and two sons who are all active in the local celebration. Born in 1947, Linda grew up in the town of Iota, across from the St. Francis School. Although her parents spoke Cajun French, she (like many of her generation) grew up speaking English. She can understand conversational French well, but responds in English.

Linda has early memories of the local men-only Mardi Gras band, which would stop at her Iota school and peep in the window. Like many children, she was terrified of the Mardi Gras, even though two of her uncles were running then. When the maskers visited her relatives' homes, Linda would lock herself in a car until they left. During a 2003 interview with Linda and her daughter Renée, I asked Linda if she could imagine her mother, Ruby Prather, running Mardi Gras when she was young. Linda laughed and then said, "I don't know. Her brothers ran, but I don't think that was an issue back then, I don't think women ran."[21] Like Miss Agnes in Basile, Mrs. Prather accepted the status quo; this was simply the way things were.

After graduating from high school in 1964, Linda traveled to Massachusetts for a summer job. The next year, having returned home, she married Gerald Frugé and moved to Tee Mamou. Not long afterward, Gerald was recruited as head *capitaine* for the Tee Mamou men's run, and this was the beginning of

Linda's own involvement. She, like other Mardi Gras wives, helped make the gumbo by slaughtering, plucking, and cooking the chickens the riders caught. For a month or two before Mardi Gras, she recalled in a 1995 interview, she and Gerald saw little of each other. He was busy with a myriad of organizational tasks, and she sewed—captain's coats for her husband, which inevitably got torn up during the run, and later suits and masks for herself and her children.

Linda's first experience of running Mardi Gras herself was in the 1970s in nearby Basile, which at that time had a separate women's run. Linda, a young mother by then, borrowed her brother-in-law's costume to join a friend in the run, since Tee Mamou had no ladies' run yet. She says, "I just ran [in Basile] that one time, I don't remember how it came about. It probably wasn't long before our group formed. [Daughter] Jeanette was young." Not long afterward, her husband, Gerald, became captain of the new Tee Mamou women's run, and Linda and her friends began masking there.

Like many women, Linda found her own style of running Mardi Gras. She says, "Now whenever I was running, I wasn't into chasing the chickens. And that wasn't my cup of tea, that was Merline and them. I liked to find me a bike, or a wheelbarrow, or a tire. And then as I got older and the younger ones started coming, the few things that were left out there for us to do, they'd get to them before me." Linda invited friends and acquaintances to join the run, which gradually grew from a dozen or so women to forty or fifty these days.

After a knee injury years ago, Linda kept running, but "I was crippled so I couldn't get around." Over the years, many of the original Mardi Gras dropped out as they got older or busier, and the experience changed for her. She says, "And then as people got older and they quit participating, you know, and I was one of the last ones of the original [group]. . . . It just changed and it wasn't the same, you know. . . . A lot of new people came in and it just never had that same feel."

All of Linda and Gerald's four children became involved in the run as soon as they were old enough. Sons Chad and Todd ran in the men's run or served as cocaptains, and daughters Jeanette and Renée joined the women's run. Usually, Linda made their suits and masks as well as her own. She kept running longer than she might have otherwise because she wanted to run with her daughters. She says, "I stuck with it because my girls got of age and I wanted to run with them, until my knee, I decided I better shut it down before I really finished it off." In the years I've been following Tee Mamou, Linda ran off and on, depending on the state of her knee, until Gerald Frugé's death in 1998. Since then, she has watched and supported from the sidelines, often accompanied by her grandchildren (whose parents are either masking or captaining).

Linda comments that family roles have changed quite a bit from her generation to her daughters'. She says, "I was more on the old-fashioned way. Gerald worked and I stayed home and raised the kids." Being a wife and mother, she says, "was my job." She laughs, "There were times I wanted to go to work to get away. And he said, 'You have your job here.'" At various times during her marriage (after Gerald's heart surgery for an aneurysm in the 1980s, for example) she had to go to work to help support the family. At one point, she lectured for Weight Watchers, and for many of the years I've known her, she worked as head waitress at D.I.'s Restaurant. Still, she had to balance domesticity and employment. She comments, "I had two jobs and I cooked in between. . . . I had an hour. I'd cook a hot meal and go to work at D.I.'s. I did it."

Linda's youngest child, Renée, now twenty-nine, belongs to the second generation of women to run Mardi Gras in Tee Mamou. She grew up immersed in the Mardi Gras tradition through both her mother's and her father's participation, but nevertheless she recalls being afraid of the male Mardi Gras as a child. She jokes, "I think because they were tall, big, and smelly. You know that mask, you breathe in it all day, and then plus the alcohol. And they come up to you, get right in your face, and they don't realize they're breathing [in your face]. And they're running around and starting to sweat, and some of them end up in the sewer ditch." The women Mardi Gras, on the other hand, did not frighten her. Perhaps they smelled better; certainly they took more care to reassure frightened children.

Renée first ran Mardi Gras herself in 1989 when she was thirteen. (This was also my own first year running with, and observing, the group.) By this time, the women's run had been in place for about fifteen years, and was older than Renée herself. Running Mardi Gras seemed only natural to her—the entire family was involved in one way or another. Renée still runs regularly with the Tee Mamou women, although she (like other family members) took a year off in 1998 when her father was critically ill. (She was sidelined again in 2005, when she gave birth to her daughter Ayda the night before the women's run.) Over the years, Renée has watched a new, younger generation of girls come into the run and become regulars, and has helped train them as Mardi Gras.

Like many Cajun women her age, Renée left home after high school to work and go to school; she moved to Lake Charles and attended McNeese State University. When her father fell ill, she returned to Tee Mamou, and she has remained there since. She and her husband, Jason, live in a mobile home next to the house that she grew up in, which Linda now shares with her second husband, Herman Doucet. At the time of our 2004 interview, Renée was working long hours as a manager at D.I.'s Restaurant (owned by her aunt and uncle) and earning most of the couple's income, while her husband was finishing nursing school.

Linda and Renée agree that young women today have a different attitude toward marriage and sharing responsibilities. Both of Linda's daughters expect their husbands to help out in ways she sometimes finds surprising. Daughter

Jeanette and her husband, for example, have two children, and "both pitch in to do whatever has to get done," Linda comments. Renée observes that women her age no longer consider men the undisputed head of the household. The assumption that "we're supposed to respect our husband . . . take care of them, and do what they say," she says, no longer works for many young women, especially those who work full-time. She says of her own marriage: "To me, we're both, we're in it together, we decide together. And you know, we make decisions together. Like right now, I'm the breadwinner. Later, Jason will be. I'm praying that he'll be graduating from nursing. So right now, it's the total opposite [of traditional gender roles]. I'm bringing home the money while he's going to school learning and, you know, I'm okay with that. Because I know later, my time's coming where I'll get to relax a little more. Or I'll have kids and get to stay home with the kids, and then when they go to school, we'll both work and make decisions together." Renée, like many young women, feels it is only fair to share the burden of housework, at least as long as both she and her husband are employed. She says, "I think for us, as long as we both have to work, then the duties go together." However, she is open to a more traditional role as wife and mother in the future. She explains, "'And then later,' I told him, 'whenever you're working and I'm at home taking care of the kids, yes, taking care of the kids is a full-time job. But I'll have the house clean—you know, if I'm staying home. That's going to be my job, keeping the house and all this other stuff.' But as long as we're both working, I don't think just because I'm a woman, that it [should be my job]. Because his hands can wash dishes just as good as mine." (Before her daughter's birth in 2005, Renée quit her job, as planned, and is now a stay-at-home mother.)

This sense of gender equity also extends to her Mardi Gras participation. In an earlier interview, in 1995, Renée mentioned that she might consider being a captain some day, although Tee Mamou has never had women captains. (Other members of the women's run have commented she has all the characteristics of a good Mardi Gras captain, except for her gender.) Eight years later, her mother and I reminded her of her remark. Although she doesn't remember this ambition, she does comment that perhaps it was because she thinks women have good organizational skills. Although she holds no official title, Renée helps her brother, Todd, now head *capitaine,* in a variety of behind-the-scenes ways—planning the route, helping to paint the Mardi Gras wagon, and ordering beer for the men's and women's runs. Like other Tee Mamou women her age, Renée takes her right to run Mardi Gras as a given. She says, "How I feel about it, we've always done it. Women, as a far as I'm concerned, we're equal with the men. I came into [the tradition] like that."

*   *   *

Some rural Cajun women I've talked with acknowledge and welcome the changes "women's lib" has brought in gender dynamics. However, few women I've interviewed really identify much with feminism, perhaps because the term has negative connotations for them. Berline Boone, for instance, says she does not consider herself a feminist, despite her groundbreaking achievements in festive and everyday life. But her actions and words fit squarely within what I consider a feminist stance—that is, one of gender equality. Berline comments, "I'm just as good as anybody else, though. Just by the way I was raised. I don't think [men are] any better than me. They're not any less than me. I can do just about anything they can do. And my girls can too. And just about any woman who puts their heart and their mind to it can." This attitude has shaped Berline's Mardi Gras involvement as well as her work and family life. She says of Basile's pioneering female Mardi Gras, "It's part of our heritage, too, and we have a lot to show how we feel inside. We got a heart. I guess [the first women Mardi Gras] had enough guts to stand up and say how they feel. It's true."

Nor do most women describe their shifting Mardi Gras roles in terms of the national feminist movement. There are exceptions, of course: Janice Ashford comments that when she was young, "the women didn't run. Of course that was before they had women's lib and everything. I mean women didn't do anything but stay home and have babies."[22] Instead, women suggest, their determination to run Mardi Gras came from other, closer sources: family ties, a sense of tradition, or a desire just to act crazy with good friends. Linda Doucet says that when she "came into" the Tee Mamou women's run in the 1970s, "It was this little handful of women, all kinfolks, that were trying to have a run, and they just needed some leadership to keep it going. . . . My personal feeling, as far as I'm concerned, it didn't have anything to do with women's lib." Within a generation, women's Mardi Gras runs and coed runs were so well established that younger women now take for granted the opportunity to run Mardi Gras.

I, on the other hand, see women's Mardi Gras runs as part of a broader, grassroots insistence on equal access in employment, education, and family life. Whatever the influences, Cajun women do see themselves and their options differently from their parents. As Suson Launey comments, "A woman [today] isn't expected just to go to school, get out of school or quit school, get married, and have kids. We can go to school. We can go to college. We can still get married and have kids, but we can be a person, not just a housewife."[23] These opportunities don't preclude being a wife and mother, of course; most women, like Kathleen Blanco, still describe themselves in terms of familial relationships. But Cajun families are less patriarchal than they were a generation ago. Mardi Gras runs, too, are a bit less patriarchal, as women runners and (in Basile) captains have made their mark on the festivities.

A persistent question in the study of festivals is whether festive inversions and subversions ultimately reinforce the existing power structure, or whether they can actually suggest a new order. Natalie Zemon Davis asserts that under certain circumstances, the festive realm can lead to social change. I don't wish to overstate the importance of Mardi Gras in creating cultural change for Cajun women, but I do see it as a portal to new possibilities for them. Likewise, changes in family life and the workplace changed women's attitudes about their place in Mardi Gras. While many older women may have wished to run Mardi Gras, women now insist on it. Male dominance has slowly been eroded in Mardi Gras as in everyday life, and women's empowerment in one area facilitated advancement in others.

Women's Mardi Gras participation has had a significant impact on the celebration itself. Throughout much of the twentieth century, and still today, Cajun women have helped keep the country Cajun Mardi Gras tradition alive—behind the scenes as cooks, seamstresses and mask makers, partners, and teachers; within Mardi Gras associations as officers and helpers; and as skilled and innovative performers themselves. Women's more active involvement over the last fifty years has played a vital role in the Cajun Mardi Gras tradition. Early ladies' runs served as bridges during the 1940s, 1950s, and 1960s, when male participation dropped. Later, women reinvigorated long-established community runs as they began masking alongside men, and Mardi Gras *courirs* became more gender-inclusive.

Women see their Mardi Gras participation not as a break from tradition but as a continuation, or perhaps an evolution, of deeply felt custom. Throughout the years, women—whether or not they run Mardi Gras—have coached their own and others' children in rural Mardi Gras customs, passing them on to the next generation. For many women, Mardi Gras represents not only an intensely enjoyable experience but also nurturing of important connections to family, friends, community, and heritage. Perhaps maintaining their local Mardi Gras traditions was so important to some women that they were willing to break with precedent and become Mardi Gras themselves, rather than see the celebration die—especially as the social climate changed and gender barriers were broken in all aspects of life.

Notes

Introduction

1. Each Mardi Gras community has its own Mardi Gras song variant. In addition, there are a number of recorded versions of "La Danse de Mardi Gras," most based on the song as it is (or was) performed in Mamou. The classic recording that introduced the hoofbeat-like percussion was recorded by the Balfa Brothers in 1972, on *The Balfa Brothers Play More Traditional Cajun Music.* This version, however, does not include an invitation for *les belles* to join them at their dance, as some community variants do.

2. The term "Creole" is understood in various ways, but on the prairies of southwest Louisiana, it generally means "Louisianians whose culture (and often whose lineage) represents a mixture of French African American, French Afro Caribbean, and White French American influences" (Lindahl, "A Note on the Range," 140–41).

3. Tallant, *Mardi Gras,* 251.

4. Post, "Acadian Mardi Gras," 31.

5. Fournet and Guidry, "Le Mardi Gras Traditionel."

6. Spitzer, "Zydeco and Mardi Gras," 417. Ancelet adopted the phrase in his commentary for the Pat Mire video *Dance for a Chicken.*

7. Lindahl, "Presence of the Past," 130.

8. Note to author from Berline Boone, 11 August 2003.

9. Here I paraphrase comments by Roger Abrahams on an earlier version of this work.

10. Nicholas R. Spitzer's comprehensive work describes the Creole Mardi Gras run. See, for example, "Mardi Gras in L'Anse de 'Prien Noir.'"

11. Fontenot, *Cooking with Cajun Women,* 12. For more on the idea of Mardi Gras as reciprocal exchange, see Ancelet, Edwards, and Pitre, *Cajun Country,* and David, "Le Voisinage." Post also describes events such as *boucheries de la campagne* and various cooperative work events during the 1930s and 1940s, in *Cajun Sketches.*

12. Quoted in Lindahl, "Presence of the Past," 101–27.

13. The importance of Mardi Gras runs in inscribing territorial bounds and defining community is explored more fully in Ancelet, *Capitaine,* and Lindahl, "Bakhtin's Carnival Laughter."

14. I am indebted to Roger Abrahams for pointing out the importance of "dizzy-making" fun and "opening of the sensorium" in the Mardi Gras bonding experience (personal communication, March 1991).

15. Agnes Miller and Helena Putnam interview, 23 July 1991.

16. Cajun Mardi Gras runs will occasionally visit Creole neighbors they know well. For example, years ago the Basile run (with Vories Moreau as *capitaine*) stopped at the home of a Creole man who worked for the town. Vories also invited the local Creole run to his home one year when Basile's Cajun run was in hiatus.

17. Boone interview, 11 August 2003.

18. Cajun French is historically an oral language, and spellings vary widely. For the Cajun contraction of *petit,* or "little," I use *tee* throughout this book, because this is the way the Tee Mamou community spells it. For other Cajun French words, I use standard French spelling whenever possible, unless there is a strong precedent for an alternative orthography.

19. Lindahl ("One Family's Mardi Gras") offers an in-depth look at three generations of Moreaus and their Mardi Gras performances. Lindahl's "Finding the Field" is an excellent account of self-discovery through fieldwork, and draws on his work with Vories Moreau.

20. Related begging quests include mumming in England and northern Ireland, Christmas-time belsnickeling in Germany, and la Chandaleur (Candelmas, celebrated on 2 February) or la Guignolée (a New Year celebration) in parts of France. Some of these house visit traditions survived in Europe well into the twentieth century, and some still take place or have been revived on a small scale. Many of these customs were carried elsewhere by settlers in the Caribbean and North America, where they were adapted to new surroundings and became localized.

21. Historically, bachelors in many cultures have been licensed to transgress social ideals from time to time, and their misbehavior often serves as social commentary. In *Society and Culture,* Davis describes medieval French youth-abbeys that provided rituals "to help [boys] control their sexual instincts and also to allow themselves some limited sphere of jurisdiction or 'autonomy' before they were married" (108). Young unmarried girls, according to Davis, "also had prescribed roles in rural festive life: they danced with the young men; they participated in May festivities, they sometimes went out with the young males on the New Year's *quête de l'aguileneuf,*" or "quest for the New Year's mistletoe," a festivity that Davis suggests derives from the Druid tradition of collecting mistletoe (105). The *quête de l'aguileneuf* gradually came to mean a quest for small gifts of money, rather than mistletoe.

22. See, for example, van Gennep, *Manuel de folklore français contemporain,* and Gaignebet and Lajoux, *Art profane.* Both mention nineteenth-century Mardi Gras enactments in places from which Cajuns came. One instance from southwestern France particularly parallels the Cajun celebration. My thanks to Carl Lindahl for pointing out these similarities (personal communication, 14 September 2004).

23. The modern Cajun Mardi Gras run shares many characteristics of twentieth-century mumming in northern Ireland (see Glassie, *All Silver and No Brass*) and Newfoundland (Halpert and Story, *Christmas Mumming in Newfoundland,* and Thomas, "Noël, La Chandaleur, Mardi Gras"); Halloween trick-or-treating in the United States and especially Canada (Santino, *Halloween,* and Taft, "Adult Halloween Celebrations"); Christmas and Carnival traditions in the West Indies (Abrahams, "Christmas and Carnival" and *Man-of-Words*); Haitian ra-ra (McAlister, *Rara!*); and Jonkonnu in the Bahamas (Bettelheim and Nunley, *Caribbean Festival Arts*). It is especially close to French American and French Canadian masking traditions at the New Year, Candelmas, and mid-Lent. (See, for example, Brassieur, "Living French Traditions," Arcenault, "Courir," Egan, "Vincennes," and Ekberg, "Colonial Ste. Genevieve"). Closer to home, Mardi Gras runs have features in common with Mardi Gras Indian masking by African Americans in New Orleans (Kinser, "Violence Ritually Enjoined," Miner, "The Mardi Gras Indians," Smith, *Mardi Gras Indians,* and Tisserand, "Street Talk").

24. Dorman (*The People Called Cajuns* and "The Cajuns"), Sexton ("Cajun Mardi Gras"), Brassieur ("Cajuns"), and others remind us that Cajun ancestry and heritage are in fact complicated, and other cultural traditions, including Continental French and Creole, are often subsumed under "Cajun."

In Louisiana, the country Mardi Gras celebration has certainly been localized and creolized to some extent. Cajuns may have borrowed aspects of their Mardi Gras festival from other ethnic groups on the prairie, although there is little documentation of this process. German settlers accustomed to *fastnacht* (Carnival) festivities would have found parallels in the *courir de Mardi Gras,* and many enthusiastically adopted the local custom. (See Tokofsky, "Fasnacht in Basel" and "A Tale of Two Carnivals," for discussions of modern-day European *fashnacht* or *fasnet* performances.)

Acadia Parish residents of German descent also made disguised house visits around the Feast of Saint Nicholas well into the twentieth century (Sexton, "Kinder, Gentler St. Nicholas"). Similarly, older residents of French German heritage in French Settlement, near Baton Rouge, recall boys and girls disguising themselves to make house visits at Christmastime during the first half of the twentieth century. The maskers were called *les cristines,* presumably from the German "Kriss Kringles." For discussion of belsnickling in other parts of the United States and Canada, see Shoemaker, "Belsnickel Lore," and Bauman, "Belsnickling." Irish immigrants to Louisiana's prairies may also have recognized elements of mumming in the Mardi Gras *courir* and added their own influences.

25. On regional subcultures, see Brasseaux, *Acadian to Cajun,* and Post, *Cajun Sketches.*

26. In the 1940s, Tallant (*Mardi Gras*) described several "picturesque Mardi Gras customs" among Cajuns, in addition to the prairie Mardi Gras run. In bayou country, he reported, "Maskers stroll through the streets and along the highways and lanes . . . playing tricks on their neighbors and indulging in all sorts of foolishness and gallic good humor" (250–51). Today, young Cajun men in two small bayou communities, Gheens and Choupique, carry switches, chase children and teen-age girls, and demand that young boys kneel to beg for pardon. This tradition is described in Pitre, "Mardi Gras Chase."

Creoles in or near Lafayette used to roam the streets in disguise on Mardi Gras, carrying switches or small whips. Patricia Rickels writes that in years past, these groups of men would "catch anyone who offended them in the past year and beat them severely" ("The Folklore of Acadiana," 160). Presumably this is the same urban Creole tradition Gaudet explores in "Mardi Gras 'Chic-a-la-Pie.'" According to Gaudet, years ago children taunted the maskers by chanting "Mardi Gras Chic-a-la-Pie," and were in turn chased and whipped. Lafayette Creoles have revitalized the celebration in recent years and toned down its potential for violence.

27. *Crowley Signal,* 23 February 1901. Twenty-one years later, the same newspaper described two days of Mardi Gras festivities "in the vicinity of Cleomere Leleux's place." According to this report, "there were more than seventy-five persons present. It took twenty-two gallons of gumbo, besides chickens, geese, and other good things to eat to take care of the crowd. On Mardi Gras night there was a grand ball. L. N. Leleux was captain in charge of the arrangements for the fun and amusement" ("Celebrate Mardi Gras").

28. Bernard, *The Cajuns,* gives a thorough account of French Louisiana's cultural renaissance or (as he argues) renaissances.

29. Discussions of Mamou's revived run can be found in Ancelet, *Capitaine,* and Oster and Reed, "Country Cajun Mardi Gras." The rebuilding of the Eunice Mardi Gras run in 1946 is described in Mire's film *Dance for a Chicken,* and in Langley, LeJeune, and Oubre, *Le Reveil des Fêtes.*

30. The effects of tourism and media attention are explored in Ancelet, "Mardi Gras and the Media," Ware, "Making a Show" and "Marketing Mardi Gras."

31. Spitzer, "Zydeco and Mardi Gras," observes that by the 1980s, women were also demanding, and being allowed, to join some Creole runs.

32. For a fuller description of differences between urban and rural Mardi Gras, see Lindahl's introduction to Lindahl and Ware, *Cajun Mardi Gras Masks.*

33. De Caro and Ireland, "Every Man a King," 26.

Chapter 1: Just Like Cinderella

1. Kane, *Bayous,* 305.
2. Ibid.
3. Hollis et al., *Feminist Theory,* 341–42.
4. Simon, "The Changing Role of Women," 87.
5. All quotations from Betty and Hugh Miller interview, 14 December 1998.
6. Quoted in Sawin, "Carnival in Grand Marais," 4.
7. Berline Boone interview, 11 August 2003.
8. Agnes Miller interview, 25 March 1993.
9. Post, *Cajun Sketches,* 146. Joel Fletcher (*The Acadians in Louisiana Today*), writing in 1947, noted that the Cajun girl "is not only fair to look upon and sweet to be around, but is also superior as a wife and mother. However gay during girlhood, she becomes at marriage the most decorous of wives, with her entire attention centered upon her home and family" (3). Acadian women, he also notes, are "very thrifty and able to make much from little" (4).

10. Elson Cart interview, 12 December 1991.

11. All quotations from Evelyn Frugé interview, 12 November 1994.

12. All quotations from Betty Pousson interview, 27 February 1990.

13. All quotations from Marion Courville interview, 25 March 1992.

14. All quotations from Vories Moreau interview, 21 December 1991, unless otherwise noted.

15. Kim Moreau interview, 15 January 2003.

16. Ibid.

17. Ibid.

18. All quotations from Janot interview, 1 April 1992.

19. See Roshto, "Georgie and Allen Manuel." Georgie Manuel, who has conducted extensive research on the early history of Cajun screen masks, discovered an 1880s advertisement for wire screen masks imported from Austria.

20. Russell "Potic" Rider and Sandy Sonnier interview, 17 March 1992.

21. Suson Launey interview, 30 July 1991.

22. Suson Launey interview, New Orleans Jazz and Heritage Festival, 26 April 1996.

23. Suson Launey interview, 13 January 1996.

24. Turner, *Beautiful Necessity*, 95.

25. Hollis et al., *Feminist Theory*, 341–42. The term "femmage" was coined by Meyer and Schapiro in "Waste Not, Want Not."

26. All quotations from Janice Ashford interview, 26 February 2001.

27. Renée Frugé Douget and Linda Frugé Doucet interview, 11 February 1996.

28. Suson Launey interview, 22 March 2002.

29. Renée Frugé Douget and Linda Frugé Doucet interview, 11 February 1996.

30. Ibid.

31. Ibid.

32. Ibid. In chapter 6, I discuss how women's traditional association with animals and nature adds another possible layer of meaning to Tee Mamou women's wild-looking masks. See Ortner, "Is Male to Female as Nature to Culture?" for example.

33. Ibid.

34. Ibid.

35. Fontenot (*Cooking with Cajun Women*), David ("Le Voisinage"), and others have pointed out that Mardi Gras runs are the largest and most dramatic of a whole cycle of traditional cooperative systems blending work and socializing, all of which depended on women's work and organization. Rushton comments that the "group visit serves as a sort of community inspection of each farmhouse in the area, to make sure that no-one will be left destitute until the spring" (*The Cajuns*, 245).

36. *Basile Weekly*, 1 March 1990.

37. "Prairie Mardi Gras Memories," Tee Mamou–Iota Folklife Festival.

38. Unless otherwise noted, all quotations from Agnes Miller interview, 25 March 1993.

39. See Gutierrez, *Cajun Foodways*, and Spitzer, "Zydeco and Mardi Gras."

40. All quotations from Anne Marie Leger and Allen Leger interview, 16 December 1988.

41. Kane, *Bayous,* 305–6.

42. Agnes Miller interview, 12 November 1994.

43. Vories Moreau interview, 17 April 1993.

44. Carl Lindahl, personal communication, 4 September 1994. On occasion, the drunken men's attentions genuinely unnerve their targets, especially those they don't know well. While coproducing a film on the Cajun Mardi Gras, Louisiana state folklorist Maida Owens was approached by a male Mardi Gras who bent down, sniffed at her, and then howled. Ancelet also describes this incident in "On the Edge of Chaos."

45. Sawin, "Carnival in Grand Marais," 6–7.

46. Lindahl, "Presence of the Past," 130.

47. Alice Janot interview, 1 April 1992; Betty and Hugh Miller interview.

48. Merline Bergeaux, Shirley Reed, and Patsy Simar interview, 20 December 1988.

49. Ibid.

50. *Basile Weekly,* 5 November 1992.

Chapter 2: Not Just the Work

1. Agnes Miller interview, 12 November 1994.

2. All quotations from Betty Pousson interview, 27 February 1990.

3. Gerald Frugé and Linda Frugé Doucet interview, 28 June 1992.

4. Mitchell, "All on a Mardi Gras Day," 133.

5. Kinser, *Carnival American Style,* 130.

6. Basile woman at Exxon Station during the 2004 Basile Mardi Gras run.

7. Davis, "Women on Top," 131.

8. All quotations from Alice Janot interview, 1 April 1992.

9. Linda Frugé Doucet and Renée Frugé Douget interview, 24 November 2003.

10. *Basile Weekly,* 23 February 1966.

11. Ibid.

12. Agnes Miller interview, 12 November 1994.

13. Tallant, *Mardi Gras,* 251.

14. Vories Moreau interview, 21 December 1991.

15. Ancelet, *Capitaine,* 7.

16. Chicoine, Grosbois, and Poirier, *Laches-lousses.*

17. Ancelet, *Capitaine,* 7.

18. Ibid.

19. Barry Ancelet, personal communication, 6 July 1993.

20. Maud Ancelet interview, 3 June 2002.

21. Ancelet, *Capitaine,* 41.

22. Norma Jean Miller and Theresa Seale interview, 11 November 1991.

23. Betty and Hugh Miller interview, 14 December 1998.

24. Lindahl, "Bakhtin's Carnival Laughter," 50.

25. Spitzer, "Zydeco and Mardi Gras," 417.

26. Agnes Miller interview, 12 November 1994.

27. Lindahl, "Presence of the Past," 51.

28. Claude Durio interview, 16 June 1992.

29. Unless noted otherwise, all quotations from Frozine Thibodeaux interview, 14 January 2001.

30. Gerald Frugé and Linda Frugé Doucet interview, 28 June 1992.

31. Boone interview, 14 May 1994.

32. See, for example, Lindahl, "Presence of the Past" and "A Note on the Festive, Cultural, and Geographic Range," Mire's film *Dance for a Chicken,* Sexton, "Germans and les Americains," and Ancelet, "Falling Apart."

33. For more on Cajun women as creative Mardi Gras performers and artists, see Onebane, "Voices of Pointe Noire," Langley et al., *Le Reveil des Fêtes,* Roshto, "Georgie and Allen Manuel," and Ware, "I Read the Rules Backward" and "Anything to Act Crazy."

34. All quotations from Marion Courville interview, 25 March 1992.

35. Women of means in the town of Crowley, at least, had access to more modern representations of gender roles and marriage. In 1921, the Acadia Theatre showed a film called *The Inferior Sex?* described as "A dramatic comparison of the sexes in a romance of modern marriage. Every wife should see that her husband sees this picture with her. A startling exposé of married life and domestic problems—in a story that shatters traditions and tells how to be happy though married" ("The Inferior Sex?" *Crowley Signal,* 19 February 1921). Of course, poor, rural, and French-speaking families may not have had much access to this kind of popular culture.

36. Ancelet (*Capitaine*) and Sexton ("Germans") discuss the decline of Cajun Mardi Gras runs in the face of Americanization.

37. Thibodeaux quoted in Onebane, "Voices of Pointe Noire," 200.

38. Supek, "Gender Inversion in the Contemporary Carnival," 27.

39. Onebane, "Voices of Pointe Noire," 200.

40. Thibodeaux quoted in Onebane, "Voices of Pointe Noire," 200.

41. Leathem, "A Carnival," 222.

42. Thibodeaux quoted in Onebane, "Voices of Pointe Noire," 200.

43. Neumeyer, "Eunice Maw-Maws' Run."

44. Ibid.

45. Ibid.

46. Manuel, in Langley et al., *Le Reveil des Fêtes,* 17.

47. Neumeyer, "Eunice Maw-Maws' Run."

48. Fontenot quoted in Chicoine et al., *Laches-lousses.*

49. All quotations from Miller and Seale interview.

50. Hillman Smith, quoted in Langley et al., *Le Reveil des Fêtes,* 14.

51. Curtis Joubert interview, 19 October 2000.

52. The Duralde women's run is mentioned in Chicoine et al., *Laches-lousses,* which quotes Berline Boone (then using her married name of Sonnier). Berline also described the run to me in an interview on 14 May 1994. In both places, she characterizes it as distinct from the later Basile women's run, although some other women see the two as the same run extending over more than a decade.

53. Berline Boone interview, 14 May 1994.

54. The chronology of the Basile women's run is murky, and no Mardi Gras ledgers are available for the years before 1974. An account in the *Basile Weekly* mentions that

women, children, and men all ran together at Mardi Gras that year (19 February 1969). This suggests that a ladies' run did exist by then, and that they (like the men's run) sometimes allowed two or three children to mask and run with their parents. That year, the *Basile Weekly* also reported: "Mardi Gras began early this year for a group of ladies of this area [Basile, Duralde, and Eunice] who were invited to Lafayette on February 3 by the KLFY-TV station. They donned costumes and Mardi Gras spirit to become part of the Mardi Gras Dance which will be telecast on Channel 10" (*Basile Weekly,* 12 February 1969). Some of these women were later active in the Basile run. Clearly, the lady Mardi Gras attracted media interest, though largely as novelties.

55. *Basile Weekly,* 4 February 1970.

56. *Basile Weekly,* 11 March 1970.

57. Lindahl, "Presence of the Past," 107.

58. Debbie Andrus and Susie Lopez interview, 5 November 1991.

59. Basile Mardi Gras Association ledgers for 1974.

60. Berline Boone interview, 14 May 1994.

61. Ibid.

62. The Basile Mardi Gras ledgers sometimes list women as head captains and men as cocaptains; in other years, men are named as captains with female cocaptains.

63. Andrus and Lopez interview.

64. Gilbert and Esther (Nin) LeBlanc interview, 8 April 1992.

65. Boone interview, 14 May 1994.

66. Ibid.

67. Ibid.

68. Ibid.

69. Andrus and Lopez interview, 5 November 1991.

70. The *Basile Weekly* announced that "the attendance at this meeting on Feb. 6 [1979] will decide whether the Mardi Gras run will be held once again in Basile. So whoever wants to keep the women's and men's Mardi-gras going in Basile, please attend this meeting."

71. Basile Mardi Gras Association ledgers for 1986.

72. Basile ledgers for 1987.

73. Ibid.

74. Russell "Potic" Rider and Sandy Sonnier interview, 17 March 1992.

75. Snookie LeJeune interview.

76. Boone interview, 14 May 1994.

77. Ibid.

78. Boone interview, 11 August 2003.

79. All quotations from Merline Bergeaux, Shirley Reed, and Patsy Simar interview, 20 December 1988.

80. Merline Bergeaux interview, 28 May 1995.

81. Ivy Deshotels interview, 23 February 1992.

82. Ibid.

83. Gerald Frugé interview, 28 June 1992.

84. Gerald Frugé interview, 8 October 1989.

85. Bergeaux interview, 28 May 1995.

86. Kane, *Bayous of Louisiana,* 305.

87. All quotations from Janice Ashford interview, 26 February 2001.

88. Davis, "Women on Top," 131.

89. Suson Launey interview, 26 April 1996.

90. Lindahl, "Presence of the Past," 107.

91. Ibid.

Chapter 3: Organizing Mayhem

1. A local woman created and administers the Internet website for the LeJeune Cove Mardi Gras Association, which holds a men-only horseback run. She has given it a distinct educational and promotional slant, and plans to post Mardi Gras lesson plans for teachers.

2. Work schedules play a part in who is available for pre–Mardi Gras work. Several core members of the Association are legally disabled and so are not employed.

3. Potic Rider did step down as Basile Mardi Gras Association president for a year in 1994.

4. The Basile association's earliest ledgers have disappeared; those still available begin in 1974 but are often sketchy. Berline Boone recalls that in 1975 (when men and women still ran separately) she was elected the Mardi Gras association's only female president. There are virtually no notes for that year, but a single notation on the ledger's cover names Berline as president. No one else seems to recall her being president for the whole group, and it seems likely that the Ladies' Mardi Gras Association was still separate from the men's at that point.

5. Boone interview, 14 May 1994.

6. All quotations from Cassie LeBlue and Laura LeBlue interview.

7. All quotations from Debbie Andrus and Susie Lopez interview, 5 November 1991.

8. Fontenot suggests that because "the heart of a Cajun resides in the home," women have always played a big part in the "development of everyday Cajun life, as well as the perpetuation of the community's heritage and family values" (*Cooking with Cajun Women,* 9). She notes, for example, that women did much of the organizational work for social gatherings such as baptisms, weddings, and Mardi Gras, by cooking food and by "perpetuating numerous cultural and familiar traditions" (14). Bodin ("The Cajun Woman as Unofficial Deacon") has argued that women were the primary caretakers of their family's religious practices. Though men were the main transmitters of public performance traditions such as dance music and Mardi Gras masking, women also had a less visible hand. The *Crowley Signal* reported in 1948 that in Church Point, a "Mardi Gras party staged by the mother's club at the convent hall was a huge success, with hundreds of children participating in the games, and the refreshments which were served" ("Church Point News," *Crowley Signal,* 19 February 1948). The image of Cajun women as cultural conservators has been contested in recent years by folklorist Barry Ancelet (*Cajun Country*), among others.

9. All quotations from Andrus and Lopez interview.

10. All quotations from Ella Ruth Young interview, 20 January 1992.

11. According to the Mardi Gras association ledgers, there was considerable doubt whether the 1979 Mardi Gras run would take place, because its membership was so low. This may have sparked interest in creating school programs, or added urgency to the desire to conserve the tradition.

12. Kim Moreau, personal communication, 23 April 2004. Kim, longtime Basile Mardi Gras and former association vice-president, took part in several of these school programs in the 1980s; he recalls more men than women helping out at that point.

13. *Basile Weekly,* 28 February 1979.

14. *Basile Weekly,* 6 February 1997. Hall of Fame members (or their descendants—many inductees are deceased) received engraved plaques during a ceremony at the Mardi Gras dance. Duplicate plaques are displayed on a wall in City Hall.

15. In 2003, Mary Moreau, Alida Young, Ida Bellon, Elvina Rider, and Agnes Vidrine, all deceased, were honored for their work as Mardi Gras cooks, and the late Agnes Miller was also recognized for her cooking contributions. Kim Moreau, Mary Moreau's son, introduced and strenuously lobbied for the nominations because he felt the women's contributions had received little recognition. (Potic Rider's mother, Elvina, was also an honoree.) Originally association officers suggested plaques of appreciation for the women, but eventually the suggestion to name them, en masse, to the Hall of Fame prevailed. The Mardi Gras Association decided to engrave one plaque with all names, and this hangs in City Hall. On his own initiative, Kim Moreau had individual plaques made up for the five women and for Agnes Miller, to be presented to their families during the Mardi Gras dance.

16. Potic Rider, 8 January 2004, from my field notes.

17. A third Tee Mamou area run, for children, takes place on Sunday, but the Mardi Gras organization as a whole is not closely involved in its production. Maskers in the Tee Mamou–Iota children's Mardi Gras are aged eight to thirteen, and are selected for participation, according to the Tee Mamou–Iota Folklore Festival website. Their Sunday run is organized and led by Sonya Miller, whose husband runs in the Tee Mamou men's run. The children ride in the same wagon used for the adult runs, and attend their own meetings (not the association's) to learn Mardi Gras traditions, including song and dance.

18. Don LeJeune interview, 18 March 1992.

19. Tee Mamou captains are not elected; they are either recruited or handpicked by their predecessors. Before his death in 1998, Gerald asked Todd, then only twenty-six years old, to take over the reins of both runs. Gerald was asked to be captain of the leaderless men's run in 1968.

20. All quotations from Linda Frugé Doucet and Renée Frugé Douget interview, 24 November 2003.

21. Most Tee Mamou Mardi Gras meetings I've attended over the years follow a similar pattern. This description is based on field notes from the 25 January 2002 meeting, the first of the year.

22. The entire song is performed only at special stops; otherwise the group omits four verses.

23. Merline Bergeaux, Shirley Reed, and Patsy Simar interview, 20 December 1988.

24. Claude Durio, Gerald Frugé, and Roonie Frugé interview, 12 December 1988.

25. Suson Launey interview, 26 April 1996.

26. Durio, Frugé, and Frugé interview.

27. Ibid.

28. Occasionally, dissatisfied members talk about splintering off and forming new Mardi Gras runs. Recently a group of Tee Mamou men revived the dormant LeJeune Cove horseback run, but so far women have not followed suit. Ryan Brasseux's essay "On the Origins of a Celebration" describes how LeJeune Cove's male riders are negotiating and reinventing their local Mardi Gras tradition.

29. Kinser, *Carnival American Style,* 136.

Chapter 4: All's Fair in Love and Mardi Gras

1. Sexton ("Germans and Les Americans") notes that post–World War II Mardi Gras runs in general "no longer reflected the social intimacy" of earlier eras, when most riders were "members of the same close social networks" (208).

2. Turner, *Ritual Process,* 9.

3. Linda Frugé Doucet in Linda Frugé Doucet and Renée Frugé Douget interview, 24 November 2003.

4. Linda Frugé Doucet in Gerald Frugé and Linda Frugé Doucet interview, 28 June 1992.

5. Gerald Frugé interview, 28 May 1995.

6. Suson Launey interview, 22 March 2002.

7. Merline Bergeaux, Shirley Reed, and Patsy Simar interview, 20 December 1988.

8. Linda Frugé Doucet and Renée Frugé Douget interview, 24 November 2003.

9. Ibid. Patricia Sawin ("Transparent Masks") points out that disguise practices in modern runs often diverge from ideals, as runners frequently unmask during or after house visits, for example. Anonymity, while still a crucial concept in Mardi Gras runs, is not always as complete or as consistent in reality as it appears in maskers' accounts.

10. Suson Launey interview, 22 March 2002.

11. Ibid.

12. Ibid.

13. Ibid.

14. Berline Boone and Madeline Reed interview, 27 November 1998. In fact, longtime cocaptain Don LeJeune says that the group has never turned away a runner for not having the right disguise.

15. Renée Frugé Douget and Linda Frugé Doucet interview, 11 February 1996.

16. Suson Launey interview, 26 April 1996.

17. Linda Frugé Doucet and Renée Frugé Douget interview, 24 November 2003.

18. Some men make their own masks, but almost all Mardi Gras suits are made by women. If men buy a mask, it is likely to be made by a woman, because women are now the most prolific mask makers.

19. Claude Durio interview, 16 June 1992.

20. Lindahl, "Presence of the Past," 129.

21. Linda Frugé Doucet and Renée Frugé Douget interview, 24 November 2003.

22. Bergeaux, Reed, and Simar interview, 20 December 1988.

23. Suson Launey interview, 22 March 2002.

24. Ibid.

25. Linda Frugé Doucet and Renée Frugé Douget interview, 24 November 2003.

26. Gerald Frugé interview, 8 October 1989.

27. Ibid.

28. Linda Hughes, in "'You Have to Do It with Style,'" points out that game rules are often those "by which people should play rather than the ones by which they do play" (134). She notes: "Players can, if they collectively want to and within important limits, selectively invoke, ignore, defend, reject, reinterpret, or simply change the rules as they mold their games to suit their own agendas and purposes" (135).

29. Gerald Frugé interview, 8 October 1989.

30. Ibid.

31. Bergeaux, Reed, and Simar interview, 12 December 1988. The preceding quotation is from Shirley Reed and Patsy Simar, whom I interviewed along with Merline Bergeaux.

32. Gerald Frugé and Linda Frugé Doucet interview, 28 June 1992.

33. Gerald Frugé interview, 8 October 1989.

34. Gerald Frugé and Linda Frugé Doucet interview, 28 June 1992.

35. Gerald Frugé interview, 8 October 1989.

36. Ibid.

37. Bergeaux, Reed, and Simar interview, 20 December 1988.

38. Suson Launey interview, 22 March 2002.

39. Walter Garber, quoted in "Cajuns Run Wild."

40. Linda Frugé Doucet and Renée Frugé Douget interview, 24 November 2003.

41. The Tee Mamou Mardi Gras song belongs to the less common of two main families of Cajun Mardi Gras songs. (See Oster, "Country Mardi Gras," and Sexton and Oster, "Une 'Tite Poule Grasse"). Only neighboring Grand Marais, Lacassine, and LeJeune Cove (an all-male *courir* recently revived by former Tee Mamou members) perform versions of this type, derived from old French and French Canadian drinking songs. The song's final verse is borrowed from a different song, one associated with la Guignolée in the French Midwest.

42. Spitzer, in "Zydeco and Mardi Gras," quotes a member of a Creole Mardi Gras run who told him, "'Them young boys has got to prove they can do it, that they can catch that chicken and kill it'" (427).

43. Bergeaux, Reed, and Simar interview, 20 December 1988.

44. Gerald Frugé and Linda Frugé Doucet interview, 28 June 1992.

45. Linda Frugé Doucet and Renée Frugé Douget interview, 24 November 2003.

46. Launey interview, 6 October 1991.

47. Gerald Frugé and Linda Frugé Doucet interview.

48. Merline Bergeaux interview, 28 May 1995.

49. Suson Launey interview, 30 July 1991.

50. Gerald Frugé and Linda Frugé Doucet interview.

51. Durio interview, 16 June 1992.

52. Gerald Frugé interview, 8 October 1989.

53. Ibid.

54. Gerald Frugé and Linda Frugé Doucet interview.

55. Suson Launey interview, 25 May 1998.

56. Bergeaux, Reed, and Simar interview.

57. Baldwin, "Cultural Tourists," 94. Ancelet writes about encounters (including his own) between Mardi Gras and their scholarly documenters in "On the Edge of Chaos."

58. Gerald Frugé interview, 8 October 1989.

59. Bergeaux, Reed, and Simar interview.

60. Suson Launey interview, 22 March 2002.

61. Ibid.

62. Ibid.

63. Linda Frugé Doucet and Renée Frugé Douget interview, 24 November 2003.

64. Suson Launey interview, 22 March 2002.

65. Ibid.

66. Gerald Frugé and Linda Frugé Doucet interview.

67. Ibid.

68. Ibid.

69. Suson Launey interview, 30 July 1991.

70. Suson Launey interview, 22 March 2002.

71. Don LeJeune interview, 18 March 1992.

72. Ibid.

73. Suson Launey interview, 22 March 2002.

74. Gerald Frugé and Linda Frugé Doucet interview.

75. Durio interview, 16 June 1992. Sexton ("Ritualized Inebriation") further discusses the roles of alcohol, violence, and social control in the Tee Mamou men's run.

76. Ibid.

77. Ibid.

78. Linda Frugé Doucet and Renée Frugé Douget interview, 24 November 2003.

79. Ibid.

80. Ibid.

81. The men's Tuesday run, however, still visits Gerald's tomb.

82. Suson Launey interview, 13 January 1996.

83. Gerald Frugé interview, 28 May 1995.

84. Bergeaux interview, 28 May 1995.

85. Janice Ashford interview, 26 February 1991.

86. Suson Launey interview, 22 March 2002.

87. Tee Mamou women and men both have had to tone down their performance at their dance in the last few years, although it is still raucous. D.I.'s has little room to wrestle and "play horse," and spectators (who include many out-of-state tourists) complain if they are accidentally struck, or if Mardi Gras snatch food from their plates or steal a beer from their table. Captains now warn the celebrants in advance, "Put on a good show but you can't get [too] rough. Go to the floor, put on a little show, and get off."

Chapter 5: Letting It Fly

1. Unless otherwise indicated, all quotations from Debbie Andrus are from Debbie Andrus, Helena Putnam, and Kerry Kim Moreau interview, 18 October 1998.

2. Abrahams, *Man-of-Words,* 2.

3. Leander Comeaux retired as men's head *capitaine* in 2004, and Potic Rider now serves as the main captain.

4. Debbie Andrus and Susie Lopez interview, 5 November 1991.

5. All quotations from Cassie LeBlue and Laura LeBlue interview, 5 August 2003.

6. All quotations from Ella Ruth Young interview, 20 January 1992.

7. All quotations from Snookie LeJeune interview, 18 March 1992.

8. Field notes on the Basile Mardi Gras Association's planning meeting, 9 January 2004.

9. For years, Potic Rider straddled the boundary between captain and Mardi Gras, wearing a Mardi Gras suit but no mask. In the last few years, he has begun wearing a red cape over coveralls, the uniform of a captain.

10. Agnes Miller and Helena Putnam interview, 23 July 1991.

11. Kim Moreau, a longtime Basile Mardi Gras and former vice-president, suggests that one factor in the run's growth is out-of-town runners, but the main reason is the success of its children's run, which typically draws over a hundred children. As these young trainees turn thirteen or fourteen, many join the adult run (personal communication, 20 April 2004).

12. Berline Boone interview, 27 November 1998.

13. When I first began visiting Basile in 1991, several women Mardi Gras commented that there was a critical age gap and stressed the importance of getting younger women interested. Longtime female Mardi Gras feared that if they quit running, the tradition might die out. This concern prompted organizers to create the local children's Mardi Gras run in 1986, to train and then funnel girls and boys into the adult run. Their strategy seems to be working; today the run does have more teen-age girls than before.

14. All Susie Lopez quotations are from Andrus and Lopez interview.

15. Ibid.

16. Berline Boone interview, 14 May 1994.

17. Andrus and Lopez interview.

18. Ibid.

19. Boone interview, 14 May 1994.

20. Russell "Potic" Rider interview, 25 July 1991.

21. Andrus and Lopez interview.

22. Boone interview, 14 May 1994.

23. Ibid.

24. Snookie LeJeune interview. Mortarboards are a traditional alternative to *capuchons* (along with a third hat type, miters) but are now rare in Cajun runs.

25. Basile men also wear "character" disguises at times, but not as often as women; male Mardi Gras partners rarely dress along a common "theme." Representational costumes were more common twenty years ago. One man in particular wore imagina-

tive disguises such as a vampire or bride for the Mardi Gras *bal*. More recently, Tony Johnson masked as Death.

26. Andrus, Putnam, and Moreau interview.

27. Russell "Potic" Rider interview, 4 November 1994.

28. Miller and Putnam interview.

29. Andrus and Lopez interview.

30. Ibid.

31. Russell "Potic" Rider and Sandy Sonnier interview, 17 March 1992.

32. The Basile run has lost a number of customary stops over the last decade as businesses such as Gene's Food Store, Manuel's Slaughterhouse, and the Bearcat Lounge have closed. One of my favorite stops was always Da Office, a highway bar that served as a social hub for many Mardi Gras members. Sadly, Da Office shut down just before Mardi Gras in 2004, leaving another gap in the Mardi Gras schedule.

33. In a 17 March 1992 interview, Potic Rider compared the Mardi Gras' fringed costumes to Native American clothing, and the maskers' singing, dancing, and whooping to a war dance.

34. Helena Putnam, "Mardi Gras Song Explained: Interpretation of the Mardi Gras Song," *Basile Weekly*, 27 February 1992.

35. The Basile song belongs to the most common type of Mardi Gras song, which describes the Mardi Gras' activity, requests specific donations for their gumbo, and extends hospitality to the hosts by inviting them to a gumbo that evening. Several other communities have similar (although not identical) songs. See Oster, "Country Mardi Gras," and Sexton and Oster, "'Une 'Tite Poule Grasse,'" for more discussion of variants and meanings.

My transcription of the Basile song draws on several sources, but most specifically on Helena Putnam and Barry Ancelet's transcription of Potic Rider's version of the Basile song, printed in Putnam's 1992 newspaper article "Mardi Gras Song Explained." My field recording of Potic singing the song during the 1995 Basile run included several repetitions not noted in Putnam's article, however, and I've added these. I also relied on Potic's performance of the song during a 1994 interview Carl Lindahl and I conducted with him, when he offered English translations of some of his own interpretations of the lyrics. Two of his unusual phrasings are briefly discussed in notes 36 and 37.

36. Older Basile Mardi Gras such as Vories Moreau understood this line to say that the Mardi Gras come from "l'Angleterre," or England. Potic sings it as "les langues de terre" (literally, "the tongues of the earth"), which he says metaphorically means "far away." I am indebted to Barry Ancelet for pointing out that the phrase "langue de terre" has a very definite meaning in Cajun French: it means "peninsula" and thus the edge of the land (personal communication, 12 April 2005). A number of other variants of the Mardi Gras song, including the Tee Mamou song, include a similar phrase that is almost always sung and written as l'Angleterre.

37. This line marks another divergence between Potic's version and those of most other singers. Previous generations of Basile singers understood this phrase as "les quémandeurs," or beggars. Potic sings it as either "les queues d'en bonheur" or "les queues de bonnes heures." In an interview some years ago, Potic explained to folklorist

Barry Ancelet that "les queues d'en bonheur" meant "good-timers" (Ancelet, personal communication, 12 April 2005). During a later (4 November 1994) interview with Carl Lindahl and me, Potic translated it as "early risers" ("les queues de bonnes heures"). Thus, an individual singer's concept of the lyrics' meaning may shift over time.

38. Andrus, Putnam, and Moreau interview.

39. Kim Moreau, personal communication, 8 May 2004.

40. Andrus and Lopez interview.

41. Miller and Putnam interview.

42. Ibid.

43. Andrus and Lopez interview.

44. Ibid.

45. Ibid.

46. Snookie LeJeune interview.

47. Andrus and Lopez interview.

48. Miller and Putnam interview.

49. Rider interview, 25 July 1991.

50. Miller and Putnam interview.

51. All quotations by Cassie LeBlue are from Cassie LeBlue and Laura LeBlue interview.

52. All quotations by Laura LeBlue are from Cassie LeBlue and Laura LeBlue interview.

53. Female Mardi Gras and their male captains seem to have very different perspectives on women's orderliness. Helena Putnam suggests that women are essentially easier to control than the men, who play more roughly, get out of hand more often, and are "a lot more determined to get at the captains," she says. Women, in her opinion, respond better to captains' attempts to "corral them back" (Miller and Putnam interview).

54. Andrus and Lopez interview. Drinking may be an accepted part of the run, but illegal drugs are not. In a recent run, leaders caught a young male Mardi Gras smoking marijuana, and Potic Rider led him directly to the sheriff's car accompanying the run. The reveler was promptly arrested and driven away, a far harsher punishment than the customary expulsion for ordinary misbehavior.

55. Boone interview, 11 August 2003.

56. Andrus and Lopez interview.

57. Ibid.

58. Susie Lopez, ibid.

59. Potic Rider quoted in Lindahl and Ware, *Cajun Mardi Gras Masks,* 61. Emphasis in original.

60. Susie Lopez, in a 1991 interview, described the criteria for best all-around Mardi Gras as "keeping the other Mardi Gras motivated, or knowing the song, or acting like a Mardi Gras, you know. . . . And acting like a Mardi Gras, that's different things that they would be judged on. Like if you would dance, like the old Mardi Gras tradition was, or if you were one that would chase the chickens, and . . . cut up . . . and singing the song, and keeping the other Mardi Gras motivated and going. Just an all-around fun guy

person." Andrus and Lopez interview. Helena Putnam says that the best Mardi Gras is typically a "troublemaker, the ones that pick more at the crowd and everything."

61. Andrus and Lopez interview.

Chapter 6: Festive Reversals

1. Babcock, *The Reversible World,* 14.
2. Davis, "Women on Top," 124.
3. Ibid., 149–50.
4. Ibid., 125.
5. Radner and Lanser, "Strategies of Coding in Women's Cultures," 3.
6. Ibid., 10. Keyes's work on women rappers ("Empowering Self") offers an excellent example of women appropriating a male performance and using it to convey their own feminist messages.
7. Radner and Lanser, "Strategies of Coding in Women's Cultures," 13.
8. Bakhtin, *Rabelais,* 19.
9. Ibid., 26.
10. Ibid., 373.
11. Leathem, "A Carnival," 31.
12. See, for example, Ancelet, "Playing the Other."
13. Lindahl comments that the ideal for the Cajun man dressing as a woman is "to appear conspicuously male . . . at the same time that he reshapes himself to caricature female form" (Lindahl, "Bakhtin's Carnival Laughter," 112). In *Vested Interests,* Garber makes a similar point about male crossdressing in a very different context. Describing a transvestite, she notes that "imperfection of imitation is what makes her appealing, what makes her eminently readable. . . . Foolproof imitations of women by men, or men by women, are curious, but not interesting. There has to be some[thing] telltale . . . something readable" (149). Cajun men's female impersonations resemble the tradition of "burlesque" drag more than "pageant" drag.

Cajun men's humorous Mardi Gras depictions of women have parallels in the once-popular local tradition of staging mock "womanless weddings," in which men played all parts. A 1921 newspaper announcement of the event commented that "this entertainment is a scream, from start to finish" ("Womanless Wedding to Be Given Here," *Crowley Signal,* 12 March 1921). Similar events are occasionally still held as fundraisers.
14. Helena Putnam, in Debbie Andrus, Helena Putnam, and Kerry Kim Moreau interview, 18 October 1998.
15. Mitchell, "Some Differences." Mitchell found that women especially value clever wordplay in jokes, because it distances jokes from aggression. Women, she argues, use jokes mainly to create harmony and break tension.
16. Merline Bergeaux, Shirley Reed, and Patsy Simar interview, 20 December 1988. The classic Mardi Gras disguise of fringed suit, screen mask, and peaked hat can perhaps be read as implicitly male, and therefore a form of gender inversion for women Mardi Gras. Female participants do not see it this way, though, and explain that sons and husbands often wear their disguises.

17. Deloria, *Playing Indian,* 115–16.

18. One of Basile's male Mardi Gras, after seeing these disguises, mentioned to me that a friend had once given him a similar apron. It lifted to show off three large penises and testicles made from stuffed pantyhose, and pockets covered smaller versions. He wore his apron only on semiprivate occasions, such as when he cooked for a party. I think it is largely the very public nature of the female Mardi Gras's play that is disconcerting for some. Rayna Green, "Magnolias Grow in Dirt," discusses the bawdy folklore that is very much a part of many Southern women's private lives but is rarely made public.

19. Hotchkiss, *Clothes Make the Man,* 86. I find Hotchkiss's historical consideration of women's crossdressing helpful in thinking about female Mardi Gras, as I did Dugas, *Warrior Women,* and Greenhill, "'Neither a Lass nor a Maid.'" There is, of course, a whole body of feminist scholarship on the construction and performance of gender that has influenced my thinking here, although I touch on it only briefly. See, for example, Butler, *Gender Trouble,* Weston, *Gender in Real Time,* and Garber, *Vested Interests.*

20. See Garber, *Vested Interests,* 16.

21. Ibid., 49.

22. I borrow the phrase "asymmetry of crossdressing" from Peter Tokofsky, who likewise comments that in various traditional carnivals, women crossdress far less often than men. Women, he suggests, "seem to prefer working creatively together to construct highly imaginative costumes over dressing as men" ("Masking Gender," 312). Gilmore (as quoted in Tokofsky) notes that women in Andalusia "have more choice and do not always choose to parade in masculine attire." Supek ("Gender Inversion") points out that in Croatian Carnival celebrations, women mask mainly as gender-neutral characters and female characters.

23. Taft, "Men in Women's Clothes," 135.

24. Tokofsky ("Masking Gender") observes that this seems to be a general characteristic of women's Carnival disguises in many different cultures.

25. Da Matta, *Carnival, Rogues, and Heroes.*

26. Margaret Mills observes that Afghan women's narratives in Afghanistan rarely include women disguised as men and concludes that "women's female characters are able to do more as females; hence they imitate men less" ("Sex Role Reversals," 196).

27. Andrus, Putnam, and Moreau interview.

28. Ibid.

29. Ibid.

30. Ibid. The Swine Festival always chooses a king and queen to head its parade, and sometimes they are elderly residents of the Basile Care Center.

31. The origins of blackface roles in Cajun Mardi Gras runs are open to speculation; certainly the *nègre* and *négresse* can be traced back to the 1950s, at least, and may well be much older. The Cajun blackface tradition is increasingly coming under fire, but because it is not a prominent part of women's Mardi Gras runs today, I do not discuss the practice in depth here. For more thoughts on Cajun racial inversions, see Lindahl, "A Note on Blackface." On blackface and minstrelsy in general, see Abrahams, *Singing the Master,* Lott, *Love and Theft,* and Toll, *Blacking Up.*

32. Frozine Thibodeaux quoted in Onebane, "Voices of Pointe Noire."

33. Debbie Andrus and Susie Lopez interview, 5 November 1991.

34. Kibler, *Rank Ladies*, 116.

35. Ibid., 121.

36. Ibid., 120.

37. Andrus and Lopez interview. Cajun women's interpretations of Indian dress draw on popular stereotypes rather than influences by local tribes like the Coushatta. These stylized versions of Plains styles of a century ago convey an image of Indians as "distant, primal Others" (Deloria, *Playing Indian*, 119) who represent nobility and savagery simultaneously. See Bellour and Kinser, "Amerindian Masking," for a discussion of Indian disguises in Trinidad's Carnival.

38. Lindahl, "Bakhtin's Carnival Laughter," 111. Symbolic connections between Cajun Mardi Gras and American Indians are rarely voiced today—I have never heard them in Tee Mamou, for example. But a few Basile participants compare the Mardi Gras' high-pitched whoops to Indian war cries, and their fringed suits to Native dress. In Potic Rider's opinion, "A Mardi Gras suit is like an Indian dress. You know, you got to have the fringe . . . down the sleeves, and across the back, the pockets, the pants legs" (Russell "Potic" Rider and Sandy Sonnier interview, 17 March 1992).

39. Stallybrass and White (*Politics and Poetics of Transgression*) examines the symbolic associations of pigs as "low" and unclean figures that can stand for other kinds of low status. In Basile, however, they are also the popular emblem of the Louisiana Swine Festival.

40. Renée Frugé Douget and Linda Frugé Doucet interview, 11 February 1996.

41. Abrahams, "Making Faces in the Mirror," 128.

42. Adams, *The Sexual Politics of Meat.*

43. Ortner, "Is Female to Male." See also Delaney, Lupton, and Toth, *The Curse*. Weltman (*Ruskin's Mythic Queen*) discusses Victorian constructions and disruptions of these gendered categories.

44. Deloria, *Playing Indian*, 119.

45. Renée Frugé Douget and Linda Frugé Doucet interview, 11 February 1996.

46. Andrus, Putnam, and Moreau interview.

47. Launey interview, 25 May 1998.

48. Boone interview, 14 May 1994.

49. J. B. LeBlue, quoted in Lindahl, "That's My Day," 127.

50. Chedgzoy, "Impudent Women," 1.

51. Bakhtin, *Rabelais*, 240.

52. Davis, "Women on Top," 129. See Ware, "I Read the Rules Backward," for more discussion of women's Mardi Gras role-playing as inversion.

53. Bergeaux, Reed, and Simar interview, 20 December 1988.

54. Definitions of leadership often imply masculinity, and in popular and folk culture, women with authority are often portrayed as unnatural and dangerous. Feminist scholar Robin Roberts, in *Sexual Generations*, notes that female leaders in the television series *Star Trek: The Next Generation* are almost invariably alien creatures who end up either destroyed or subjugated.

55. Lindahl, "Bakhtin's Carnival Laughter," 54.

56. In *Handmaidens,* Lawless explores how Pentecostal women preachers use maternal strategies to explain and justify their leadership positions in a male-dominated religious culture.

57. Nicholas R. Spitzer, personal communication, 12 March 2000.

58. All quotations from Ancelet, "On the Edge of Chaos" (7–9), available at the website of the Center for Cultural and Eco-Tourism at the University of Louisiana at Lafayette: http://ccet.louisiana.edu/Mardi_Gras_Chaos.html. Used with his permission.

59. Gerald Frugé interview, 8 October 1989.

60. Ibid. After the 1990 Mardi Gras, the Tee Mamou Mardi Gras and captains were invited to perform at Eunice's Liberty Theater for a live radio show that Barry Ancelet hosts. During the performance, Barry asked cocaptain Claude Durio if similar attacks happen often. Claude answered, "Just if you get in the truck." Asked why he let Barry get in the women's wagon, Claude said with a straight face, "We all got to learn." (Tape recording of *Rendez-vous des Cadiens,* show, Liberty Theatre, 26 February 1990.)

61. Gerald Frugé interview, 8 October 1989.

62. Paul E. McGhee, "The Role of Laughter and Humor in Growing Up Female," in *Becoming Female,* edited by Claire Kopp (New York: Plenum Press, 1979), quoted in Barrecca, *They Used to Call Me Snow White,* 107. Barreca argues that women's humor is often secret and inherently subversive.

63. Spitzer, "Zydeco and Mardi Gras," 502.

64. Lindahl, "Presence of the Past," 134.

65. Abrahams and Bauman, "Ranges of Festival Behavior," 204.

66. Renée Frugé Douget and Linda Frugé Doucet interview, 11 February 1996.

67. Barreca, *They Used to Call Me Snow White,* 108. Throughout this paragraph I paraphrase some of her observations on women's humor in general, which ring true to me.

Epilogue

1. "Inauguration 2004," *Baton Rouge Advocate,* 13 January 2004.

2. The prospect of a woman governor would have seemed almost unimaginable to Louisiana women in the 1920s, who (like other American women) were still struggling for the right to vote. Members of the Louisiana branch of the National Women's Party told Crowley women's club members in 1922 that "women citizens in the state of Louisiana have not the same rights, privileges, and immunities under the laws as have men citizens." The meeting was held under the auspices of the League of Women Voters, which was "working solely to remove the legal and civil discriminations against women" ("Women Score Laws of State," *Crowley Signal,* 28 January 1922).

3. Davis, "Women on Top," 142.

4. Ibid., 143.

5. See, for example, Bernard (*The Cajuns*), Fontenot (*Cooking with Cajun Women*), Collard ("The Cajun Family"), and Bodin ("The Cajun Woman") on women as cultural conservators.

6. Several authors suggest that adaptation to mainstream American culture has meant that Cajun women have relinquished their roles as conservators or "guardian[s]" of

NOTES TO PAGES 172–84 · 207

traditional culture (Collard, "The Cajun Family," 16). Esman, for example, writes that Cajun women are generally more concerned with "bettering themselves" and "making it" and with conspicuous consumption than men are ("Celebration of Cajun Identity," 71–72). Despite a revival of ethnic pride among Cajuns in the last two or three decades, many aspects of middle-class American society (representing status and material security) are favored over those of traditional Cajun culture (signifying a lower socioeconomic status). Women, it has been suggested, have been apt to encourage their children to acculturate rather than to maintain their traditional culture. Cajun French is rarely spoken at home, and Cajun mothers do not teach their children to speak French. (See, for example, Collard, "The Cajun Family," Esman, "Celebration," and Ancelet et al., *Cajun Country.*) Other discussions of changing family structure and gender roles among Cajuns include Allain, "Twentieth Century Cajuns," Del Sesto and Gibson, *The Culture of Acadiana,* and Edwards, "Family Organization."

7. Snookie LeJeune interview, 12 November 1991.

8. Don LeJeune interview, 18 March 1992.

9. Kinser, *Carnival American Style,* 136.

10. See Bernard, *The Cajuns.*

11. In 1970, about 28 percent of Acadiana's white females worked outside the home (about 12 percent less than the national average). By 1980, the figure was about 36 percent (Bernard, *The Cajuns*). In Basile, 54.6 percent of women with children between the ages of six and sixteen work outside the home; in Iota, it is 61.9 percent, according to the 1990 U.S. Census. For more socioeconomic and historical data on Acadia and Evangeline Parishes, see Chauvin, *Socioeconomic Profile of Acadia Parish,* Fontenot and Freeland, *Acadia Parish,* vol. 1, Freeland and Fontenot, *Acadia Parish,* vol. 2, Gahn, *Opelousas Country,* and Baker and Kreamer, *Louisiana Tapestry.*

12. Bernard, *The Cajuns,* 74–75.

13. Unless otherwise noted, all quotations from Agnes Miller interview, 12 November 1994.

14. Agnes Miller's formal education was cut short in the sixth grade, although she later earned a GED once all her children were grown. Typically, she interrupted her studies as an adult to care for her oldest daughter's children, so her daughter could complete her GED; then she finished her own requirements.

15. Agnes Miller interview, 25 March 1993.

16. Unless otherwise noted, all quotations from Boone interview, 11 August 2003.

17. Boone, note to author, 11 August 2003.

18. Ibid.

19. Ibid.

20. Boone interview, 27 November 1998.

21. Linda Frugé Doucet and Renée Frugé Douget interview, 24 November 2003.

22. Janice Ashford interview, 26 February 2001.

23. Suson Launey interview, 13 September 2003.

Bibliography

Abrahams, Roger D. "An American Vocabulary of Celebrations." In *Time out of Time: Essays on the Festival,* edited by Alessandro Falassi, 63–77. Albuquerque: University of New Mexico Press, 1987.

———. "Christmas and Carnival on St. Vincent." *Western Folklore* 31 (1972): 275–89.

———. "The Language of Festivals." In *Celebrations: Studies in Festivities and Ritual,* edited by Victor Turner, 161–77. Washington, D.C.: Smithsonian Institution Press, 1982.

———. "Making Faces in the Mirror: Playing Indian in Early America." *Southern Folklore* 52, 2 (1995): 121–35.

———. *The Man-of-Words in the West Indies: Performance and the Emergence of Creole Culture.* Baltimore: Johns Hopkins University Press, 1983.

———. *Singing the Master: The Formation of African-American Culture on the Plantation.* New York: Oxford University Press, 1993.

———, ed. *Fields of Folklore: Essays in Honor of Kenneth S. Goldstein.* Bloomington, Ind.: Trickster Press, 1995.

Abrahams, Roger D., and Richard Bauman. "Ranges of Festival Behavior." In *The Reversible World: Symbolic Inversion in Art and Society,* edited by Barbara A. Babcock, 193–208. Ithaca, N.Y.: Cornell University Press, 1978.

Adams, Carol. *The Sexual Politics of Meat: A Feminist-Vegetarian Critical Theory.* New York: Continuum, 1990.

Allain, Mathé. "Twentieth Century Cajuns." In *The Cajuns: Essays on Their History and Culture,* edited by Glenn Conrad, 129–41. Lafayette: Center for Louisiana Studies, University of Southwestern Louisiana, 1978.

Ancelet, Barry Jean. "Falling Apart to Stay Together: Deep Play in the Grand Marais Mardi Gras." *Journal of American Folklore* 114, 452 (2001): 144–53.

———. "Mardi Gras and the Media: Who's Fooling Whom?" *Southern Folklore* 46, 3 (1990): 211–19.

———. "On the Edge of Chaos: The Relationship between the Mardi Gras and Its Observer." Available at the website of the Center for Cultural and Eco-Tourism, University of Louisiana at Lafayette: http://ccet.louisiana.edu/Mardi_Gras_Chaos.html.

———. "Playing the Other: Ritual Reversal in the South Louisiana Country Mardi Gras." Paper presented at the annual meeting of the American Folklore Society, Jacksonville, Florida, 15 October 1992.

———. "Singing Beggars and Outlaws with Whips: Mardi Gras in Three Louisiana French Communities." Paper presented at the annual meeting of the American Folklore Society, St. John's, Newfoundland, 19 October 1991.

Ancelet, Barry J. *Capitaine Voyage Ton Flag: The Traditional Cajun Country Mardi Gras.* Lafayette: Center for Louisiana Studies, 1989.

Ancelet, Barry J., Jay Edwards, and Glen Pitre, eds. *Cajun Country.* Jackson: University of Mississippi Press, 1991.

Arsenault, George. *Courir le Chandeleur.* Moncton, Canada: Editions d'Acadie, 1984.

Babcock, Barbara, ed. *The Reversible World: Symbolic Inversion in Art and Society.* Ithaca, N.Y.: Cornell University Press, 1978.

Baker, Vaughn B., and Jean T. Kreamer, eds. *Louisiana Tapestry: The Ethnic Weave of St. Landry Parish.* Lafayette: Center for Louisiana Studies, 1982.

Bakhtin, Mikhail M. *Rabelais and His World.* Cambridge: MIT Press, 1968.

Baldwin, Karen. "Cultural Tourists at Mardi Gras: On the Cajun Prairie in Louisiana and 'Downeast' in Carolina." *North Carolina Folklore Journal* 50, 1–2 (2003): 62–91.

Balfa Brothers. *The Balfa Brothers Play More Traditional Cajun Music.* Swallow LP 6019, 1972.

Barreca, Regina. *They Used to Call Me Snow White . . . But I Drifted.* New York: Viking Penguin, 1991.

Bauman, Richard. "Belsnickling in a Nova Scotia Island Community." *Western Folklore* 31 (1972): 229–43.

Bellour, Helene, and Samuel Kinser. "Amerindian Masking in Trinidad's Carnival: The House of Black Elk in San Fernando." *Drama Review* 42, 3 (1998): 147–69.

Bernard, Shane K. *The Cajuns: Americanization of a People.* Jackson: University Press of Mississippi, 2003.

Bettelheim, Judith, and John Nunley, ed. *Caribbean Festival Arts: Every Little Piece of Difference.* Saint Louis: Saint Louis Art Museum, 1988.

Bodin, Ron. "The Cajun Woman as Unofficial Deacon of the Sacraments and Priest of the Sacramentals in Rural Louisiana, 1800–1930." *Attakapas Gazette* 25 (1990): 2–13.

Brasseaux, Carl A. *Acadian to Cajun: Transformation of a People, 1803–1877.* Jackson: University Press of Mississippi, 1992.

Brasseaux, Ryan. "On the Origins of a Celebration: The Genesis of Tradition in the L'anse LeJeune Mardi Gras." Unpublished paper. Baton Rouge, Louisiana, spring 2003.

Brassieur, C. Ray. "Cajuns." In *American Folklore: An Encyclopedia,* edited by Jan Harold Brunvand, 109–12. New York: Garland, 1996.

———. "Living French Traditions of the Mid-Mississippi Valley." Missouri Heritage Fair Program. Columbia: Missouri Historical Society, 1993.

Broussard, René. *Pardon, Pardon: The Cajun Mardi Gras Chase.* Documentary videotape. Zeitgeist Multi-Disciplinary Arts, New Orleans, 2002.

Butler, Judith. *Gender Trouble: Feminism and the Subversion of Identity.* New York: Routledge, 1990.

Bynum, Victoria E. *Unruly Women: The Politics of Social and Sexual Control in the Old South.* Chapel Hill: University of North Carolina Press, 1992.

Cagle, Madeline Domangue. "Neither Spared nor Spoiled: The Mardi Gras Chase in Choupic, Louisiana." *Louisiana Folklore Miscellany* 11 (1996): 17–28.

Caillois, Roger. *Man, Play and Games.* New York: Free Press of Glencoe, 1961.

"Cajuns Run Wild for Mardi Gras." *New Orleans Times-Picayune,* 7 February 1993, p. E1.

Chauvin, James. "A Socioeconomic Profile of Acadia Parish." M.A. thesis, Louisiana State University, 1969.

Chedgzoy, Kate. "Impudent Women: Carnival and Gender in Early Modern Culture." *Glasgow Review* 1 (2004): 1–9. Available at the website of STELLA (Software for Teaching English Language and Literature and Its Assessment): www.arts.gla.ac.uk/SESLL/STELLA/COMET/glasgrev/issue1/chefgz.htm.

Chicoine, M., L. de Grosbois, E. Foy, and F. Poirier, eds. *Laches-lousses: Les fêtes populaire au Quebec, en Acadie et en Louisiane.* Montreal: vlb éditeur, 1982.

Collard, Clyde V. "The Cajun Family: Adjustment to Modern Trends." In *The Culture of Acadiana: Tradition and Change in South Louisiana,* edited by Steven L. Del Sesto and Jon L. Gibson, 111–19. Lafayette: University of Southwestern Louisiana Press, 1975.

Conrad, Glenn R., ed. *The Cajuns: Essays on Their History and Culture.* Lafayette: Center for Louisiana Studies, 1983.

Da Matta, Roberto. *Carnivals, Rogues, and Heroes: An Interpretation of the Brazilian Dilemma.* Notre Dame, Ind.: University of Notre Dame Press, 1991.

David, Dana. "Le Voisinage: Evolution of Community in Cajun Country." In *Louisiana Folklife Festival Program Book,* 13–15. Monroe: Louisiana Folklife Festival, 1999.

Davis, Natalie Zemon. *Society and Culture in Early Modern France.* Stanford: Stanford University Press, 1975.

———. "Women on Top: Symbolic Sexual Inversion and Political Disorder in the Early Modern World." In *The Reversible World: Symbolic Inversion in Art and Society,* edited by Barbara Babcock, 147–90. Ithaca, N.Y.: Cornell University Press, 1978.

Davis, Susan. *Parades and Power: Street Theater in Nineteenth-Century Philadelphia.* Philadelphia: University of Pennsylvania Press, 1986.

De Caro, Frank, and Tom Ireland. "Every Man a King: Worldview, Social Tension, and Carnival in New Orleans." In *Mardi Gras, Gumbo, and Zydeco: Readings in Louisiana Culture,* edited by Marcia Gaudet and James C. McDonald, 26–41. Jackson: University Press of Mississippi, 2003.

De Lauretis, Teresa. *Feminist Studies/Critical Studies.* Bloomington: Indiana University Press, 1986.

Del Sesto, Steven L., and Jon L. Gibson, eds. *The Culture of Acadiana: Tradition and Change in South Louisiana.* Lafayette: University of Southwestern Louisiana Press, 1975.

Delaney, Janice, Mary Jane Lupton, and Emily Toth. *The Curse: A Cultural History of Menstruation.* Urbana: University of Illinois Press, 1988.

Deloria, Philip J. *Playing Indian.* New Haven: Yale University Press, 1998.

Dorman, James. "The Cajuns: Ethnogenesis and the Shaping of Group Consciousness." In *The Cajuns: Essays on Their History and Culture,* edited by Glenn R. Conrad, 233–51. Lafayette: Center for Louisiana Studies, 1983.

———, ed. *Creoles of Color of the Gulf South.* Knoxville: University of Tennessee Press, 1996.

———. *The People Called Cajuns: An Introduction to an Ethnohistory.* Lafayette: Center for Louisiana Studies, 1983.

Dorson, Richard M. *Buying the Wind: Regional Folklore in the United States.* Chicago: University of Chicago Press, 1964.

Dugas, Dianne. *Warrior Women and Popular Balladry 1650–1850.* Cambridge, England: Cambridge University Press, 1989.

Edwards, Jay. "Family Organization." In *Cajun Country,* edited by Barry J. Ancelet, Jay Edwards, and Glen Pitre, 69–76. Jackson: University of Mississippi Press, 1991.

Egan, Thomas Joseph. "Vincennes, Indiana: Echoes of French Popular Culture." Doctoral thesis, Monash University, Clayton, Victoria, Australia, 1990.

Ekberg, Carl. *Colonial Ste. Genevieve: An Adventure on the Mississippi Frontier.* Gerald, Mo.: Patrice Press, 1985.

Esman, Marjorie. "The Celebration of Cajun Identity and the Crawfish Festival." Ph.D. diss., Tulane University, 1981.

Falassi, Alessandro, ed. *Time out of Time: Essays on the Festival.* Albuquerque: University of New Mexico Press, 1987.

Firestone, Melvin M. "Mummers and Strangers in Northern Newfoundland." In *Christmas Mumming in Newfoundland,* edited by Herbert Halpert and G. M. Story, 62–75. Toronto: University of Toronto Press, 1968.

Fletcher, Joel L. *The Acadians in Louisiana Today.* Lafayette: Southwestern Louisiana Institute, 1947.

Fontenot, Mary Alice, and Paul B. Freeland. *Acadia Parish, Louisiana.* Vol. 1. *A History to 1900.* Baton Rouge: Claitor's, 1976.

Fontenot, Nicole Denée. *Cooking with Cajun Women: Recipes and Remembrances from South Louisiana Kitchens.* New York: Hippocrene Books, 2002.

Fournet, Nadine, and Richard Guidry. "Le Mardi Gras Traditionnel." *Louisiane* 54 (1982): 1.

Freeland, Paul, and Mary Alice Fontenot. *Acadia Parish, Louisiana.* Vol. 2. *A History to 1920.* Baton Rouge: Claitor's, 1976.

Gahn, Robert, Sr. *Opelousas Country: A History of Evangeline Parish.* Baton Rouge: Claitor's, 1972.

Gaignebet, Claude, and Jean-Dominique Lajoux. *Art profane et religion populaire au Moyen Age.* Paris: Presses Universitaires de France, 1985.

Garber, Marjorie B. *Vested Interests: Cross-Dressing and Cultural Anxiety.* New York: Routledge, 1992.

Gaudet, Marcia G. "'Mardi Gras Chic-a-la-Pie': Reasserting Creole Identity through Festive Play." *Journal of American Folklore* 114, 452 (2001): 154–72.

———. "The World Downside Up: Mardi Gras at Carville." *Journal of American Folklore* 111, 439 (1998): 23–38.

Gaudet, Marcia, and James C. McDonald, eds. *Mardi Gras, Gumbo, and Zydeco: Readings in Louisiana Culture.* Jackson: University Press of Mississippi, 2003.

Geertz, Clifford. *The Interpretation of Cultures.* New York: Basic Books, 1973.

Gibson, Jon L., and Steven Del Sesto, eds. *The Culture of Acadiana: Tradition and Change in South Louisiana.* Lafayette: University of Southwestern Louisiana Press, 1975.

Gilmore, David D. *Carnival and Culture: Sex, Symbol, and Status in Spain.* New Haven: Yale University Press, 1998.

Glassie, Henry. *All Silver and No Brass.* Bloomington: Indiana University Press, 1975.

Green, Rayna D. "Magnolias Grow in Dirt: The Bawdy Lore of Southern Women." *Southern Exposure* 4 (1977): 29–33.

Greenhill, Pauline. "'Neither a Lass nor a Maid': Sexualities and Gendered Meanings in Cross-Dressing Ballads." *Journal of American Folklore* 108, 428 (1995): 156–77.

Guttierrez, Charlotte Paige. *Cajun Foodways.* Oxford: University of Mississippi Press, 1992.

Halpert, Herbert, and G. M. Story, eds. *Christmas Mumming in Newfoundland: Essays in Anthropology, Folklore and History.* Toronto: University of Toronto Press, 1968.

Hollis, Susan Tower, Linda Pershing, and M. Jane Young, eds. *Feminist Theory and the Study of Folklore.* Urbana: University of Illinois Press, 1993.

Hotchkiss, Valerie R. *Clothes Make the Man: Female Cross Dressing in Medieval Europe.* New York: Garland, 1996.

Hughes, Linda. "'You Have to Do It with Style': Girls' Games and Girls' Gaming." In *Feminist Theory and the Study of Folklore,* edited by Susan Tower Hollis, Linda Pershing, and M. Jane Young, 130–48. Urbana: University of Illinois Press, 1993.

"Inauguration 2004." *Baton Rouge Advocate,* 13 January 2004.

Jordan, Rosan, and Susan Kalcik, eds. *Women's Folklore, Women's Culture.* Philadelphia: University of Pennsylvania Press, 1985.

Kane, Harnett T. *The Bayous of Louisiana.* New York: Morrow, 1943.

Keyes, Cheryl L. "Empowering Self, Making Choices, Creating Spaces: Black Female Identity via Rap Music Performance." *Journal of American Folklore* 113, 449 (2000): 255–69.

Kibler, M. Alison. *Rank Ladies: Gender and Cultural Hierarchy in American Vaudeville.* Chapel Hill: University of North Carolina Press, 1999.

Kinser, Samuel. *Carnival American Style: Mardi Gras at New Orleans and Mobile.* Chicago: University of Chicago Press, 1990.

———. "Violence Ritually Enjoined: The Mardi Gras Indians of New Orleans." *Cahiers de Littérature Orale* (Centre de Recherche sur la'Oralite, Institute National des Langues et Civilisations Orientales) 37 (1995): 115–50.

La France, Siona. "A Mardi Gras of Their Own." *New Orleans Times-Picayune,* 8 March 2003, p. E1.

Langley, Linda, Susan G. LeJeune, and Claude Oubre, eds. *Le Reveil des Fêtes: Revitalized Celebrations and Performance Traditions.* Louisiana State University at Eunice Folklife Series, vol. 3. Eunice: Louisiana State University at Eunice, 1997.

———. *Les Artistes: Crafters Tell Their Tales.* Louisiana State University at Eunice Folklife Series, vol. 2. Eunice: Louisiana State University at Eunice, 1996.

Lawless, Elaine. *Handmaidens of the Lord: Pentacostal Women Preachers and Traditional Religion.* Philadelphia: University of Pennsylvania Press, 1988.

Leathem, Karen Trahan. "A Carnival According to Their Own Desires: Gender and Mardi Gras in New Orleans, 1870–1941." Ph.D. diss., University of North Carolina, 1994.

LeRoy Ladurie, Emmanuel. *Carnival in Romans.* New York: Braziller, 1979.

Levi-Strauss, Claude. *The Savage Mind.* Chicago: University of Chicago Press, 1969.

Lindahl, Carl. "Bakhtin's Carnival Laughter and the Cajun Country Mardi Gras." *Folklore* 107 (1996): 49–62.

———. "Finding the Field through the Discovery of the Self." In *Working the Field: Accounts from French Louisiana,* edited by Jacques Henri and Sara LeMenestral, 33–50. Westport, Conn.: Praeger, 2003.

———. "A Note on Blackface." *Journal of American Folklore* 114, 452 (2001): 248–54.

———. "A Note on the Festive, Cultural, and Geographic Range of This Issue." *Journal of American Folklore* 114, 452 (2001): 140–43.

———. "One Family's Mardi Gras: The Moreaus of Basile." *Louisiana Cultural Vistas* 9, 3 (1998): 46–53.

———. "The Presence of the Past in the Country Cajun Mardi Gras." *Journal of Folklore Research* 33, 2 (1996): 101–27.

———. "'That's My Day': Mardi Gras in Basile, Louisiana." In *Carnaval!* edited by Barbara Mauldin, 121–24. Seattle: University of Washington Press, 2004.

Lindahl, Carl, and Carolyn Ware. *Cajun Mardi Gras Masks.* Jackson: University Press of Mississippi, 1997.

Lott, Eric. *Love and Theft: Minstrelsy and the American Working Class.* New York: Oxford University Press, 1993.

Louisiana State University College of Commerce, Division of Research. *An Economic Survey of Acadia Parish Prepared for the Texas and Pacific Railway Company.* Baton Rouge: Louisiana State University, 1950.

Lovelace, Martin J. "Christmas Mumming in England: The House Visit." In *Folklore Studies in Honour of Herbert Halpert,* edited by Kenneth S. Goldstein and Neil V. Rosenberg. St. John's, Newfoundland: Memorial University of Newfoundland, 1980.

McAlister, Elizabeth. *Rara! Voudou, Power, and Performance in Haiti and Its Diaspora.* Berkeley: University of California Press, 2002.

McConnaughey, Janet. "Mardi Gras Run Uses Trucks, Not Horses." *Lafayette (La.) Daily Advertiser,* 7 February 1989, 5–6.

McMahon, Felicia Faye. "The Aesthetics of Play in Reunified Germany's Carnival." *Journal of American Folklore* 113, 450 (2000): 378–90.

Meyer, Melissa, and Miriam Schapiro. "Waste Not, Want Not: An Inquiry into What Women Saved and Assembled." *Heresies* 4 (winter 1978): 66–69.

Mills, Margaret. "Sex Role Reversals, Sex Changes, and Transvestite Disguise in the Oral Tradition of a Conservative Muslim Community in Afghanistan." In *Women's Folklore, Women's Culture,* edited by Rosan A. Jordan and Susan J. Kalcik, 187–213. Philadelphia: University of Pennsylvania Press, 1985.

Miner, Allison. "The Mardi Gras Indians." *Louisiana Folklore Miscellany* 3, 3 (1973): 48–50.

Mire, Patrick. *Dance for a Chicken: The Cajun Mardi Gras.* Film. Eunice, Louisiana, 1993. Distributed by Attakapas Productions, P.O. Box 821, Eunice, La., 70535.

Mitchell, Carol. "Some Differences in Male and Female Joketelling." In *Women's Folklore, Women's Culture,* edited by Rosan A. Jordan and Susan J. Kalcik, 187–213. Philadelphia: University of Pennsylvania Press, 1985.

Mitchell, Reid. *All on a Mardi Gras Day: Episodes in the History of New Orleans Carnival.* Cambridge: Harvard University Press, 1995.

"Mrs. Agnes Miller Is Parade Marshall." *Basile Weekly,* 5 November 1992.

Noyes, Dorothy. "Façade Performances: Public Face, Private Mask." *Southern Folklore* 52, 2 (1995): 91–95.

Neumeyer, Kathy. "Eunice Maw-Maws' Run." *Eunice News,* 10 February 1988.

Onebane, Donna Magee. "Voices of Pointe Noire: A Study of Place and Identity." Ph.D. diss., University of Southwestern Louisiana, 1999.

Ortner, Sherry. "Is Male to Female as Nature Is to Culture?" In *Women, Culture and Society,* edited by Michelle Zimbalist Rosaldo and Louise Lamphere, 67–87. Stanford: Stanford University Press, 1974.

Ortner, S. B., and H. Whitehead, eds. *Sexual Meanings: The Cultural Construction of Gender and Sexuality.* Cambridge, England: Cambridge University Press, 1981.

Oster, Harry. "Country Mardi Gras." In *Buying the Wind: Regional Folklore in America,* edited by Richard M. Dorson, 274–81. Chicago: University of Chicago Press, 1964.

Oster, Harry, and Revon Reed. "Country Cajun Mardi Gras." *Louisiana Folklore Miscellany* 1, 4 (1960): 1–17.

Pershing, Linda. "Peace Work out of Piecework: Feminist Needlework Metaphors and the Ribbon around the Pentagon." In *Feminist Theory and the Study of Folklore,* edited by Susan Tower Hollis, Linda Pershing, and M. Jane Young, 327–57. Urbana: University of Illinois Press, 1993.

Pitre, Glen. "Mardi Gras Chase." *Louisiana Life* (February–March 1992): 54–60.

Post, Lauren C. *Cajun Sketches.* 2nd ed. Baton Rouge: Louisiana State University Press, 1962.

Radner, Joan N., ed. *Feminist Messages: Coding in Women's Folk Culture.* Urbana: University of Illinois Press, 1993.

Radner, Joan N., and Susan S. Lanser. "Strategies of Coding in Women's Cultures." In *Feminist Messages,* edited by Joan N. Radner, 1–29. Urbana: University of Illinois Press, 1993.

Regis, Helen A. "Second Lines, Minstrelsy, and the Contested Landscapes of New Orleans Afro-Creole Festivals." *Cultural Anthropology* 14, 4 (1999): 472–504.

Rickels, Patricia K. "The Folklore of Acadiana." In *1776–1976: Two Hundred Years of Life and Change in Louisiana,* edited by Patricia K. Rickels, 143–73. Lafayette, La.: Lafayette Natural History Museum, 1977.

———. "The Folklore of the Acadians." In *The Cajuns: Essays on Their History and Culture,* edited by Glenn Conrad, 240–54. Lafayette: Center for Louisiana Studies, 1978.

Roberts, Robin. *Sexual Generations: "Star Trek: The Next Generation" and Gender.* Urbana: University of Illinois Press, 1999.

Rosaldo, Michelle Zimbalist, and Louise Lamphere, eds. *Women, Culture and Society*. Stanford: Stanford University Press, 1974.

Roshto, Ronnie E. "Georgie and Allen Manuel and Cajun Wire Screen Masks." *Louisiana Folklore Miscellany* 7 (1992): 33–49.

Rushton, William Faulkner. *The Cajuns: From Acadia to Louisiana*. New York: Farrar, Strauss and Giroux, 1979.

Russo, Mary. "Female Grotesques: Carnival and Theory." In *Feminist Studies/Critical Studies*, edited by Teresa de Lauretis, 213–29. Bloomington: Indiana University Press, 1986.

Santino, Jack, ed. *Halloween and Other Festivals of Death and Life*. Knoxville: University of Tennessee Press, 1994.

Savoy, Ann Allen. *Cajun Music: A Reflection of a People*. Eunice, La.: Bluebird Press, 1984.

Sawin, Patricia. "Carnival in Grand Marais: The Strength of Women and the Fragility of Tradition." Paper presented at the annual meeting of the American Folklore Society, Portland, Oregon, 30 October 1998.

———. "Transparent Masks: The Ideology and Practice of Disguise in Contemporary Cajun Mardi Gras." *Journal of American Folklore* 114, 452 (2001): 173–203.

Saxon, Lyle, Edward Dreyer, and Robert Tallant, eds. *Gumbo Ya-Ya: A Collection of Louisiana Folktales*. New York: Bonanza, 1945.

Saxon, Lyle, Edward Dreyer, and Harvey W. Wixon. *Louisiana State Guide*. New York: Hastings House, 1941.

Sexton, Rocky L. "Cajun Mardi Gras: Cultural Objectification and Symbolic Appropriation in a French Tradition." *Ethnology* 38, 4 (1999): 297–313.

———. "Germans and les Americains: A Historical Anthropology of Cultural and Demographic Transformations in Southwest Louisiana, 1880 to Present." Ph.D. diss., University of Iowa, 1996.

———. "A Kinder, Gentler St. Nicholas: Transformation and Meaning in a 'Louisiana German' Tradition." *Southern Folklore* 56, 2 (1999): 149–60.

———. "Ritualized Inebriation, Violence, and Social Control in Cajun Mardi Gras." *Anthropological Quarterly* 74, 1 (2001): 28–38.

Sexton, Rocky L., and Harry Oster. "'Une 'Tite Poule Grasse ou la Fille Ainee': A Comparative Analysis of Cajun and Creole Mardi Gras Songs." *Journal of American Folklore* 114, 452 (2001): 204–24.

Shoemaker, Alfred L. "Belsnickel Lore." *Pennsylvania Folklife* 46, 3 (1997): 109–12.

Shuler, Marsha. "Women Lawmakers Enjoying New Powers." *Baton Rouge Advocate*, 4 February 2004, p. 8B.

Simon, Anne L. "The Changing Role of Women." In *1776–1976: Two Hundred Years of Life and Change in Louisiana*, edited by Patricia K. Rickels, 87–91. Lafayette, La.: Lafayette Natural History Museum Association, 1977.

Simoneaux, Angela. "Courir de Mardi Gras Keeps Cajun Heritage Alive." *Baton Rouge Advocate*, 2 March 1992, B1.

Smith, Lynn T., and Vernon J. Parenton. "Acculturation among the Louisiana French." *American Journal of Sociology* 44 (1938): 355–64.

Smith, Michael P. *Mardi Gras Indians.* Gretna, La.: Pelican, 1994.

Soileau, Jeanne. "Children's Observance of Mardi Gras in Ville Platte, Louisiana, in the Early 1950s." *Louisiana Folklore Miscellany* 3, 2 (1971): 50.

Spitzer, Nicholas R. "Mardi Gras in L'Anse de 'Prien Noir': A Creole Community Performance in Rural French Louisiana." In *Creoles of Color of the Gulf South,* edited by James H. Dormon, 87–125. Knoxville: University of Tennessee Press, 1996.

———. "Zydeco and Mardi Gras: Creole Identity and Performance Genres in Rural French Louisiana." Ph.D. diss., University of Texas, Austin, 1986.

St. George, Robert Blair. "Ritual House Assaults in Early New England." In *Fields of Folklore: Essays in Honor of Kenneth S. Goldstein,* edited by Roger Abrahams, 253–72. Bloomington, Ind.: Trickster Press, 1995.

Stallybrass, Peter, and Allon White. *The Politics and Poetics of Transgression.* Ithaca, N.Y.: Cornell University Press, 1986.

Supek, Olga. "Gender Inversion in the Contemporary Carnival: Saturnalia or an Echo of a Changing Reality?" *Contributions to the Study of Contemporary Folklore in Croatia* 9 (1988): 23–34.

Sutton-Smith, Brian. *The Ambiguity of Play.* Cambridge: Harvard University Press, 1997.

Taft, Michael. "Adult Halloween Celebrations on the Canadian Prairie." In *Halloween and Other Festivals of Death and Life,* edited by Jack Santino, 152–69. Knoxville: University of Tennessee Press, 1994.

———. "Men in Women's Clothes: Theatrical Transvestites on the Canadian Prairie." In *Undisciplined Women: Tradition and Culture in Canada,* edited by Pauline Greenhill and Diane Tye, 131–38. Montreal: McGill–Queen's University Press, 1997.

Tallant, Robert. *Mardi Gras . . . As It Was.* Gretna, La.: Pelican, 1976.

Thomas, Gerald. "Noel, La Chandeleur, Mardi Gras: Begging Rituals in French Newfoundland." In *Fields of Folklore: Essays in Honor of Kenneth S. Goldstein,* edited by Roger Abrahams, 300–310. Bloomington, Ind.: Trickster Press, 1995.

Tisserand, Michael. "Street Talk with Tootie Montana: An Offbeat Interview with the Oldest Active Mardi Gras Indian Chief." *Offbeat* 7, 2 (1994): 34–47.

Toelken, Barre. *The Dynamics of Folklore.* Logan: Utah State University Press, 1996.

Tokofsky, Peter. "Fasnacht in Basel, Switzerland: A Carnival of Contradictions." In *Carnaval!* edited by Barbara Mauldin, 93–120. Seattle: University of Washington Press, 2004.

———. "Masking Gender: A German Carnival." *Western Folklore* 58 (summer–fall 2000): 299–318.

———. "A Tale of Two Carnivals: Esoteric and Exoteric Performance in the Fasnet of Elzach." *Journal of American Folklore* 113, 459 (2000): 357–77.

Toll, Robert. *Blacking Up: The Minstrel Show in Nineteenth-Century America.* New York: Oxford University Press, 1974.

Turner, Kay. *Beautiful Necessity: The Art and Meaning of Women's Altars.* New York: Thames and Hudson, 1999.

Turner, Victor, ed. *Celebrations: Studies in Festivities and Ritual.* Washington, D.C.: Smithsonian Institution Press, 1982.

———. *The Ritual Process.* Ithaca, N.Y.: Cornell University Press, 1969.
U.S. Census Bureau. *Census of Population and Housing, 2000 Census.* Washington, D.C.: U.S. Department of Commerce, May 2003.
———. *Census of Population and Housing, 1990 Census.* Washington, D.C.: U.S. Department of Commerce, August 1993.
———. *Census of Population and Housing, 1980 Census.* Washington, D.C.: U.S. Department of Commerce, December 1983.
van Gennep, Arnold. *Manuel de folklore français contemporain.* Vol 1. *Les ceremonies périodique cycliques et saisonnières.* Pt. 3. *Carnaval/Carême—Pâcques.* Paris: Picard, 1937–38.
Voorhies, Felix. *Acadian Reminiscences.* New Orleans: Rivas, 1907.
Ware, Carolyn E. "Anything to Act Crazy: Cajun Woman and Mardi Gras Disguise." *Journal of American Folklore* 114, 452 (2001): 225–47.
———. "I Read the Rules Backward: Women, Symbolic Inversion, and the Cajun Mardi Gras Run." *Southern Folklore* 52, 2 (1995): 137–60.
———. "Making a Show for the People: Cajun Mardi Gras as Public Display." In *Signifying Serpents and Mardi Gras Runners: Representing Identity in Selected Souths,* edited by Celeste Ray and Luke Eric Lassiter, Southern Anthropological Proceedings, no. 36, 19–37. Athens: University of Georgia Press, 2003.
———. "Marketing Mardi Gras: Heritage Tourism in Rural Acadiana." *Western Folklore* 62, 3 (summer 2003): 157–87.
Weltman, Sharon Aronofsky. *Ruskins's Mythic Queen: Gender Subversion in Victorian Culture.* Athens: Ohio University Press, 1998.
Weston, Kath. *Gender in Real Time: Power and Transience in a Visual Age.* London: Routledge, 2002.

Archival Sources

Basile Mardi Gras Association ledgers, 1974–87. Basile Mardi Gras Association, Basile.
Basile Mardi Gras Association meeting. 3 January 2003. Audiotape recording and field notes by author. Basile.
Basile Weekly, 1965–72. Special Collections, Hill Memorial Library, Louisiana State University, Baton Rouge. Available on microfilm.
Crowley Signal, 1921–48. Special Collections, Hill Memorial Library, Louisiana State University, Baton Rouge. Available on microfilm.
Post, Lauren C. "Acadian Mardi Gras." *Louisiana State University Alumni News* 12, 1 (January 1936): 8–10, 31–32. Special Collections, Hill Memorial Library, Louisiana State University, Baton Rouge. Available on microfilm.

Interviews

Unless indicated otherwise, I conducted all of the following interviews. Cities named, except where indicated, are in Lousiana.

Ancelet, Maude. 3 June 2002. Scott.
Andrus, Debbie, and Susie Lopez. 5 November 1991. Basile.

Andrus, Debbie, Helena Putnam, and Kerry Kim Moreau. 18 October 1998. Basile.

Ashford, Janice. 26 February 2001. Basile.

Bergeaux, Merline. "Country Mardi Gras," session, Tales 'n' Talk Stage, Louisiana Folklife Festival. 28 May 1995. Monroe.

Bergeaux, Merline, Shirley Reed, and Patsy Simar. 20 December 1988. Tee Mamou.

Boone, Berline. 14 May 1994. Basile.

———. 11 August 2003. Basile.

Boone, Berline, and Madeline Reed. 27 November 1998. Basile.

Cart, Elson. 12 December 1991. Iota.

Courville, Marion. 25 March 1992. Eunice.

Deshotels, Ivy. 23 February 1992. Eunice. Notes only.

Doucet, Linda Frugé, and Renée Frugé Douget. 24 November 2003. Tee Mamou.

Doucet, Stanley, and Gerald Cormier. 14 December 1988. Iota.

Douget, Renée Frugé, and Linda Frugé Doucet. 11 February 1996. Interview by Carl Lindahl and Carolyn Ware. Tee Mamou.

Durio, Claude. 16 June 1992. Tee Mamou.

———. 5 March 2000. Tee Mamou.

Durio, Claude, Gerald Frugé, and Roonie Frugé. 12 December 1988. Tee Mamou.

Frugé, Evelyn. 12 November 1994. Eunice.

Frugé, Gerald. 8 October 1989. Tee Mamou.

———. 28 May 1995. "Country Mardi Gras," session, Tales 'n' Talk Stage, Louisiana Folklife Festival. Monroe.

Frugé, Gerald, and Linda Frugé Doucet. 28 June 1992. Tee Mamou.

Janot, Alice. 1 April 1992. Eunice.

Joubert, Curtis. 19 October 2001. Eunice.

Launey, Suson. 30 July 1991. Iota.

———. 13 January 1996. New Orleans.

———. 26 April 1996. New Orleans.

———. 25 May 1998. Iota.

———. 22 March 2002. Baton Rouge.

———. 13 September 2003. Monroe.

———. 17 February 2004. Baton Rouge.

LeBlanc, Gilbert and Esther (Nin). 8 April 1992. Basile.

LeBlue, Cassie, and Laura LeBlue. 5 August 2003. Basile.

Leger, Anne Marie, and Allen Leger. 16 December 1988. Iota.

LeJeune, Don. 18 March 1992. Rayne.

LeJeune, Mary Jane (Snookie). 12 November 1991. Basile.

Manuel, Georgie. 23 March 1993. Eunice.

———. 2 November 1994. Phone interview by Carolyn Ware. Notes only.

Miller, Agnes. 25 March 1993. Interview by Carl Lindahl and Carolyn Ware. Basile.

———. 12 November 1994. Basile.

Miller, Agnes, and Helena Putnam. 23 July 1991. Basile.

Miller, Betty and Hugh. 14 December 1998. Interview by Larry Miller and Carolyn Ware. Iota.

Miller, Jackie. 15 January 1996. Iota.

Miller, Norma Jean, and Theresa Seale. 11 November 1991. Eunice.

Moreau, Kerry Kim. 10 June 1999. Hattiesburg, Mississippi.

———. 20 March 2002. Baton Rouge.

———. 15 January 2003. Baton Rouge.

———. 21 March 2003. Baton Rouge.

Moreau, Vories. 21 December 1991. Interview by Carl Lindahl. Lawtell.

———. 31 October 1992. Lawtell.

———. 17 April 1993. Interview by Carl Lindahl and Carolyn Ware. Lawtell.

———. 25 August 1994. Lawtell.

———. 12 March 2001. Interview by Barry J. Ancelet and Carl Lindahl. Lawtell.

Pousson, Betty. 27 February 1990. "Prairie Mardi Gras Memories," narrative stage session, Tee Mamou–Iota Folklife Festival. Iota.

Rider, Russell "Potic." 25 July 1991. Basile.

———. 4 November 1994. Interview by Carl Lindahl and Carolyn Ware. Basile.

Rider, Russell "Potic," and Sandy Sonnier. 17 March 1992. Basile.

Thibodeaux, Frozine. 14 January 2001. Richard.

Young, Ella Ruth. 20 January 1992. Basile.

Index

Italicized page numbers refer to illustrations.

havior, 51, 145–46; traditional roles by, 176, 177–78, 181–82, 184; women runners' wrestling with male captains as transforming, into comic theater, 120–21, 128; women's Mardi Gras performances as challenging associations with, 2–3, 46–48, 52, 153–70. *See also* genitalia; men; women

Gene's Food Store (Basile), 68, 201n32

genitalia: exposure of actual, 40; and "grotesque body" concept, 154, 157, 162, 163; symbolic, 40, 142, 145, 155–57, 159–60

German Americans, 13, 189n24

Germany, 188n20

Gilmore, David D., 204n22

Godot, Violet, 176, 180

Gott's Cove (Louisiana), 109

Grand Marais (Louisiana), 16, 20, 41, 198n41

Grand Prairie (Louisiana), 16

Great Britain. *See* England; Ireland

Green, Rayna, 204n18

"grotesque body," 154, 157, 162, 163. *See also* genitalia; "ugly" effects (of masks)

Guidry, Richard, 2

la Guignolée festival (France), 188n20

la Guillonée festival (Illinois and Missouri), 13

gumbo: awards for cooks of, 37, 38, 44, 84; begging for ingredients for, as part of Mardi Gras runs, 2, 11, 114–15; commercial ingredients for, 37, 38, 65, 80, 114; cooking of, by men, 35, 38, 61; cooking of, by women, 1, 9, *18*, 20, 35–38, 44, 45, 51, 56, 84, 150, 180, 181, 185, 196n15; etiquette of serving, after a run, 18, 37, 38, 124, 150; original purpose of, 4, 35, 36, 191n35; as post-run community Mardi Gras feast, 1, 4, 18, 20, 35–38, 58, 65–69, 72, 96, 124, 149–50, 190n27. *See also* chickens; rice; sausage

gypsies, 56, 161

Halloween, 189n23

hats: captains', 5; switching of, by maskers, 42, 47; women's sewing of, 20, 22, 23, 25–26; women's wearing of, 56, 135. See also *capuchons*

"Hee-Haw Breakdown" (tune), 125

hogs. *See* pigs

horses: blankets for, 26; Eunice women as riding, 62, 64; in Mardi Gras runs, 13–16, 19, 57; men as riding, 13, 52, 55, 62, 64, 177, 195n1, 197n28; men's charging of houses using, 52, 62, 109; men's dancing on, as part of Mardi Gras runs, 2, 52, 116; women as catching, 116–17. *See also* wagons or trucks

hoses, *31*, 121, 165

hosts (of house visits): of family runs, 49, 51; as introducing their children to Mardi Gras traditions, 43, 175; invitations extended to, 1, 40, 124, 149; role of, in Mardi Gras run, 1–2, 4, 11, 20, 38–39, 53, 55, 114–15, 141–44; trickery once directed toward, now aimed at captains, 146; as turning Mardi Gras runners away, 13; of women's Mardi Gras runs, 51, 57–58, 67, 71, 72. *See also* children; house visits; spectators

Hotchkiss, Valerie R., 157

house visits: to ailing Merline Bergeaux, 75; booking, 85, 87; children's reactions to Mardi Gras, 39, 71, 118, 145, 164, 169, 170, 177, 180, 182; and children's runs, 82; men on horses charging houses during, 52, 62, 109; as part of Mardi Gras runs, 1, 6, 7, 8–9, 17, 20, 38–41, 109, 137, 139–43; rules about, 40, 104–5; as symbolic raids on women's domestic realm, 39, 168–69; women's avoidance of, 57; women's interest in toilets during, 67. *See also* hosts (of house visits); performances; spectators

Hughes, Linda, 198n28

Iberia Parish (Louisiana), 171

Illinois, 13

impersonation. *See* clowning; crossdressing; disguises

Indians (Native Americans): African Americans masking as, 13, 189n23; in Basile Mardi Gras song, 140; Cajuns disguising themselves as, 56, 158, 160–62; Mardi Gras practices likened to practices of, 137, 205n38; significance of, to Cajun Mardi Gras celebrants, 161

The Inferior Sex? (film), 193n35

Internet, 15, 195n1

Iota (Louisiana), 13, 15, 29, 72, 98, 124, 180; Mardi Gras parades in, 74, 94, 97, 119, 126. *See also* Tee Mamou–Iota Mardi Gras Folklife Festival

Ireland (northern), 188n20, 189nn23–24

Ireland, Tom, 17

Janot, Alice, 25, 26, 41–42, 47

Jeff Davis Parish, 15

Jennings (Louisiana), 5, 10, 88, 98

Johnson, Renos, 23

Johnson, Tony, 160–61, 201n25

Joubert, Curtis, 64

juxtaposition (artful), 154, 169

182–84, 207n1; World War II shift in rural, 13–14, 61, 173, 177
Onebane, Donna, 57, 160
Opelousas (Louisiana), 178, 180
Ortner, Sherry, 162
Ossun (Louisiana), 49
Owens, Maida, 192n44

parades (Mardi Gras): in Basile, 17, 65, 68, 149; in Eunice, 26, 63, 74; in Iota, 74, 94, 97, 119, 126; in New Orleans, 17
Pecanière (Louisiana), 16, 75
performances: as coded acts, 154–56, 163, 164, 169, 170; of cultural memory, 3; men's, 19; pulling of spectators into, 4, 20–21, 38, 43, 44, 51, 89, 107, 114, 118, 166–67, 192n44; standard elements of, in Mardi Gras runs, 2; women's, 2–3, 6–7, 10, 46, 115–18, 132, 137, 139–43, 153–70, 185. *See also bal de Mardi Gras;* begging; clowning; dancing; disguises; house visits; mischief making; parades; pre–Mardi Gras performances; singing (of Mardi Gras song)
photographers (of Mardi Gras runs), 98, 118, 140, 166–67
"picking at," 4, 16, 17, 40, 69, 105–6, 117, 126, 128, 143, 149, 168; as enhanced by theme costumes, 135, 152, 159. *See also* captains and co-captains: runners' "wrestling" with; mischief making
Pig Barn. *See* Town Park Barn (Basile Pig Barn)
pigs (hogs), 4, 161
Pitre, Glen, 189n26
Pointe Noire (later, Richard, Louisiana), 50, 53, 55–59, 160
Ponderosa Club (Tee Mamou), 72
Post, Lauren C., 2
potato salad, 35, 96, 124
Pousson, Betty, 19, 22, 45
Pousson, Mrs. (of Arcadia Parish), 25
power: challenging of men's, by women runners, 165–68; crossdressing as emphasizing differences in, 157–58; disguises associated with female, 158–59, 161; inversions of, enacted by Mardi Gras women, 153–70, 185; performing humor as a kind of, 168, 170; wearing masks as a kind of, 46, 48. *See also* captains and co-captains
Prather, Ruby, 180
pre–Mardi Gras performances, 80–83, 88, 91. *See also* education: about Mardi Gras traditions

punishments (for Mardi Gras rules violations), 40, 67, 105, 106, 141, 202n54
Putnam, Helena Miller: awards for, 84; as Basile Mardi Gras runner, 70, 132–33, 143–45, 149; being "picked at," 69, 144; on captains, 146; on criteria for great Mardi Gras runners, 203n60; and disguises, 60, 135, 156, 160–61; as fieldwork informant, 7; on male Mardi Gras runners, 40, 142, 144–45; on Mardi Gras, 1, 4–5, 131; on Mardi Gras begging, 141; on Mardi Gras rules, 135; on Mardi Gras song, 139, 201n35; on women runners, 202n53
Putnam, Mike, 161

quémandeurs. See begging
Quick-Trip grocery (Tee Mamou), 87
Quincy's Club, 48, 175

Rabelais and His World (Bakhtin), 154
race: segregation of Mardi Gras runs by, 5. *See also* African Americans; Asians; Creole communities; Indians
Radner, Jo, 154
reciprocity. *See* community
Reed, Carol, 47
Reed, Revon, 14, 49
Reed, Sam, 71–72
Reed, Shirley, 43, 104, 118; as Mardi Gras runner, 70–73, 91, 99, 105, 115, 164
Reed family, 70, 107, 124
release forms, 76, 85, 106, 129
rice, 35–38, 80, 114, 124, 150
Richard (Louisiana). *See* Pointe Noir
Richard, Enos, 66
Richard family, 65
Rickels, Patricia, 190n26
Rider, Elvina, 196n15
Rider, Russell ("Potic"): and Basile children's runs, 81; as Basile Mardi Gras Association president, 78, 80, 84, 130–31, 137, 147, 202n54; as Basile Mardi Gras captain, 200n3, 200n9; and disguises, 134, 135, 159, 205n38; on Mardi Gras, 4, 76, 149; on Mardi Gras dancing, 137; and Mardi Gras song, 137, 139, 201nn35–37; Mardi Gras suit of, 27–28; on mixed-sex Mardi Gras runs, 68, 145
Rider family, 65
Roberts, Robin, 205n54
rules (Mardi Gras): of Basile Mardi Gras Association, 135–36; punishments for violations of, 40, 67, 105, 106, 141, 202n54; of Tee

CAROLYN E. WARE is an associate professor of folklore and English at Louisiana State University. Her publications include *Cajun Mardi Gras Masks,* coauthored with Carl Lindahl (University Press of Mississippi, 1997), and numerous journal articles and essays on Cajun Mardi Gras, French Louisiana "treating" (healing), Croatian folklife in southeast Louisiana, and public presentation of folk culture. Previous positions include director of the Pine Hills Culture Program at the University of Southern Mississippi, research fellow and programs coordinator for Newcomb College Center for Research on Women, and programming coordinator for the Louisiana Folklife Festival. As a public folklorist, Ware has worked with the New Orleans Jazz and Heritage Festival and many other community festivals and organizations.

The University of Illinois Press
is a founding member of the
Association of American University Presses.

———————————————

Composed in 10.5/13 Adobe Minion
with Meta display
by Jim Proefrock
at the University of Illinois Press
Manufactured by Thomson-Shore, Inc.
University of Illinois Press

1325 South Oak Street
Champaign, IL 61820-6903
www.press.uillinois.edu